The Philosophical Imaginary

The Philosophical Imaginary

Michèle Le Dœuff

Translated by Colin Gordon

Stanford University Press
Stanford, California
1989

Stanford University Press
Stanford, California
© 1980 Éditions Payot
English translation © 1989 by The Athlone Press
Originally published in French in 1980 by Éditions Payot as
    L'Imaginaire philosophique
Originating publisher of the English edition: The
    Athlone Press, London
First published in the U.S.A. by Stanford University Press,
    1989
Printed in Great Britain
ISBN 0-8047-1619-6
LC 88-63325

Contents

Translator's Note

Although recent years have seen a number of English translations of works by French feminist writers translated into English, along with a number of works by male French theoreticians who have influenced or preoccupied Anglophone feminist culture, it is rather less common to encounter translations of books by French feminist writers who are professional philosophers. Michèle Le Doeuff's *The Philosophical Imaginary* (which was her first book, and is her first to be translated) belongs to this latter, rarer category; piecemeal translations of her work over the past decade have, nevertheless, already gained a significant audience in Britain, America and Australia. Where, then, one must perhaps unavoidably ask, is Michèle Le Doeuff to be located on the maps of contemporary French philosophy and feminism?

The shortest answer, and one which the author might herself favour, would be: elsewhere, or nowhere. Her writing is singularly bare of the period's usual fashionable impedimenta; it shows no systemic affiliation, no signs of a formative debt or repudiation. Politically and affectively, Le Doeuff belongs to the generation of May 1968: stylistically, she is an unseasonable classicist; philosophically, she affiliates herself to an honoured and (in her view) now largely abandoned French tradition which she defines as critical epistemology: that of the *Lumières* and, in this century, of Koyré and Bachelard. Le Doeuff develops, out of this tradition, a novel critique of philosophy itself: where Bachelard undertook a kind of philosophical iconography of error in the prehistory of the physical sciences, *The Philosophical Imaginary* provides an iconography of philosophy's own surreptitious traffickings in the world of images. It would be insufficient to say that this venture also happens to encompass a feminist critique, via the observation that Woman-as-Other figures as a main and perennial denizen of this peculiarly masculine philosophical reverie. For, through this latter critique, Le Doeuff's venture widens, here and in her subsequent writing, into a theory of phenomena of philosophical closure and exclusivity, accompanied by a countervailing effort to envisage what a philosophy would be like which would not, in its treatment of women, systematically violate its own standards.

 If feminism acts as a fulcrum in Le Doeuff's work of philosophical criticism (not least, it may be said, through the medium of some superbly gritty vignettes of academic life and mores), her philosophy articulates, though it certainly does not found, her conception of and commitment to feminism. In philosophy, Le Doeuff is a universalist but also an anti-foundationalist: philosophy cannot countenance the sacralization of arbitrary differences, but neither can it fetishize its own difference, seal off its frontiers and function as a self-judging and exclusive autarchy-patriarchy. Its work is in the world. Feminism's work, for Le Doeuff, is properly and truly philosophical in just this sense, as the rational criticism of actually existing injustice. 'For feminism does not create its object itself. Sexism comes first.' Feminist criticism, pursued collaboratively across a multitude of different domains and disciplines, moreover offers a model and an inspiration for 'something new under the philosophizing heavens', a 'philosophy without borders'; 'thanks to feminism, philosophy is more widely practised, and philosophical reasoning is expressed in more diversified forms than it would be if it were limited to departments of philosophy or professional philosophers.'

 No doubt it is considerations similar to these which disincline Le Doeuff from engagement in forms of feminist theoretical controversy which would, in her view, tend towards the closure of a domain or the attempted enforcement of an orthodoxy. So far as the role of philosophy itself is concerned, she sees feminist engagement and feminist criticism as furthering and demanding a reform of its practice which abandons all claims to a hegemonic, adjudicating status and offers instead the prospect – of interest by no means only to feminists – of a different way of doing philosophy, one which can accept more frankly and freely the uncertainty of its resources and purposes, and their problematic relationship with the experiences and desires of those who practise it.

 This 'something new' is allied, at its deepest level, to an idea which

Michèle Le Doeuff perceives as against the post-modern times: the notion that critique has an ethical end. 'When feminists think that Simone de Beauvoir's work mattered for the emancipation of at least a part of humankind, and that we must carry it on, most of our up-to-date colleagues at best smile, find us serious-minded, lacking a sense of playfulness, in short adopting an attitude which is neither up-to-date nor feminine. But we think we have to hold our heads above a stream of oppressive nonsense. Perhaps this is an eighteenth-century conception of philosophy – but, as the saying goes, he or she who will not live at all in the eighteenth century will never know what happiness is.'

*All quotations are from 'Ants and Women, or Philosophy without Borders' (cited below).

Chapter Six of this book previously appeared in earlier translated versions under the title 'Women and Philosophy', in *Radical Philosophy* 17 (Summer 1977), and in *French Feminist Thought*, edited by Toril Moi, Basil Blackwell, 1987.

Chapter Eight previously appeared in translation in *I&C* 9, Winter 1981–82. It is reproduced here, with minor amendments, by permission of I and C Publications Ltd.

The present translation of Chapter Six is the work of Debbie Pope, Michèle Le Doeuff, Margaret Llasera, myself, and others.

Minor modifications have been made by the author to some Chapters for the English edition, and linking passages between Chapters in the French edition have been deleted.

Other articles by Michèle Le Doeuff published in English translation include 'Operative philosophy: Simone de Beauvoir and existentialism' (*I&C* 6, Autumn 1979), and 'The Public Employer' (*m/f* 9, 1984). An interview with Michèle Le Doeuff and an account of a collective research project on philosophy teaching in which she took part appeared in *Radical Philosophy* 16, 1977. Her 'Ants and Women, or Philosophy without Borders', a lecture delivered in 1986 at the Royal Institute of Philosophy, is published in *Contemporary French Philosophy*, edited by A. Phillips Griffiths, Cambridge University Press, 1987. A major new book, *L'Etude et le Rouet: Des Femmes, de la philosophie, etc.* (1989), is published by Editions du Seuil, Paris.

Subsequent writings by Michèle Le Doeuff which develop themes explored in *The Philosophical Imaginary* include 'Utopies scolaires' (*Revue de Métaphysique et de Morale*, 1983); *La Nouvelle Atlantide: Voyage dans la pensée baroque*, Payot, Paris, 1983 (in collaboration with Margaret Llasera: a translation of and extended commentary on Francis Bacon's *New Atlantis*); and numerous articles on the philosophy of Bacon, including a Preface to Bacon, *Le 'Valerius Terminus' (ou de l'interprétation de la nature)*, translation with notes and commentary by François Vert.

Michèle Le Doeuff participated in the creation of the Théâtre de l'Aquarium's play *La Soeur de Shakespeare* (*Shakespeare's Sister*), which has been performed since 1977 in eight languages, including English. Her French performing version of Shakespeare's *Venus and Adonis* was produced in 1984 by the Compagnie de l'Orient Express in La Rochelle and Fort-de-France, Martinique, and is published together with her accompanying commentary, 'Genèse d'une catastrophe', by Alidades-Distique (Paris, 1986).

1
Preface: The Shameful face of Philosophy

In fact, Socrates talks about laden asses, blacksmiths, cobblers and tanners[1]

Whether one looks for a characterization of philosophical discourse to Plato, to Hegel or to Bréhier, one always meets with a reference to the rational, the concept, the argued, the logical, the abstract. Even when a certain coyness leads some authorities to pretend that they do not know what philosophy is, no agnosticism remains about what philosophy is not. Philosophy is not a story, not a pictorial description, not a work of pure literature. Philosophical discourse is inscribed and declares its status as philosophy through a break with myth, fable, the poetic, the domain of the image. Hegel says, in effect, that the form of thought is the sole form of philosophy, after first remarking that 'opposition and struggle between philosophy and so-called popular notions conveyed through mythology is an old phenomenon.'[2] It is, indeed, a very old commonplace to associate philosophy with a certain *logos* thought of as defining itself through opposition to other types of discourse.

If, however, one goes looking for this philosophy in the texts which are meant to embody it, the least that can be said is that it is not to be found there in a pure state. We shall *also* find statues that breathe the scent of roses, comedies, tragedies, architects, foundations, dwellings, doors and windows, sand, navigators, various musical instruments, islands, clocks, horses, donkeys and even a lion, representatives of every craft and trade, scenes of sea and storm, forests and trees: in short, a whole pictorial world sufficient to decorate even the dryest 'History of Philosophy'.

But only to decorate, nothing more. If someone set out to write a history of philosophical imagery, would such a study ever be as much an accepted part of the historiography of philosophy as histories of philosophical concepts, procedures or systems? If one further argued that existing histories of philosophy are at the very least incomplete, not to say mutilating, in that they never present us with any individual philosopher's image-album, would such a reproach be deemed worthy of serious consideration? The images that appear in theoretical texts are normally viewed as extrinsic to the theoretical work, so that to interest oneself in them seems like a merely anecdotal approach to philosophy.

It is of course well known that women can only ever look at history in terms of little stories, through the wrong end of their opera glasses! Obviously I am not aiming to justify my present undertaking in these terms, but it seems advisable to mention these prejudices so that the critique of the allegedly complete rationality of theoretical work which I am going to develop here is not too easily dismissed later on with judgements such as: 'There are no great texts for little Thracian servant-girls'.

Now that the notion of *thinking in images* has come to acquire a degree of cultural respectability it is no longer feasible to go on ignoring the importance of imagery in philosophy, but this does not mean that its theorization becomes an easy task. Our time has seen major studies of myth and dream, locations where thought in images is in some sense at home. Bachelard, conversely, has offered analyses of the imaginary component within scientific work, whose final aim is to extradite an element judged alien and undesirable, and assign it a residence *elsewhere*. The perspective I am adopting here differs, as will be seen, from both these approaches, since it involves reflecting on strands of the imaginary operating in places where, in principle, they are supposed not to belong and yet where, without them, nothing would have been accomplished. My book does not attempt a full treatment of this problem; rather it is a series of essays, perhaps the only format allowing one not to close a question reductively before it has even been posed.

Collecting articles whose original place of publication was, for various circumstantial reasons, widely varied implies some possibility of indicating ways in which they connect or converge.

Six or seven years passed between the writing of the first piece (on Thomas More) and the last. In that span of time one evolves, even if one does not produce very much. Consequently, to try to construct retrospectively some close theoretical linkage between these studies would amount to destroying what seems to me, with hindsight, their most important feature: the fact that the monographic style I had chosen of working on particular texts and themes came to modify the perspectives within which I had started. I take responsibility for the scattered quality of my work as reflecting the necessity of feeling one's way in a field of research which offers large scope for empiricism.

It is true that all the articles which follow start from the same interest in the occurrence, in texts regarded as theoretical, of a form of thought in images. And I cannot claim to have begun these studies without some preconceived ideas about the functioning of imagery in texts where its presence is supposedly abnormal.

Among these initial hypotheses, one still seems to me essential and serviceable. It can be expressed in either a minimalist or a maximalist form:

The narrow version states that the interpretation of imagery in philosophical texts goes together with a search for points of tension in a work. In other words, such imagery is inseparable from the difficulties, the sensitive points of an intellectual venture.

The broader version states that the meaning conveyed by images works both for and against the system that deploys them. *For*, because they sustain something which the system cannot itself justify, but which is nevertheless needed for its proper working. *Against*, for the same reason – or almost: their meaning is incompatible with the system's possibilities.

The real work of these essays takes place, each time, somewhere between these two extremes: between the location of a difficulty and that of a contradiction.

While this overall perspective was not invalidated by these exercises in using it (though each study gives it a particular inflection), there is, however, a more particular direction of enquiry which I have found only along the way. I shall call this here the notion of the 'philosophical imaginary'. And since it is what I have learnt during the writing of these different essays, I am allowing it to provide their collected title.

I began thinking about images in philosophical texts without at first recognizing their specificity. I tried to interpret the insular theme of *Utopia* using a method which would have been just as well (or badly) suited to the study of a deam, a painting, a legend, a play. I do not disown this method: a minimal understanding of a primary symbolic meaning is an almost indispensable starting-point. Images generally need to be decoded before one can relate their meaning to the thought made explicit in the text, in order afterwards to reintroduce into the discourse the question which the image both resolves and helps to evade. But this reinsertion allows the hypothesis of a converse: if the images of philosophical texts are so functional, so organic in their very dysfunctionality, might we not guess that they are made to measure, that there is not just an imaginary *in* philosophy but a properly philosophical imaginary, whose specificity might be determined by a combination of a traditionally textual approach and a sociological one?

It is certainly not coincidental that I came to formulate these ideas more clearly through my work on women and/in philosophy. The icon of the feminine in philosophical texts is not a universal notion. It is indeed formulated in conjunction with some rather common phallocratic prejudices, found in opinions, everyday behaviour and social practices extending far beyond the sphere of the learned few, but its specificity – not to say strangeness – seemed clear to me, no doubt because my personal sociological trajectory has also taken me through places in society where another image of the feminine is proposed for, or imposed upon, women's self-identification.

Thinking out this specificity did not mean drawing an absolutely rigorous line of demarcation: to consider imagery as a cultural product naturally involves looking for its variations across different periods, social categories and fields of knowledge without, however, forgetting that culture is something which circulates *between* different groups, fields, practices and knowledges. Certainly this circulation is not an undifferentiated diffusion: what it imposes is rather the requirement, at each stage, to think through the transformations which are produced in a borrowed element by virtue of the act of borrowing itself. This must be done without postulating the closure of discourses or fields of knowledge in a way which would relegate us directly to a pre-Feuerbachian idealism; though by itself a mere postulate of openness would hardly advance us either.

From here on it became possible to notice things which had already long been evident, though unperceived. There was, for example, Plato's extraordinary output of fables. Plato's need to construct myths – among them perhaps even the myth of Atlantis – or strikingly to refashion mythic elements drawn from the Greek poetic heritage is something which has been known about for ages and yet never properly studied, in spite of the hints provided by the historians and especially, in the Greek domain, by Jean-Pierre Vernant. A comparative study of the myth of races, and especially of the theme of the Island of the Blessed in Hesiod and Plato, would serve to illustrate old Diès's remark that Plato gave back even more than he took from the mysticism of his time; though the audience of those who received and recognized this output of fables was surely not that of Plato's time. In any case, we need to draw the consequences of the fact that the philosopher reworks elements of a mode of discourse which philosophy elsewhere repudiates.

There is not *one* reason, or *one* imaginary – one may wonder today whether this assertion is self-evident or inaudible. When one states it as a principle, everyone is willing to accept cultural variation as a truism needing no further scrutiny; yet as soon as it comes to putting it into effect, almost everyone abandons the principle in favour of a preponderant reference to 'the imaginary' – and Jung remains the great provider of tools for interpretation. One thus begins to suspect that what is referred to as the imaginary is basically seen as extra-cultural, infra-cultural or pre-cultural, and so (why not?) uncultured.

At this point it became necessary to define my work against the Bachelardian (and broadly psychoanalytic) problematic on which I had initially relied at least for an understanding of primary symbolic material. The simple idea that imagery has a relation to what we call 'conceptualized' intellectual work, or at least that it occupies the place of theory's impossible, was already enough to distance me from a perspective which assumes the radical heterogeneity of reverie and objective knowledge. When one realizes that imagery copes with problems posed by the theoretical enterprise itself, it is no longer thinkable to attribute it to some primitive soul which, endlessly reworking the same themes, produces analogies, arbitrary valorizations and seductive images whose sweet solicitations abstract knowledge must absolutely oppose. And when one is led to postulate the existence of images specific to a work, denying precisely that there are themes that are everywhere 'the same', then one can no longer subscribe to Bachelard's poetics. Even so, in practice some of Bachelard's analyses still seem illuminating to me. I shall try later on to do justice to the decisive contribution of his poetics, which lies in the reintroduction of the dimension of affectivity into the analysis of reverie.

But the suggestion that the imaginary which is present in theoretical texts stands in a relation of solidarity with the theoretical enterprise itself (and with its troubles) – that it is, in the strict sense of the phrase, *at work* in these productions[3] and is specific in character – implies a break not only with Bachelard but with the kind of misconception fostered by the notion of a 'common mythical background', also termed the 'collective imaginary' and, in franker moments, 'the whole body of popular prejudices': a notion not unconnected with the position assumed by the learned themselves and the allurements this stance lends to itself in order to remain tenable – not unrelated, that is, to the founding misconceptions of philosophy. When the learned theorize the imaginary, theirs is always a theory of the Other, of the people which lives off legends, as if this undifferentiated entity called the 'people' (or that other one called 'folklore') had an independent reality outside the ideas of a caste which asserts its own existence through opposition to this other, blanket category.

Philosophy has always arrogated to itself the right or task of speaking about itself, of having a discourse about its own discourse and its (legitimate or other) modes, writing a commentary on its own texts.[4] This metadiscourse regularly affirms the non-philosophical character of thought in images. But this attempted exclusion always fails, for 'in fact, Socrates talks about laden asses, blacksmiths, cobblers, tanners'[5]. Various strategies have been pursued to exorcize this inner scandal. One of them consists in projecting the shameful side of philosophy on to an Other. This denegation (in which the writing subject disavows what he himself writes) is simple in its mechanism and variable in its forms. In rough terms one can say that the occurrence of a discourse in images can be despatched either upstream or downstream.

The upstream hypothesis is the resurgence of a primitive soul, of archaic or infantile thought, of an uneducated or ineducable part of the mind. Paradigms of this projected Other are the child (in that we have all been one, before becoming . . . a man!), nursery stories, the people (irrational by nature), old wives' tales, folklore, etc. As Couturat puts it,[6] we rock the child who is still within us, even in the philosopher; and as this child is none other than the irrational part of the soul which Plato compares to the common crowd, myths will always serve 'to enchant what there is of the common people in us'. As it happens, this is not so much Couturat's personal view as virtually everyone's, as though here utterance belonged no longer to individual speakers but to the whole corporation.

In the downstream variant of the idea, recourse (here termed didactic or pedagogic) to imagery is seen more in terms of an adaptation to the intended recipient of a discourse. Imagery speaks directly, with intuitive clarity, to a destined interlocutor who is still uncultivated by concepts and ignorant of philosophy, or at any rate of this philosophy. The image is a gangway, a mediation between two theoretical situations: the speaker's and the recipient's.

Here then are two possible *alibis*, two in fact diametrically opposite conceptions of the meaning within theoretical texts of thought in images, which nevertheless lead to the same result. Either one maximizes the image's heterogeneity – as Bachelard did for scientific thought, and Condillac before him for philosophies which he 'blamed'[7] – or one absorbs the image completely into the conceptualized problematic, its meaning being considered as congruent with the theoretical results which it simply translates or illustrates. A dross coming from elsewhere, or a duplicate, serviceable to the reader's deficient culture yet dispensable, if philosophers were left free to speak only to other philosophers! In each case there is a common failure of recognition: whether the image is seen as radically heterogeneous to, or completely isomorphous with, the corpus of concepts it translates into the Other's language, the status of an element within philosophical work is denied it. It is not part of the enterprise. In either case it falls within what Foucault calls the teratology of a knowledge – and the good reader, who has passed through the philosophical discipline, will know he should pass it by.

In case some readers of the following studies should be prompted, in their turn, to derogatory judgement (although the transgressive value of these analyses should not be overstated), this presentation will conclude with a few methodological propositions – accompanied, again, by the proviso that these do not encapsulate a method systematically deployed in these essays but are rather their result, a concluding appraisal designed to help outline a programme for further work.

One may appropriately begin by noting the mark of denegation which is carried by thought in images. We have seen the workings of the paradigm of childhood, and of adaptation to the uncultured reader. Here is another example of denial:

> We have now not merely explored the territory of pure under-standing, and carefully surveyed every part of it, but have also measured its extent, and assigned to everything its rightful place. This domain is an island, enclosed by nature itself within unalterable limits. It is the land of truth – seductive name! – surrounded by a wide and stormy ocean, the native home of illusion, where many a fog bank and many a swiftly melting iceberg give the deceptive appearance of farther shores, deluding the adventurous seafarer ever anew with empty hopes, and engaging him in enterprises which he can never abandon and yet is unable to carry to completion. Before we venture on this sea, to explore it in all directions and to obtain assurance whether there be any ground for such hopes, it will be as well to begin by casting a glance on the map of the island which we are about to leave, and to enquire, first, whether we cannot in any case be satisfied with what it contains – are not, indeed, under compulsion to be satisfied, inasmuch as there may be no other territory upon which we can settle; and, secondly, by what title we possess even this domain, and can consider ourselves as secured against all opposing claims. Although we have already given a sufficient answer to these questions in the course of the Analytic, a summary statement of its solutions may nevertheless help to strengthen our conviction, by focusing the various considerations in their bearing on the questions now before us.[8]

Twice in this passage Kant resorts to an evasion. First by insisting that he will be saying nothing new, that he will only be reiterating what the Analytic has established: a review which is to fortify conviction, not to create it. He is adding no new meaning here. Interpreters will, inevitably, suppose the contrary.[9] Moreover, he, Kant, is on his guard against his own text, and distances himself from it; it is the land of truth (seductive name. . . .) The text presents itself along with its own censoring, for to announce a seduction is also to denounce it – and enjoy dispensation to let the seduction work, 'even so'. Thus between the writing subject and his text there is a complex negating relationship, which is a sign that something important and troubling is seeking utterance – something which cannot be acknowledged, yet is keenly cherished. As far as I am concerned, taking an interest in images and enquiring into this sort of evasion are one and the same activity.

What is next required is an iconographic investigation[10] to establish whether or not this image is a *hapax*, an isolated feature in the text: a kind of study altogether comparable to what would be required in the analysis of a concept. In the case which I have chosen and will now follow through, this would show that there are a considerable number of islands in Kant's work, from the first edition of the *Critique of Pure Reason* to the publication of the *Critique of Practical Reason*. It would show, for instance, that the northern isle in the quoted passage, the island one must content oneself with, has its symmetric antithesis in the island of the South Seas, the seat of the Golden Age, which must be utterly renounced.[11] So far this investigation generates no interpretation, but it enables us to specify the image of the island of the Analytic and its distinctive traits,[12] embedded in a system of opposition between islands in the South which must be abandoned and islands in the North which must not be left. And the path is traced out of a journey whose end is a repetition, in radical difference, of its starting-point. From a lost island to another one needing to be settled. . .

The next stage is that of erudition. In my essay on Descartes I put forward the idea that images in philosophical texts regularly turn out to have been taken over from precise earlier sources, making their study into part of a history of learning's fabulous motifs. May I refer the reader to *Red Ink in the Margin*,[13] and content myself here with repeating its main principle: it is a good thing not only to bear in mind all the earlier usages of an image by philosophers[14] but also to locate a precise source, an image which, at the level of the signifier, is close to the one being studied. In our case it is not without interest that the metaphor elaborated by Kant is copied from two pages of Bacon. In *Temporis Partus Maximus*, we read: 'Indeed, if political conditions and projects had not put an end to these mental trips, these mariners would have touched on many another shore of error. For the island of truth is surrounded by a mighty ocean in which many an intelligence will drown in storms of illusion.' And Bacon goes on to speak of the insufficiency of the sceptical solution, for the sceptics 'waver from one side to the other, like an orator speaking from a ship-deck, and they behave towards their idols like lunatic lovers who curse their loves but can never leave them.'[15]

All this is useful in allowing us to see what it is in the Kantian system that hangs on this seductive passage about the land of truth. It prepares the ground for a structural analysis which is, for me, the essential stage of the study. It is in fact often difficult to see what sensitive or problematic theoretical point an image bears on. Here, having recognized the Baconian link, we know where to look. We must turn immediately to the epigraph to the second edition of the *Critique of Pure Reason*:[15a]

BACO DE VERULAMIO
Instauratio Magna, Praefatio, etc.

and we can guess that what is at issue in this third chapter of the Analytic is the question of the Great Instauration. *Instauratio* has a repetitive, reiterative meaning: it is the reconstruction, the great renewal, the recovery of the lost origin, but subject to difference; more precisely, for the Puritans of the early seventeenth century, it was the act of reconstructing, with human means (notably including the progress of sciences of nature), the earthly paradise. Here we have the articulation of the two islands. As this analysis is offered here only by way of an example, I shall limit myself to a brief outline of its direction without going into detail.

To interpret this northern isle, we need to look at the gap between Kant's claims and the theoretical possibility of justifying these claims *as they relate to the historic import of the critical enterprise*.[16] To put it schematically: in the perspective of the Great Instauration, the progress of the sciences is essential, whereas the importance of philosophy, in the sense Kant understands it, is altogether doubtful. In Bacon's time it was theoretically possible to give a role to philosophy in the strict sense. Since the sciences were not yet constituted, Baconian philosophy took on the historic task of clearing the ground for them by combating idols and illusions, its role being that of a propaedeutic (and a programme, calling upon the best minds to devote themselves to the knowledge of nature), a bellringer who rises earlier than others. [17]

But Kant's historical situation and viewpoint are those of the constituted sciences. The sciences of nature have found their path, and the programme of the House of Solomon is under way.[18] From the point of view of the Great Instauration, the need for philosophical assistance is no longer a tenable claim. Yet this need is what is affirmed in the third chapter of the Analytic – and what underlies the entire critical endeavour: to establish the conviction that we should fix our dwelling in the land of understanding, and prevent the understanding, which has at last applied itself to its proper, empirical employment, from wandering off elsewhere. It is thus on this terrain that one can place the conflict which generates the long metaphor of the Analytic: the occlusion (allowing it to be settled, meanwhile, in an oblique and dogmatic manner) of the question of philosophy's role in the global project of Restoration and the usefulness, for the progress of the sciences, of philosophical intervention. The understanding 'must be prepared for many a humiliating disillusionment, whenever, as must unavoidably and constantly happen, it oversteps the limits of its own domain, and loses itself in opinions that are baseless and misleading.'[19] The words 'as must unavoidably and constantly happen' are wonderful here, since they are to be understood as saying: 'if I were not there to prevent it'.

This island of the *Critique of Pure Reason* is thus the emblem of the Kantian enterprise (an emblem unthinkable in the logic of the Great Instauration), the self-justification of a project which is, for good measure, conducted on the very terrain where that project could least readily be defended: that of the pleasure principle. Reflecting on the pertinence of his own intervention in the domain of his object, introducing into the question of the functioning of the understanding the operator called 'critical philosophy', Kant takes a further step (beyond the idea of a use, for the progress of the sciences, of a philosophical work): he constructs a self-justification centred on a discrimination of pleasures and pains. Without the critical theory, the understanding 'must unavoidably' court the worst reverses. It is so cold on this sea of illusion, and the water is so choppy . . . Whereas, with the Kantian philosophy, the understanding will learn to stay on the island – of whose charms, incidentally, nothing is said to us, except that it is a place where one can stay, which does not seem much unless one happens to have been caught by a squall in the Irish Sea or the Baltic![20]

Now this evaluation and discrimination of pains lacks all supporting evidence, unless one is to take the *Critique*'s amphibolies, for example, as portraying the rollings of a swell guaranteed to produce a severe case of seasickness. This announcement of the sufferings which the understanding will face once it lets itself wander among illusions amounts to no more than an arbitrary decree, one so weakly grounded that Kant is obliged to reinforce (natural) suffering with punishment ('many a humiliating disillusionment'). Only a terroristic *mise en scène* can justify Kant's threats about these pains. Images are the means by which every philosophy can engage in straightforward dogmatization, and decree a 'that's the way it is' without fear of counter-argument, since it is understood that a good reader will by-pass such 'illustrations' – a convention which enables the image to do its work all the more effectively.

So this page does not just carry the emblem of critical philosophy. Playing on a calculus of pains, a distribution of affective values, it also works a seduction, produces and structures a fantasy. At this point interpretation cannot do without a poetics, a psychoanalysis in the loose sense of the term; or, putting it more simply, commentary must answer the question: how does this island work, on the subjective level?

The promise of the island of the understanding is balanced by some terrifying dangers. Its security value is hardly explained, and can be grasped only through contrast: the island is a good object only by being excepted from an uninhabitable world. The text is hardly gratifying, at least in any direct way: 'whether we cannot in any case be satisfied with it – are not, indeed, under compulsion to be satisfied'. One may wonder what kind of subjective satisfaction such a text – a discourse laden with typically parental warnings – is capable of offering, and whether its seduction amounts to any more than the (equally parental) promise of pains avoided. All the more so in that at this level the proposal is a double-edged one: one avoids the discomfort of the icy fogs but at the cost of renouncing the dream of discovery, the call of new lands, and hope.

To understand the affective charge of this island it is best to juxtapose it with the one I have called its symmetric counterpart:

Vain regrets for a golden age promise us unalloyed enjoyment of a carefree life, dreamt away idly, or trifled away in childish play. Such yearnings have been stimulated by stories such as *Robinson Crusoe* and reports of visitors to the South Sea Islands. The existence of such yearnings proves that thoughtful persons weary of civilized life, if they seek its value in pleasure alone.[21]

Anyone who knows a little psychoanalysis will doubtless guess that what is being talked about here is castration; and that symbolic castration has compensations which are effective only if left unspoken. When you have accepted it, then . . .: but it is essential not to say what, the formulation of the happy consequence of libidinal sacrifice must be left in eternal suspense, for no determinate – that is to say, finite – compensation could match the sacrifice in question. Every stated benefit is necessarily a partial one. The infinite perspective of desire can be set up only on the express condition that it is a simple perspective, not to be obstructed by some partial object. From this point of view Kant's text is entirely coherent and its non-gratifying character is its main seduction.

Nevertheless this grand problematic allows itself a few respites or resting-points from which better to espy the infinite. The most primary promise is to make an end of problems of frustration and fear. Another is tautological: after this, you will be yourselves: castration, it seems, allowing the individual to constitute him- or herself as subject and found his or her identity.

Perhaps it is thus that the event described in Kant's 'summary recapitulation' can work as more than the simple avoidance of displeasure: the pleasure of *ascesis*, the iconoclastic gratification of detaching oneself from imaginary satisfactions (pleasing images and 'illusions'), so as to espouse only a single image – that of the break marked as constitutive: a map of the land, a title of ownership and the vague fantasy of bodily integrity, all so many threads binding together the project of constituting oneself as subject.

Having once recognized the inner logic of this fantasy-figure, the link between the jubilation of libidinal sacrifice, the unspoken compensation promising an indefinite field for desire and the staging points that mark out this infinite perspective, it must be emphasized that the desire which is thus structured is a desire of a particular type: the emblem inaugurates an erotics of action and work (strictly in line with the ethic of the Baconian appeal cited in Kant's epigraph). More precisely, it does not strictly so much inaugurate it as formalize or symbolize a sacrifice which the reader has doubtless already made.[22] Whom is such a figure designed to gratify? Whom can it satisfy? Kant, no doubt, in so far as it valorizes his intervention in the domain of his object, but also a whole circle of bystanders marked by the experience of schooling, scholastic asceticism and the instinctual and imaginary sacrifices which our education system exacts. This page speaks to us of a subjective situation in which we are placed or through which we have passed.

In the first scene of *Love's Labour's Lost*, the King of Navarre fails to convince Biron that in order to study, to live in philosophy, one must vow complete abstinence, make war on all one's passions, die to love and fast weekly, for to Biron 'study's godlike recompense' is only a hollow phrase. Yet he has no choice, since he has sworn to remain with the king and share his life. One might regret on his behalf that the king is unable to offer him a good myth which would justify what he cannot in any case escape. The Kantian passage would have filled the bill, resolving the issue and ending the play without more ado.

It follows that the fantasy-function of the image cannot be separated from the emblematic function, except provisionally for purposes of analysis, since what one finally finds in examining the affective dimension is yet again emblematic – not, strictly, the emblem of this philosophy but the emblem of a more widespread psycho-theoretical situation.

That situation is, furthermore, necessarily that of a social and cultural minority. Only in this light can an other than classical sense be given to the idea of 'fantasy sacrifices': it is not a question of the sacrifice of fantasies in general (as is claimed by the classic interpretation which says that 'rationality' – in the singular – is created by separation from myth in general, from an infantile and popular mode of consciousness) but of a break with a shared imaginary in favour of the imaginary of a corporate body – here, an imaginary of the learned. This exchange (or moulting of plumage) is well illustrated by Pierre Roussel's book,[23] which renounces one imaginary in favour of another – with this other being an *imaginary* in the inseparably double meaning of the term: a thought in the service of desire and instinctual malaise, and the imaginary *of* one's theoretical situation – the emblem of its truth.

To return to Kant, the subjectivity which finds pleasure in the passage of the *Critique of Pure Reason* is a subjectivity which is sociohistorically determinate. Psychoanalysis, in so far as it obscures every determination of this kind, cannot claim the last word about this figure. The island of castration dates from the eighteenth century, and marks an epoch: philosophers had previously been in the habit of offering us more joyful and directly desirable things at the end of the path of knowledge – holding out in their discourse a prospect of islands to which we might more happily transport ourselves. In considering, then, the historical singularity of the Kantian island, one should also not forget the historical situation of psychoanalysis, which is also that of a dated historical formation which strives to think – whatever it may say about this itself – on questions which are those of an epoch, and of a social category.

The last word ought rather, in my view, to belong to a historicizing intertextuality: Freudianism theorizes castration and says, among other things, that the subject of science is the subject which is crossed through, a notion which in my view intuitively summarizes the content of the passage in Kant which has been used for this methodological outline. In speaking of the crossed-through subject, the analysts are returning, without necessarily knowing it, to a Kantian formulation. This does not mean that Kantain philosophy possesses some privilege of oversight over psychoanalytic theory. The two discourses have the same standing, as sciences constituted and transmitted by the school institution. Each confronts the same question: that of the subjective conditions for an abandonment of the right to dream.

Kantianism meets this question among the ruins of an old notion, itself just as mythic as the one coined by the Moderns, which we still like to rediscover nostalgically while reading some Greek author: knowledge is delightful, the search for truth has an erotic motive, love of wisdom is first of all love, one must seek the good with all one's soul, and the possession of truth produces a harmony where everything, including sensibility, finds its place. Wisdom or Sovereign Good, those old emblems in the form of happy isles, islands on a midday sea, were based in a psychology itself also founded by a distribution of images – and this psychology, too, could convince only those already in a theoretico-subjective situation such that the shaping offered by the image could answer to something within them.

This ancient happiness is no longer thinkable in the eighteenth century, as Kant does not fail to acknowledge, closing the *Critique of Pure Reason*, for example, with some thoughts on nature as cruel stepmother, and on the veneration we owe the creator 'as much for what he has refused us as for what he has given us in recompense'. The castrating dimension of the passage in the *Critique of Pure Reason* points in this direction, but at the same time its metaphor annuls this and organizes a seduction into renunication by depicting an island already discovered, recalling, via the book's epigraph, the Baconian Utopia. A restoration of paradise on earth, through the work and progress of the sciences, is declared possible and even already begun, despite and notwithstanding everything – even if the system cannot found this hope on reason. But without this hope, can there be a *Critique of Pure Reason?* Why write this work, if it can have no positive action on the workings of the understanding? Moreover, what good is there in making sure that the understanding devotes itself to its legitimate use if this use has no existential value?

The known history of the drafts of this book indicates that this page belongs among the earliest written passages. Without trying to exaggerate this fact's importance, one must still take it into account – not just in order to emphasize once again that the true function of this running metaphor is clearly not limited to the 'summary recapitulation' of the solutions given in the Analytic, but rather to situate the metaphor as a dialectical presupposition of the theory. In so far as it sets up a distinction (the foggy ocean/the island where one can remain), it is indeed an allegory of the basic distinction between the legitimate (empirical) use of the understanding and its confusing (amphibological) use. But it departs already from this simple allegorical function by adding to the pure spatialization of division a meaning of a different order: an imposition of existential values. Lastly it is a counter-allegory, to the degree that it founds the possibility of retrieving the myth of an earlier philosophical practice. When one closes the *Critique of Pure Reason* everything will, in the short ending of a chapter,[24] have been recovered which makes up a Platonic conception of philosophy: the hegemonic or governmental function of philosophy relative to other knowledges;[25] the idea that without metaphysics the essential part of particular knowledges would remain eternally inactive or virtual.[26] Or, again, the idea that it is only under the auspices of metaphysics that the scientific republic can work towards eternal happiness.

For this closing recovery of a primacy of philosophy and of a totality in which knowledge, concord and happiness converge, no proof is or can be offered. In fact all Kant's theorizing is based on the disjunction of these three registers (the speculative, the moral, the pleasing). We need, in order to identify the theoretical tension corresponding to this recovery which the *mise en scène* of the island of understanding and its settlement foreshadows, to return to the three questions Kant calls fundamental. The first question (What can I know?) has its answer in the *Critique of Pure Reason*; the second (What must I do?) is the object of the *Critique of Practical Reason*. But the third (What may I hope?) seems to elude the critical enterprise – there is no Critique of Hopeful Reason, a critique which ought to have answered the question: under what conditions can a being worthy of being happy hope to be so indeed?

Now if this question is the stumbling-block of the critical method, this is directly on account of the division laid down by the geography of the Analytic: 'reason cannot discern the necessary connection' of the state of worthiness (as a moral being) of happiness, with the state of actually being happy (in this life), because 'the senses present to us only a world of phenomena' (the island) and the latter does not offer us an instance of this connection. This is for a good reason: the hope in question would be the hope of a synthetic unity between the moral (intelligible or supra-sensible) world and the sensible world – which is to say that to justify this hope one would need to establish a continuity between the island and the foggy ocean, to suppress the insularity of the island, which is precisely what the fable of the Analytic and the whole *Critique* forbid. This synthetic unity could be argued for only by a sort of amphiboly. Its theorization would weaken the rigorous demarcation of the world of phenomena and the clear distinction between the speculative and the practical.

The lack of an answer to the third question is thus an inescapable aporia, since otherwise the foundations of the critical enterprise would be compromised. Yet a positive answer to this question is dogmatically put forward in the figure of a scientific republic which, kept on the right path by metaphysics, works towards universal happiness. And this same figure has been outlined three hundred pages earlier, in the fable we have been examining, by the reuse of a mythic theme traditionally allied to the idea that knowledge, good conduct and the delightful life can somewhere converge.

The image of the northern isle is thus indeed a precondition of the Kantian theory: in one way it works towards the coherence of the system – we meet in it the major theses of the theory, even down to some of its details.[27] But, in a contradictory sense, it reinstates everything which the work of critique tends to empty or to disavow, it cancels the renunciations demanded by the theory. Decoding it, and reintroducing into the discourse its latent meaning, make apparent the troubles of the system.

The island of the Analytic compensates for the recognition of the vanity of regrets for South Sea islands – regrets which belong not to some popular mythology but to the pre-critical practice of philosophy. And one finds this double movement of repudiation and return again in a passage not yet mentioned here. A note in the *Conflict of the Faculties*[28] starts by describing as sweet contradictory reveries the (insular) hopes imagined by Plato, by More's *Utopia* and Harrington's *Oceania*, only to conclude that it is still a duty to think such thoughts!

One might have been afraid; one might have feared having to repudiate this powerful mythology of the learned tradition and to lose, with it, the certainty of the value of learned work itself. But there was no need to worry: 'we shall always return to metaphysics as to a beloved one with whom we have had a quarrel'.[29]

Barthes attributes to language as a whole the paradoxical status of an institutionalization of subjectivity. It is almost in this way that I currently understand the philosophical imaginary: totally philosophical, in so far as it is ruled by the needs and lacunae of the theoretical enterprise it serves – which justifies an intellectualist analysis, a reading which absorbs imagery entirely into the system's theoretical problems but at the same time accommodates its full and particular affective resonance. Here one can give Bachelard's poetics its due: imaged texts are, indeed, charged with intimate valorizations, affects and desires. Bachelard simply overlooked the fact that this affectivity was that of an educated subjectivity and that, for the apprentice philosopher, there are classical images – images in which he or she learns philosophy, as one learns Latin in a Cicero constituted as a reference work, because desire structures itself into the desire to philosophize. Which explains why the imaginary is as difficult to pass on as knowledge.[30]

It is as much possible to have a dialogue of the deaf in a purportedly 'concrete' debate using picturesque comparisons and an abundance of images, as in the 'argued' encounter of two exponents of different knowledge. The ending of the dispute between Socrates and Callicles serves to capture this: Callicles will not accept the images Socrates offers him, filled barrels fail to stimulate his fantasy, or more exactly they mean nothing to him. Just as, likewise, leaky barrels mean nothing to Socrates. Far from constituting a universal imaginary, or a residue of collective popular thought, the Platonic album finds no ready taker: even the fable of Atlantis had to undergo major modifications before becoming a fairly widespread myth. Or, more exactly, it broke up into as many different figures as it found receptive cultural groups.[31]

Let us stress once more that imagery and knowledge form, dialectically, a common system. Between these two terms there is a play of feedbacks which maintains the particular regime of the discursive formation. Philosophical texts offer images through which subjectivity can be structured and given a marking which is that of the corporate body. In turn, the affectivity which is thus moulded sustains the effort of philosophic production and the system of presuppositions which govern the distinction between the thinkable and the unthinkable for a consciousness attached to settled loves. But since the relationship between the content of these two modes of writing is always marked by negativity, there can be no question of reducing one term to the other. Philosophical work is not the mechanical prolongation of fantasy – nor vice versa. Hence there can be no question of returning to the views of Lanson, even in a psychoanalysed version,[32] nor of joining hands with a monism of the *logos* which posits that even what I dream is the effect in me of the metaphysics I live by. The idea of a dialectical solidarity between reverie and theoretical work must, in my view, necessarily lead to a study of the particularism of a social minority and its problematic encounter with other thought and other discourses – and also to an appreciation of the tension between what one would like to believe, what it is necessary to think and what it is possible to give logical form. There is no closure of discourse, discourse only ever being a compromise – or bricolage – between what it is legitimate to say, what one would like to contend or argue, and what one is forced to recognize.

A last word about the restricted range of circulation of the learned imaginary. This range is far from being rigidly fixed, and it may happen that a learned fable leaves the limited circuit where it has been produced and long consumed, suddenly to assume meaning and value in a more global cultural field. Island enthusiasts will excuse me for once again choosing an insular example, that of the constitution of the character of Robinson Crusoe. In the very beginning there was an Andalusian *Riçala*, a philosophical novel written in the twelfth century by Ibn Tufayl.[33] The seventeenth century saw the enthusiastic reception of a Latin translation of this novel, published under the title of 'Philosophus Autodidacticus'.[34] Three English translations were made from this in the space of twenty years (the second was probably the one used by Defoe), followed by a French version. So before the real adventure of the Scotsman Selkirk, stranded on the island of Juan

Fernandez,[35] a philosophical *robinsonnade* fashionable among the intelligentsia had created the mythic framework within which this adventure could be at least partially reinterpreted. In fact this framework is still remarkably legible in Defoe's novel: before his shipwreck Robinson Crusoe was 'the most hardened, unfeeling and profane of sailors',[36] which is saying a good deal; his stay on the island leads him from moral unreason to wisdom, and brings him into contact with God; when he returns to England, one of his first acts is . . . to write a book of philosophy.

As an autodidactic initiation into wisdom – if such is the benefit of Crusoe's stay on the island – Defoe's novel remained very close to the philosophical figure which partly inspired it.[37] Yet it had a diffusion which no philosophical text has ever known; it became in the proper sense a popular book. Through such intermediaries there is sometimes a passage of learned images into common culture – culture shared, that is, by wider social groups. However, it is highly doubtful whether this should be viewed as a form of cultural imperialism.[38] In its trans-mutation into an adventure story, the fable of Ibn Tufayl is considerably modified. One may also suppose that the reasons why this narrative canvas was adopted by a different public are not necessarily the reasons why the 'original' had been produced and appreciated among the original circle of listeners. More generally, it seems doubtful to me whether any political or social force has ever had the power to make any circle of listeners whatsoever adopt a cultural product which did not answer a *question* meaningful to that social group. It was not coercion by Jhdanov's cultural apparatus that caused Jules Verne to be taken up by the Soviet peoples. The influence of the economic and social situation created by Stalinism would be another matter.

There is no reason for postulating that 'dominant imaginary is the imaginary of the culturally dominant class' – even supposing that there is such a thing as a 'culturally dominant class'[39] – just as there is no reason for interpreting Plato's reutilization of certain elements of Greek mythology as a 'survival', a residue of popular thought. If no inertial influence of 'affectivity', no lingering pull of a 'popular soul', has ever been a cause of the survival of a so-called 'popular mythology' in the field of learned productions – if, that is, we reject this ethnocentric temptation to attribute the shameful face of philosophy to an Other – we must be equally on guard against the converse, equally philo-sophicocentric proposition which regards 'popular culture' as a by-product of the degradation of products of learning.

2

Daydream in *Utopia*

It is possible that *Utopia* is a political work 'showing by which causes European States are corrupt'. It may be a 'treatise on the best constitution of a republic'. It may be a serious book. But it is also a daydream and, as such, a thought in the service of a far from political desire. Here the private man is speaking, an individual is soliloquizing, the servants having been strictly instructed to keep intruders out. It is an after-dinner dream, an 'afternoon discourse' in a closed garden.

I refer here, of course, to Book II of *Utopia*, in which Raphael, at More's request, describes 'the fields, the rivers, the towns, the men, the customs, the institutions and the laws' of the happy island of Utopia. And it is indeed a description, not an analysis. There are far more images than concepts in Book II; and the geography of the island is as important in Raphael's account as the consideration of its institutions. That is why I propose to analyse the imaginary material this dream works with – and who knows whether, beneath these images, we may not find a philosophy with nothing politicial about it at all.

Utopia is an island, but a very particular island:

The island of Utopia containeth in breadth in the middle part of it (for there it is broadest) two hundred miles. Which breadth continueth through the most part of the land, saving that little and little it cometh in and waxeth narrower towards both the ends. Which fetching about a circuit or compass of five hundred miles, do fashion the whole island like to the crescent moon. Between these two horns the sea runneth in, dividing them asunder by the distance of eleven miles or thereabouts, and there surmounteth into a large and

wide sea, which by reason that the land on every side compasseth it
about and sheltereth it from the winds, is not rough nor mounteth
not with great waves, but almost floweth quietly, not much unlike a
great standing pool, and marketh wellnigh all the space within the
belly of the land in the manner of a haven.[1]

In the standard French version, the Latin original 'circumjecta
undique terrae prohibitis ventis' is translated as 'the adjacent lands,
stretching out like the tiers of an amphitheatre, break the fury of the
winds'.[2] Of course many modifications of More's text were made by
different publishers in the sixteenth century. I have never found,
however, a Latin edition which authorizes the use of the word
'amphitheatre'. Yet it is not out of place here. What in plane geometry
figures as a crescent moon becomes in three-dimensional geometry a
theatre. If we stop at the image of the crescent, this description has to be
connected with the cult of the moon which More mentions later on.
Geography would then take on a mystical meaning. But the theatre
image is more fundamental, even if it is held back, arising in the
reader's imagination only when More mentions the lands which break
the wind. An amphitheatre is completely closed – a crescent is not.
There is also a feature that distinguishes the crescent shape from the
antique theatre: the theatre has a back wall. But such a wall exists:

> The forefronts or frontiers of the two horns, what with fords and
> shelves and what with rocks, be very jeopardous and dangerous. In
> the middle distance between them both standeth up above the water
> a great rock, which therefore is nothing perilous because it is in sight.
> Upon the top of this rock is a fair and a strong tower builded, which
> they hold with a garrison of men. Other rocks there be lying hid
> under the water, which therefore be dangerous.

The back wall is therefore represented by the line of the sandbanks, the
rock of the citadel and the reefs. It is indeed a rampart, represented on
the symbolic level by the visible rock, and on the level of actual efficacy
by all the invisible parts. The symbolic level seems to have the upper
hand on the illustration which accompanies the Basle edition: the rock
on which the citadel stands occupies the whole entrance to the gulf,
which itself can hardly be seen behind it.
    The island image and the theatre image are, in a way, alike, in that

both are closed spaces, but the theatre image conveys the idea of closure much more strongly. An island is surrounded by sea, and the sea invites navigation. The barrier created by the sea is not a final one, for 'man, finding himself in the middle of this infinity, is given courage to go beyond the limited'.[3] An island has a present and visible exterior, which is not the case with a theatre. However, the combination of the island and theatre themes tends to prove that the notion of closure and the denial of exteriority form an important aspect of the work. If this were not so, More would not have felt the need to dwell so much on Utopia's insularity. But the theatre image reveals another latent factor, which I shall try to explore in a moment.

For there is more to this imaginary geography than the notion of closure. If, for an island, the sea represents exteriority, then, for Utopia, the outside is inside. The sea is not around the island, it is present only in the form of the inland gulf. Utopia is like a Leibnizian monad. In Leibniz, no influence is exerted by a created substance upon another substance, and our inner feelings are but dreams well attuned to external beings. In Leibniz, too, the outside is inside and the monad can be viewed as a little theatre, a world of its own.

The inland gulf is, as we have said, a stage. Now in a theatre the stage is the interior representative of exteriority, since what takes place upon it is supposed to take place somewhere else and at another time. If the gulf is a stage, a space for performance, then what is happening on it? Nothing, apparently. More says, it is true, that this basin 'to the great commodity of the inhabitants enables boats to move about in all directions', but he immediately adds that the narrow entrance to the harbour is impassable, so that its function as a harbour seems to remain only a possibility. Nowhere in More's book is the gulf described as crowded with ships.[4] This calm and peaceful water, this tranquil lake, does not suggest the fresh breeze propitious to trade and navigation, but rather Narcissus's pool, whose surface would be dulled by the least breath of wind. The inland lake is not a harbour but a mirror, and what is performed on the stage is the life of the island: the adjoining land overhangs the pool and gazes at itself therein, like the moon in the water.

But it is time now to ask what is at issue in this geography, what desire is revealed by this daydream? The Utopians live in the best form of commonwealth. Now among this people, who live in perfect harmony, a heated debate once arose: a debate about philosophy. In brief, Utopians divide bodily pleasures into two kinds. The first is pleasure coming from without: all those pleasures felt when something stirs our senses with a certain efficacy, when an object acts agreeably on the sensibility. The second is inner pleasure, the enjoyment of a quiet and tranquil state of the body in undisturbed good health, an ease unrelated to any external pleasure. What was this debate about? A few Utopians claimed that this second, autarchic pleasure did not exist, because it could not be perceived. Some claimed that a steadfast and quiet health should not be deemed a pleasure, since it does not cause a present and distinct enjoyment to be perceived. The crux of the discussion is the question of whether the healthy man is aware of his state. The answer is yes, but the psychological proof is weak: 'There is no man insensitive enough not to find health delectable.'

My interpretation of this would be as follows. What More is unable to read where it is written in the minute characters of the individual soul, he reads instead in the large characters of the commonwealth. For the definition of health as a stable, perfect equilibrium of all the parts of the body has its equivalent in the political harmony of the island. The question thus becomes: is an island with the best possible constitution, an island living in political harmony, aware of its state? To this question, which is never explicitly formulated, imaginary geography gives a positive, if indirect answer: the island is aware of its harmony because the island is a theatre, the stage of which is a lake, and reflected in this lake it perceives its state. It has a mirror (*lacus stagnans*) in its belly (*alvum*).

Such are the dream and the anxiety underlying More's work: a dream of the self-sufficiency of the subject, expressed through the economic autarchy of the island and the closure of its space; but a disquieting question soon arises: does internal harmony give rise to voluptuous perception? One could imagine that it causes only an emotionally neutral state – indeed, a 'stupor' or lethargy. Such a fear is phantasmagorically appeased by the presence of the tranquil lake, the 'eye of the world', as Bachelard would have put it.

Utopia is a spectacle, but one in which only the self is staged; any spectacle performed for others, exhibitionism, or dramatic representation of an Other is rejected. Exhibitionism is criticized through the condemnation of the Anemolian ambassadors. Anemolia is 'the country of the wind', and More does not like the wind. The island has high ground sheltering the inland gulf. Its houses have glass windows to 'keep the wind out'. Sometimes an oiled material is used instead of glass to 'let the light in and keep the wind out'. Why does More expatiate on such details?

The wind is the great foe because it always comes from somewhere else; it is a foreigner *par excellence*. And the wind may be, like the sea, an inducement to travel, to leave oneself. The Anemolian ambassadors (pleonasm indeed!) could not be welcomed in Utopia. Actually these ambassadors are like stage characters. Their costume is magnificent; they are clad in cloth of gold. Their pomp is meant to catch the eye, to attract attention. Their outfit is as showy as a buffoon's.

Philosophy's attitude to the theatre is always ambiguous: part acceptance, part refusal. Thomas More uses the image of the theatre to think something: political perfection can be perceived; but what he borrows from it is immediately denied, and the theatrical model is rejected through the condemnation of exhibitionism. Thus the theatre is diverted from its direct meaning, to become a metaphor; it is accepted as a model only after it has been crossed out and corrected.

Besides, the Anemolian ambassadors' exhibitionism is useless, since the island is blind. 'Amaurosis' is an old medical term which in More's time denoted a kind of blindness. (In the Bible, Raphael – the name of More's narrator – is an angel who leads Tobias on a journey through which the father's blindness is cured. But the equivalent blindness in More is England's, not Utopia's.) So Amaurot, the capital of Utopia, is 'amaurotic'. This name might be taken in a mystical manner; God is said to be 'eternal, unknown, inaccessible to the human mind'. Before Raphael's arrival Utopians had not heard of Christianity; they have not received the Christian Revelation. Is not this island, in a way, closed to God? The entrance to the gulf is so difficult that one cannot pass through it without the help of a Utopian pilot who fetches one from outside. If God were outside, if he were perceived as an exterior power, Utopia would be atheistic. But God is within. The temples of Utopia are rather dark; this was not done out of architectural ignorance but, so it is said, on the advice of the priests who thought that 'overmuch light doth disperse men's cogitations whereas in dim and doubtful light they be gathered together, and more earnestly fixed upon religion and devotion.'

Amaurot is blind so as not to allow exteriority to distract it from itself. And it is in itself, through meditation and no doubt reflection too, that Utopia finds God.[5]

Exteriority is rejected once again; a mystical interpretation seems then only partial: the amaurosis of Utopia is general. Blind to all things, it contemplates itself, but only metaphorically.

The second book of *Utopia* is thus another version of the myth of Narcissus. But what kind of narcissism is involved here? Psychoanalysis has taught us to distinguish two sorts (and had it not provided this distinction, there would be reason to cite it here). One is primary or non-object-related narcissism, which is characterized by a total lack of relation to the environment. Pleasure is produced by the mere relation to the body of the self, without external stimulus. The other is secondary narcissism, which relates more precisely to the myth of Narcissus and is a form of love attached to the image of the self.

In the passage about pleasure one cannot doubt that primary narcissism is at work. More, of course, admits that there is, besides autarchic pleasure in the inner harmony of the body, a form of external pleasure, caused by the present action of an object on the body; eating and drinking when one is hungry or thirsty are the examples he gives. But the first type acts as a basis for the other: health is the foundation and basis of true happiness; without it no voluptuous pleasure is possible; it must be added that the Utopians think that fleshly pleasures should be valued only in so far as they are necessary and useful to life, 'considering that such things are not delightful in themselves' but only as the means to preserve health. Without health no pleasure is possible, and things are enjoyable when they restore health; narcissistic pleasure is at once the foundation and the purpose of the other form of pleasure; which amounts to saying that the latter does not exist. Exteriority is efficacious only when called upon by interiority; and to reach the island, one has to be guided by a Utopian pilot.

However, if the island gazes at its reflection in the water, then it seems that the classical image of Narcissus prevails and that the island is in love with its own reflection. But the gulf is an inner one, and the notion of theatrical staging is rejected. No staging of an other, no exhibitionism; there remains only the self-show, but this is not even a show: the mirror is not before but within. Although the imaginary geography seems to establish a form of secondary narcissism, this is only as a way to justify the primary narcissism which More was unable to found through theory.

This interpretation may involve greater issues than might be apparent. If More's work is a dream, if its focus is a certain conception of happiness, then it is clearly not a work of politics. Happiness is not found here in relation to the world, but in the relation to oneself. Hence the world around one does not matter. If the subject is self-sufficient and blind to everything, what will it care about politics? The private man is speaking here, the solitary man whose introversion verges on autism. Friendship is not even mentioned.

But things are not so simple. Utopia produces all that it consumes. In a certain way Utopia is an image of the individual, but the image fails in that the individual is, on the contrary, not materially self-sufficient: health, this source of voluptuous pleasure, must be constantly restored. The mere act of living, as Gide said, is eminently voluptuous, but as soon as the umbilical cord has been cut, one has to eat in order to live. I mention the umbilical cord for a reason: the island of Utopia was once linked to the continent by an isthmus. The founder, Utopus, had it cut through. Amaurot is *in umbilico terrae sita*, situated in the navel of the land. After the cord was cut, Utopia survived as an autarchy: what nature denies the individual, More grants his island.

But the individual cannot be independent, he has to eat, and this is why the central problem of Book I of *Utopia* may be not so much the injustice or absurdity of English institutions as simple poverty. The institutions are unjust because theft is punished by death; but theft exists only because of poverty: the real injustice is that of a social organization that causes starvation. It is not from the world that I derive my pleasure, but the world can deprive me of the enjoyment of myself: by this indirect way we pass from More's dream to his practical criticism: that is to say from Book II to Book I, following the chronological order of composition. But one has a right to deplore the negative aspect of this passage: social life can have only a negative effect, that of interfering with the relationship of the subject to himself, and this is why one has to concern oneself with the world. If his conception of pleasure had been different, More might have had a different conception of politics. Social life can of course steal my inner tranquillity; but it can also provide me with something better than tranquillity.

But it would, after all, be showing a lack of historical sense to reproach More for missing a dialectical reversal and presenting the best of commonwealths in such a light that it appears no more desirable than a mere state of nature. But had the idea of a 'state of nature' been invented then? Or should we say that it is through enquiries like More's that this concept came to emerge? More's daydream perhaps inaugurated more than could then be foreseen.

3

Galileo or the Supreme Affinity of Time and Movement

It is in obscurity and confusion that thought progresses.

For this study of the problem of time in Galileo, I shall extensively raid the work of Koyré[1] – not only for his conclusions but also, or so I would like to think, for his perspective. Hence this epigraph.

The speed of a freely falling body is proportional to the elapsed time. $V = gt$ is a formula which seems simple and clear, a law that can be taught to children. One of the aims of this study will be to show the difficulties encountered, in the earlier part of the seventeenth century, in establishing and afterwards accepting this law. Such difficulties are frequently glossed over by triumphalist histories of science, which repeatedly fail to mention the wanderings, failures and errors of those whom it is deemed necessary to treat as heroes. Where a problem develops, only those instances where positive is added to positive are remembered. Thus if one takes, for example, Mouy's *Manual of Logic* or Lalande's *Lectures on the Philosophy of the Sciences*,[2] when we look up Galileo's name in the index we are inevitably referred to the trio of Galileo, Torricelli and Pascal, and to the question of atmospheric pressure. Primary rationalism is even more manifest in Mouy's catalogue of modes of discovery in the physical sciences. Galileo serves to illustrate the fifth of these, that of 'simplicity accepted on grounds of likelihood': 'It is a well-known fact that falling bodies accelerate. The simplest form of this acceleration is a constant one. This is what Galileo recognizes.'

Certainly. But this was neither the difficult nor the revolutionary part of Galileo's achievement, since constancy has always counted as a characteristic of intelligibility. Besides, this principle of constancy is in no way violated by the false law of motion: 'When a certain distance has been travelled, movement has a certain intensity. When twice the distance has been travelled, the speed is double. When the distance is triple, it is triple; and so on.' This is very simple too. Keeping, in the 'story' of a discovery, only to things that are transparently clear, to simplicity and likelihood, is to be almost sure of missing the point. The question concerning us here is the treatment of time as a parameter, and I shall attempt to show that the inclusion of time in the formulation of a law was a difficult step to take in Galileo's time, even if it seems self-evident to us. Thus the guiding principle of this work is the (by now banal) idea that what is evident or easy to accept is historically variable, that the 'simple' is simple only within a certain system of constructed and acquired representations.

If one compares the first, erroneous formulations of the law of falling bodies with the 'definitive' law, the heart of the problem can easily be located.

A certain number of savants – among them Galileo at the outset of his work – said that the speed of a body was a function of the distance it fell.[3] A Bachelardian epistemology might read the origin of this error as a misinterpreted intuition, a knowledge which immediately functions as an obstacle. When a body strikes the ground, the higher it falls from, the greater its impact and the greater its speed. One might perhaps stop there for an explanation of the error. But one should always mistrust anything attributed to so-called immediate experience, just as one should be suspicious of explanations in terms of what is supposedly easiest to imagine. One can certainly say – and Koyré indeed said this of Galileo – that it is easier to imagine things in space, and in terms of space, than to think of them as in time. But a thing is easy when it fits into pre-existing structures – and supposedly immediate experience is always lived through a system of beliefs and things already known, through conceptual schemes, and through a language.

So Leonardo, Benedetti, Varro and the earlier Galileo treat as relative to space, to the distance fallen, what ought to have been treated as relative to time. I am inclined to infer, beneath this error, all the weight of a cultural tradition which extends – broadly speaking, and allowing for the blurring unavoidable in such vast synthetic generalizations – from the Greeks to the Middle Ages: the double tradition of a negative valuation of time and a positive valuation of space.

So far as the devaluation of time is concerned, it is best not to look here for evidence of a permanent devaluing theory, but rather for the signs of a certain implicit conception of temporality. One might already meditate on the mythical figure of Kronos, the god devouring his children: on the scandal of a time which produces, and destroys what it produces. According to Aristotle, popular tradition lays much greater stress on time's destructiveness than on its productivity. Aristotle writes, reporting the common received opinion in *Physics*, IV, 221a:

> We are accustomed to say that time consumes, that everything ages under the action of time, but not that one learns because of time, or becomes young or beautiful; for time in itself is rather a cause of destruction, since it is the number of movement, and movement undoes what is.

The Platonic tradition is completely in harmony with this view. The dignity of philosophical study consists in turning the spirit away from that which changes towards that which is: that which is immovable and eternal. The world of becoming is the world in which things are subject to generation and corruption, and the becoming of things is the mark at once of their unintelligibility and of their imperfection:

> ... the past and future are created species of time, which we unconsciously but wrongly transfer to eternal being; for we say that it 'was', or 'is', or 'will be', but the truth is that 'is' alone is properly attributed to it, and that 'was' and 'will be' are only to be spoken of becoming in time, for they are motions, but that which is immovably the same for ever cannot become older or younger by time; nor can it be said that it came into being in the past, or has come into being now, or will come into being in the future; nor is it subject at all to any of those states which affect moving and sensible things. (*Timaeus*, 37e ff.)

The only time which is saved is astral time, 'days, nights, months and years', a circular time which returns always to identity and is thus the 'moving image of eternity'. The demiurge creates time and the heavens together, and creates the planets 'for the determination and guard of the numbers of time'. The only philosophically recognized time is therefore astral time, accepted because it is circular and identified with the trajectory of moving things.

Aristotle, for his part, asks whether time even exists:

> . . . that first of all it absolutely does not exist, or has only an obscure and imperfect existence, may be supposed from the following; one part of it has been and is not more, while the other will be and is not yet . . . now what is composed of non-being seems incapable of participating in substance. (*Physics*, IV, 217b)

The formula of 219a, 'time does not exist without movement', leads to a conception of time as derivative, especially if juxtaposed with the famous doctrine that time is an affection of movement, which prepares the way for the scholastic definition of time as an accident.

In *Physics*, 219b one finds the best-known definition: time is the number of movement in relation to the before and the after. But to appreciate this definition suitably one must recall the ontological status of number in Aristotle.

> The much-vaunted character of numbers, and of mathematical realities in general, as conceived by certain philosophers who make them the causes of nature, seem to vanish away altogether; for no mathematical object can be a cause in any of the senses of that term. (*Metaphysics*, N, 6)

The *Metaphysics* lays great stress on the fact that number does not exist in separation from perceptible things. To say that time is the number of movement amounts to saying that time does not exist without movement. But that opens up another problem: does not the existence of time depend on the soul? This would lead to its complete ontological disqualification.

> One might find it a difficult question to answer whether, if there were no soul, time would be time or not; for if there is nothing to do the counting, there can be nothing countable, so it is clear that there can be no number either; for number is either that which has been counted or that which can be counted. But if nothing by its nature can count except the soul (and nothing in the soul except the intellect), it is impossible that there should be time if there is no soul, except for what is the subject of time, as when it is said for example that there can be change without soul. (*Physics*, IV, 223a)

One should not forget that Aristotelianism was still alive in Galileo's time, since it remained a contested issue among the proponents of the false hypothesis whether one should say that speed increased with increasing distance from the starting-point or with decreasing distance from the point of arrival: the stone accelerating as it approached its natural place, like a horse which smells the stable. And the Aristotelian conception of time was all the more acceptable because it nowhere contradicted the Christian tradition drawn from Saint Augustine. The standard citation here is the well-known admission of impotence in Book XI: 'What is time? I know well enough what it is, provided that nobody asks me; but if I am asked what it is and try to explain, I am baffled.' I prefer the question in chapter XV: 'My Lord, my Light, does not your truth make us look foolish in this case too?'

To my mind this gives a better idea of the tone of this Book, which has to do with the construction of a series of paradoxes about time which are designed to strip time of all reality, to make time appear derisory, to mock any idea of time as real. The passages where Augustine explains why one cannot speak of long or short times irresistibly reminds one of a certain tortoise which Achilles was unable to catch. The result of these paradoxes is to accord time an ontological status which is, precisely, paradoxical: 'We cannot rightly say that time *is*, except by reason of its impending state of *not being*.' For if the present ceased to annul itself by becoming past it would no longer be time, but eternity.

The two salient points emerging from this are, first, that time exists only in a derived manner: there can be no time where there is no created being. Before God created heaven and earth, there was no time. And second, that time is fundamentally a subjective mode:

> There are three times, the present of pasts, the present of presents and the present of futures. These things are in the soul; I do not see them anywhere else. The present of past things is memory, the present of present things is direct perception, and the present of future things is expectation. (Chapter XX)

Lastly, concerning the representation and devalorization of time in Antiquity, we may note that when Plotinus writes that every thought is timeless, he is only theorizing an implicit primacy given by all Greek thought to contemplation. See, for example, *Metaphysics*, L, 9.

If time was regarded as a factor of non-intelligibility, a subjective mode of the apprehension of things, etc., space tended conversely to be positively valorized. I say 'tended to be' rather than 'was', since one could easily find counter-examples. One ought, for instance, to examine the Greek philosophers' debates on the existence of the void, which covered the issue of whether one should speak in terms of space or of place. It is clear that in the seventeenth century, when an effort is made to valorize time, this is done by making it akin to space; as witness this remark in a letter from Leibniz to Clarke: 'I have noticed more than once that I was treating space as something purely relative, like time'; and, conversely, Gassendi who, in order to save time, insists on the 'remarkable parallelism of time and space'.

With these exceptions, it is generally space which is made a principle of order and a factor of intelligibility, and this for the 'simple' reason that geometry exists; for in speaking of valorized space one must of course specify that the space in question is that of Euclidean geometry. The importance of mathematization needs to be emphasized here, not only on its own account but because of the way it makes possible a univocal model of space. Leroi–Gourhan, the historians of art, and Bachelard (to mention only them) have shown that there is a plurality of ways of representing and organizing space, or more exactly that there is a plurality of spaces. For example, the space of medieval painting is characterized by its non-homogeneity: high and low, left and right are invested with different symbolic values. The space of some mythologies is non-continuous; when Tristan goes from Cornwall to Ireland, he loses consciousness during the voyage, there is a hole in space, so that Ireland becomes a utopian or atopian place outside the main space of the myth; Bachelard has shown that the acts of entering and leaving a place are not operations which can be treated as identical except for a directional sign. When an individual imagines his own place in society, his operation is more one of topology than of metric geometry; and when he builds a house he is in a space whose homogeneity he affirms by shifting bricks around, but which is far from isotropic. Such examples could easily be multiplied.

The importance of Euclidean geometry is thus not just that it mathematizes space but that it imposes *one* definite model of space against the chaotic plurality of representations of different spaces. Now, before time has been scientifically defined, before *a* time has been defined for purposes of science (we shall see later what this entails), a multiplicity of representations can compete with one another. If one takes the example of a Christian individual in modern times, one can say that he is involved in:

— an astral, circular time similar to the one in Plato which we mentioned above, which is also a sacred annual time since the religious year repeats a cycle of feast-days.

— the ascending and descending time-profile of human life, as described in various proverbial formulae.

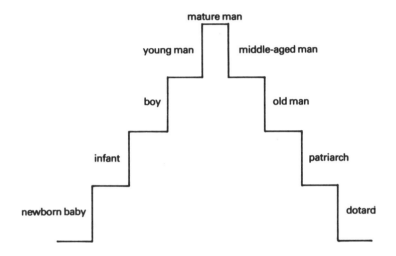

— a historico-religious time which is more complex and dialectical since the Fall is designated as '*felix culpa*', the happy fault which gained us our Redeemer.

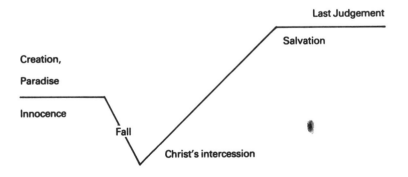

– in a time of varying speeds, passing sometimes quickly, sometimes slowly: as Shakespeare has it, time passes like a stately senator for the lover awaiting his love, at a march for the soldier awaiting the fray, at a trot for the man growing old, and at a gallop for the condemned man waiting to be hanged.

– and sometimes even a time which obeys no law of addition. As Jankélévitch says in *The Metaphysics of Boredom*, one wonders how such short years can be made out of such long days.[4]

One begins here to understand more easily how time could have seemed a challenge to rationality and provided a theme of reverie; one sees also that none of the above varieties of time could be of the slighest use to physics. One may as well say straight away that what caused a break with these reveries was the social diffusion of instruments for measuring time. I do not think the gradual perfecting of the clock can be seen purely as a form of technical progress, since that would mean assuming that the instruments were improved in order to achieve a purpose clearly envisaged beforehand. I would say rather that the perfecting *and diffusion* of the instruments contributed towards imposing a certain conception of time.

If I am right in saying that the Graeco-Christian tradition viewed time as a non-intelligible thing and a factor of non-intelligibility – while geometry, on the other hand, conferred a great dignity on space – it would follow that when it came to formulating the law of acceleration of falling bodies, it would have seemed perfectly '*natural*' to think this in terms of space, and stunningly unnatural to relate acceleration to time alone. To make time a parameter of speed meant breaking with solidly rooted mental structures. But – and this is a point on which one ought to dwell – this break which takes mechanics into a modern era is not made in the name of a rational principle but rather of one which is extremely obscure and suspect: that of affinity. I cite the text in the original Latin first, since it is its literal content which demands commentary:

Dum igitur lapidem ex sublimi a quiete descendentum nova deinceps velocitatis acquire incrementa animadverto, cur talia addimenta simplicissima atque omnibus magis obvia ratione fieri non credam? Quod si attente inspiciamus, nullum addimentum, nullum incrementum magis simplex inveniemus quam illud quod semper eodem modo superaddit. Quod facile intelligemus maximam temporis atque motus affinitatem *inspicientes.*

Therefore, when I observe that a stone which falls starting from rest continually acquires additional increases in speed, why should I not believe that these increases take place in the simplest and most obvious manner? If we examine the matter carefully we find no addition or increment more simple than that which repeats itself always in the same manner. Now just what this manner is we will easily understand if we fix our attention on the extreme *affinity of time and movement*.[5]

Now affinity is a two-sided alchemical notion: it can designate either the analogy between two things, or their aptness to combine. For example, there are three analogous series: those of the planets, the metals and the organs:

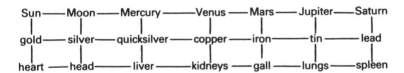

Thus the heart has an affinity with gold and the sun, affinity being a term-by-term relationship between elements of the three series. In these cases, affinity is analogy. But two substances also have an affinity when they attract each other and combine well. This theme has echoes extending as far as Romantic literature – and everyone knows it is a bad sign for a notion to find its place interchangeably in a scientific text or a novel. I allude to Geothe's *Elective Affinities*, where the *'laws of the chemical world'* are all the more easily transposed to cover human sentiments, since affections have already been lent to chemical bodies: *'Think only of lime, which evidences a great inclination, a decided desire for union with acids of every kind'*.[6] The concept of affinity seems to us a double one, but alchemical thought habitually conjoins these two modes, analogy and combination: things unite by analogy because like attracts like. Here, for example, is how the 'attraction' of iron and magnet is explained: 'The nature of iron is thus inclined towards the nature of the magnet, because iron carries in itself a resemblance to magnetic nature.' In the accompanying note I attempt an explanation of this unacknowledged duality.[7]

In correctly formulating the law of acceleration, Galileo is thus invoking an extremely obscure form of relation inherited from a tradition of entirely non-scientific speculation. But it is this notion of affinity which makes the choice of the time parameter psychologically possible and plausible. There is already time within movement, since speed is measured in terms of time. Hence it is normal that time should mix well with movement: like attracts like. One does not need to put Galileo on trial for resorting to occult and mysterious forms of reasoning in order to make sense of this change of perspective. I am tempted to say that it could not have happened any other way. Once one has seen the pre-eminence of space and the low standing of time in Western thought, one can see what an upheaval was entailed by saying that $v = gt$. The idea was so impossible to fit into the mental structures of the time that one can understand its having been formulated in a vocabulary bordering on the mystical – and this is for me a powerful reason not to follow Bachelard in his description of the decrepitude of scientific ideas.

Bachelard says[8] that in the course of time, by acquiring a sort of familiarity, the scientific idea gradually loses it 'vector of abstraction', overloading itself with psychological concreteness and amassing an excessive repertoire of analogies, images and metaphors. Galileo's case might lead us to say, instead, that a revolutionary scientific idea may, precisely because of its unfamiliarity, be born among metaphors and confusion and attain its 'fine abstract pointing' only afterwards, by integration into a scientific system not yet constituted at the time of its initial appearance. Admittedly, Bachelard is probably thinking of the case of constituted science, where problems are posed on the basis of a knowledge, whereas I am looking here only at a moment of beginning.

My study might well stop at this point, since the aim of this chapter was to bring out the astonishing character of this one step in science by showing how Galileo's discovery went against a millennial system of representations and had recourse to formulation in an occult vocabulary. But stopping here would, in the first place, be to play Galileo's own game, telling the story of his conceptual inversion while carefully obscuring the paths it took from what it was acceptable to think to what demanded, 'contrary to all expectation', thought.[9] Galileo's '*Quod facile intelligemus inspicientes*' reads like a precursor of 'Elementary, my dear Watson'. He admits in one of his letters that this discovery cost him great effort; but as far as I know he nowhere provides any information about how he proceeded, which is something which we must nevertheless endeavour to reconstruct if we are to avoid the risk of creating a notion of a 'Galilean miracle' comparable with that of the 'Greek miracle', an idea which is no more than an avowal of incomprehension.

The hypothesis which will probably occur to you[10] is that having first accepted the false law, Galileo tested it experimentally and found that the result did not match its predictions. This hypothesis must be set aside, for two reasons: first because Galileo's experiments, as Koyré very rightly stresses, took place most often only on paper: he represents things in a diagram, and then tries to work out how they happen; and secondly because in order to confront the results of the experiment with the consequences of the law, it would first have been necessary to calculate those consequences. But that was just what Galileo would not have been able to do, since if acceleration were a function of distance traversed the formula would have had to be exponential – requiring, that is, a mathematical tool not yet then discovered; whereas in the case of the time parameter, the formula is a quite trivial second-order equation. The commentators agree that mathematical difficulty was a decisive factor in Galileo's abandonment of the false law. Here the idea emerges that in the development of the sciences, the negative (in this case the incomplete development of mathematics, but in others the impossibility of precise measurement) can work as a positive factor.

Another reason seems important to me in explaining the false law, a reason I will designate by the term 'physicalism'. If indeed mechanics stands in need of the fullest possible mathematization, one can find in Galileo the idea that the laws of mechanics are not reducible to geometry. In the *Dialogue of the New Sciences*,[11] for example, he shows that in geometry one deals only with proportions and not with orders of magnitude. Now one finds that a larger machine, constructed in the same proportions as a smaller one, does not have the same properties of solidity and resistance. This is because there is a specificity of *matter* as such which means that it cannot be reduced to the space it occupies. This understanding of the extra-geometrical character of the physical object probably contributed towards Galileo's abandonment of a viewpoint centred entirely on the *trajectory* of moving objects, for expressing the law of acceleration in terms of the distance traversed amounted to reasoning solely in terms of trajectory.

Lastly, one must allow room for speculation about causes. Galileo is seeking a descriptive formula (cf. the phrases *simplicissima ratione* and *eodem modo* in the text cited above), but he remains preoccupied with the search for explanations. We know that the idea of terrestrial attraction had been formulated a few years earlier by Gilbert, an English physicist whom Galileo greatly admired. Once one refers to a cause, the problem of acceleration is reformulated, since the question now becomes how a constant cause produces a constant effect. The solution consists of saying that if the body accelerates its movement, this is because at each instant (T) it is affected by the same cause, namely attraction, while at the same time retaining all the effect of that cause's operation at moment (T-1). The ideas of conservation and reiteration require expression in terms of time, not of space. Reflections on causes which a positivist epistemology would discount as merely metaphysical would thus seem to have been of capital importance in orientating Galileo's thought and providing its rational kernel.

But all the foregoing remarks have two defects. First, they treat Galileo as an isolated individual, and by presenting only his own distinctive reasons for rectifying his problem they are liable to encourage an idea of genius which offers an easy refuge for ignorance. Secondly, they fail to reach the heart of the problem. It is not enough to trace the route by which it became possible for Galileo to consider time as a parameter; one must also know what species of time this is, and how it came to be constructed. These two failings are interconnected, and what we now need to show, in order to correct them, is how Galileo's revolution constitutes a reduced model or a component of a cultural mutation which exceeds the strict framework of a local problem in mechanics. This is not a trivial problem, and I do not claim to offer here anything more than the sketchy beginnings of an answer.

One may first of all note that Galileo inaugurates the extraordinary attentiveness of modern thought to time and temporal phenomena. History, notions of progress and decadence, questions of evolution, problems of genesis, origin and formation, become privileged objects of intellectual work, escaping the domain of narrative to which they had previously been confined. The immovable and the eternal give way to becoming, and this reversal comes into operation from the beginning of the seventeenth century – not the eighteenth, as is often said. Here are a few indications. Gassendi[12] writes, among other things, that 'Of the things of nature we can know only their history', a formula which is still ambiguous because it is restrictive. But in a fragment of a *Treatise on the Void*, Pascal opposes the realm of animal instinct which 'remains always in an equal state' – in the domain, that is, of the same and repetition – to the reason of man, who 'is made only for infinity'. One should quote this whole passage, since it is remarkably similar to the Galilean formulation: increase of knowledge relates to the fact that man 'retains always in memory the knowledge which he has once acquired', as the stone retains the effect of the impulse it has already received.

Now this continual progress, this mobility of humanity, is positively valued; it is a 'particular prerogative'. One need not underline the revolutionary nature of this passage, but it is worth clarifying its relation with Galileo's work. I do not think a causal argument is required here to the effect that once time has attained scientific dignity, this valorization afterwards takes effect in the philosophical domain also. Nor need one say – though this might be more acceptable – that once a linear, cumulative model of time had been worked out in the field of mechanics, this then came to be transposed into the field of philosophy. For an external element is readily integrated into a system only if the latter already possesses all the means needed to produce it itself. I prefer, then, to say that Galileo, Gassendi and Pascal are joint witnesses to and agents of a more fundamental cultural mutation whose effects are more easily traced than its causes. But I will venture to assert that this linear and continuous model of time – within which specific operations, particularly those of addition, can be defined – is one which was laboriously worked out in a plurality of different domains.

Let us return to the clock. There is a great difference between a clock-face and a sundial. The latter is composed of lines which are non-equidistant, encouraging a non-homogeneous conception of time. One says here 'the first hour', 'the second hour', and not 'one hour', 'two hours', etc.; that is, one defines a relationship of order, not of addition. The clock, in contrast to the sundial, contains in its very functioning a linear conception of time. Sometimes it is an easy leap from technology to theology: Nicholas of Cusa[13] offers a remarkable spatial image, or geometrical representation of the relations between time and eternity:

> Let us not forget to note that when a circle rolls along a straight line it touches it only at one point; its circumference is everywhere at an equal distance from the centre; when a straight line touches it, it

therefore touches it only at one point. From this one may derive another consideration regarding time, which moves, so to speak, in a circle, and whose figure is like the circle. Constituted in some sense by the movement of the heavens, it is the measure of movement. The revolution of time is thus the image of eternity and resembles the revolution of a circle *along an infinite straight line*. Time, indeed, does not subsist in itself, but only through its revolution along the infinite line which corresponds to Eternity. Hence it can and does subsist in virtue of its being tangential at a single point to Eternity.

One need only read 'time' in place of 'Eternity' and one obtains the adequate model for representing a linear, infinite, continuous time, whose homogeneity is guaranteed by the continuous tangency of the circle, and upon which the rotation of the circle measures out a series of equal segments. All these expressions will seem redundancies to a mathematician, but redundancy is permissible when one is seeking to think through the history of representations.

There is still something missing from this explanatory schema: the notion of the capitalization of the past; this notion is not explicit in Cusa's text because here the straight line is the image Eternity; although the straight line is in fact given its orientation in this image by the circle's rotation.

The Galilean law assumes a capitalization of the past, the falling body cumulatively acquiring further degrees of speed, or undergoing a perpetual augmentation of its previous speed. It is correct to say that the law of falling bodies implicitly contains the principle of inertia,[14] since this latter principle explains why the body does not immediately lose the effect produced on it by attraction. But from the point of view I have adopted here, something else can be read in this: a new social use of time. Here again I am not looking for a relation of cause and effect, especially as in the present instance this would lead one into a mechanistic materialism of the most disreputable kind. But one must observe that the social practice of time makes this idea of accumulation transparent.

Let us think of the way a loan at simple interest is defined (I will not talk here of compound interest, since that would again involve exponentials): rate x per cent per annum means interest of x per cent on a one-year loan, $(2x)$ per cent on a two-year loan, etc. Labour hired by the hour obeys the same schema, as do all our practices of rent, hire, etc. It is not difficult to satisfy oneself that this social use of time is a strictly modern one. *The Merchant of Venice* is still used as a reference in commentary on Galileo.[15] Shylock lends 300 ducats for three months. This is a fixed-length loan with a fixed deadline, lacking any idea of a progressive quality of time. Day-labour wages belong, for their part, to a circular conception of time; one receives at the end of the day what is needed to restore labour-power: that is to say, to restore the labourer to the identical state by the following morning. As for piecework wage rates, these operate without any reference to time. I am not an expert in these questions, but I notice that in Molière's *L'Avare* the loan is defined by its rate: that is, in the modern manner.

A modification in the social usage of time took place, similar to the one which can be seen in the Galilean revolution and associated with a technological revolution. This sufficiently attests, I think, the solidarity of a scientific work with a whole culture. This solidarity explains why a school pupil has less difficulty in accepting the rule '1/2 $gt2$' than did Descartes. But it also explains why we have so much difficulty in understanding why the men of the Renaissance had so much difficulty in formulating this law.

A last remark: the divorce in ancient thought between the astral and sublunary worlds was in keeping with the Platonic opposition between circular time and inchoate becoming. If it was left to Newton to declare the identity of these two worlds, it was Galileo who began breaking down the old philosophy by producing a form of time sufficient in dignity to make a sublunary mechanics thinkable.

In trying to show how Galileo arrived at his law in polemical contention with a whole tradition and the quality of strangeness this gave to his thought, I have attempted to demonstrate the sundering force of a scientific discovery. But this sundering must not be thought of in terms of a rigorously scientific break, an act by which the scientific detaches itself radically from the non-scientific, from reverie, the imaginary, the obscure and the confused. The obscure and the confused remain, under the form of the notion of affinity which I have been analysing. Further, it is not only within the scientific field that this break is made; a whole civilization makes a revolution which can be discerned as much outside the scientific field as inside it. But if it is important to insist on the deep linkage which exists between a moment of science and a cultural reality, there is no need to make this linkage into a relation of dependence, least of all one of definitive dependence. I have been examining here an inaugural discovery, an initial move which shifts mechanics into a scientific era, meaning that after Galileo, problems will be posed on a basis of knowledge, within a knowledge, something which is a minimal condition for the autonomous development of a scientific discourse. The break is epistemological not in the way it takes place, but in its effects. But nothing here justifies one in claiming that the autonomous development of scientific discourse is an assured fact from the instant its possibility conditions are in place. For a long time afterwards there will be a place in science for the non-scientific, a place still not necessarily lost for the exercise of a role which is perhaps not always condemned to be that of an obstacle.

4

The Polysemy of Atopian Discourse

A contingent starting-point: the analogy between the composition of *Utopia* and that of *The Fable of the Bees*. Thomas More begins by writing a description of a virtuous island which, if we limit ourselves to classical categories, may be called a fiction, and which becomes Book II of *Utopia*. Then he writes another, second text which can be roughly termed the critical analysis of a reality (the England of his time), a reality against which the fiction is then, but only then, to be taken as a polemic; this text becomes Book I of *Utopia*. Mandeville first writes a fiction, the poem *The Grumbling Hive*, and then seven years later re-publishes it in a new edition comprising a preface, an introduction, a dissertation on the origin of moral virtue and, above all, extensive notes. So, at first sight, both the genre-inaugurating *Utopia*, text and source for the common noun 'utopia', and a work which is explicitly an anti-Utopia[1] share the same property of being double texts.

It is a platitude to remark that the category 'utopia' cannot be properly defined. Is a given description of a marvellous city or reflection on the legitimacy of power to be called a utopia? Is it pertinent to group under the same rubric Rabelais's abbey of Thélème, Plato's *Republic* or the community of Clarens in Rousseau's *La Nouvelle Héloïse*, not to speak of *The Social Contract*, The Declaration of the Rights of Man, or May 1968? The most sensible answer to this sort of question is probably the conventionalist one: a discourse is utopian if it is classed as such by book catalogues and library indexes – that is, by academic

*This chapter originated as a paper written for the conference on Utopian Discourse held at Cérisy-la-Salle in July 1975.

and publishing institutions. Unless, that is, the very vagueness of the
notion ought not to be taken as constitutive for the repeated renewal of
a discourse whose life and utterability depend on its unfixable nature.
My procedure will be to take advantage of this category's lack of
consistence to set it on one side: to construct within its flux, but without
its encumbrance, the formal model of something which I will term an
atopia. It will become apparent, once this model is outlined, that a
number of texts considered as utopian do not fit within it, whereas
conversely a number of texts seldom considered by the critics and never
categorized by them as utopian can be designated as atopian.

More and Mandeville, as we saw, first of all write a fiction and then
effect a *reprise* of their text in a mode which is less fictional, more
theoretical. But I prefer to leave aside the question of chronological
order of composition, which can all too easily lead to a trite psychoanalytical stereotype of fantasy and secondary rationalization or a
return to an opposition cherished by classical criticism: the moment of
inspiration or vision, followed by the moment of work. That procedure
might also fail to distinguish *Utopia* and the *Fable* clearly from a number
of other works which have the same dual quality but whose order of
composition is known to have been the opposite. I am thinking here
first of Plato; the *Republic* was written before the *Laws*, the work which
one can crudely term theoretical before the fiction of the Cretan city.
Moreover, the *Laws* themselves subdivide in two: the first three books
are a critical analysis of existing constitutions, while the description of
the future city begins only in Book IV. Then there is Rousseau. First
comes a theoretical work, *The Social Contract*, and then afterwards a
Projet de constitution pour la Corse.

With More and Mandeville there is a conceptual, analytical and
critical reprise of a prior fiction; in Plato and Rousseau, the reprise is a
quasi-fiction of principles worked out by a critical theory. *Whichever end
one starts from, there always has to be a fresh beginning, without it being possible
to amalgamate the reworking into the initial text.* Thus I shall examine the
question of reprise without concern for the order of priority. The
underlying reason for this is that I want to show that the reprise is made
necessary by the polysemy of the text which was written first. To look
only at texts where the order of composition is from fable to theoretical
reflection (More and Mandeville) and to lay stress on that order would
entail reviving old prejudices about the polysemy of fable: the *mythos*
says too much, and therefore has to be reworked in a conceptual – that

is, univocal – language. I hope to avoid this trap by allowing for the possibility of a bidirectional play of polysemy.

The most readily discernible and explicit function of the reprise is to impose one single reading on the initial text. Mandeville himself explains this: he tells how after the first publication of *The Grumbling Hive*, a pirated edition appeared; he says he is taking up his pen once more to explain clearly what his true intention had been. So one is not surprised to find in the Preface a phrase such as: 'the general design of the *Fable* is to show that . . .' I do not know if there are surviving copies of the pirated edition; one may suppose that this must have been a caricature: a rewriting which highlighted one possible meaning of Mandeville's text. Mandeville's own reprise reflects an analogous purpose: the need to highlight 'the true intention', the authentic design: the *Fable*, by its very nature, is polysemic, it admits of a plurality of readings; the reprise determines for it one meaning at the expense of others – if it is true that every determination is a negation. *Except that the polysemy is maintained, since the original text is not retouched.* (This aspect of the question is surely fundamental and it may well be that the seductive power of the meanings marginalized by the reprise is all the greater, just because these meanings have been marginalized.)

The same is more or less true of *Utopia*. Consider Book II, the only one commonly cited, since More's name is primarily linked to the portrayal of the perfect island. This dominance of the code of political perfection is, moreover, inscribed in one of the titles which More himself gave to his book, *The Best State of a Commonwealth*, a title apparently referring to Book II which describes, among other things, the best of all possible constitutions. When one talks of *Utopia* one seldom has in mind the contents of Book I, yet without Book I, Book II would not have been read as it has. For if we play its own game, if we isolate or insularize Book II without taking account of the first, a plurality of meanings is restored. This is not necessarily or only a description of the best government. It could equally well be a pleasantry in the manner of Lucian, a reverie, a pastiche of Pythagoreanism (as in its abundant mention of numbers), a questioning of Christianity (the Utopians are not Christians), an illustration of the parable of the sower (Utopia is a good ground where the Christian seed sprouts immediately), or again the illustration of a most ancient and very new idea, that of the Antipodes.

I am no partisan of this last reading, and I outline it here only to show its possibilities as a competitor with the others. One could read Book II of *Utopia* as a long metaphor of antipodeity. The Antipodes, a commonplace topic of ancient literature, are a people who live on the earth's underside and do everything upside-down. One finds mention of them almost everywhere: in Plato (*Timaeus*, 63a), Aristotle (*De Caelo*, IV), Strabo, Cicero (*Second Analytics* and *De Finibus*, II), Quintus Curcius, Seneca, Virgil, Plutarch, etc. The term is connected with a solar myth (the Antipodes live by night and sleep by day) – a mytheme which also occurs in Book II of *Utopia* – and with frenzied search for pleasure: it is used familiarly to mean revellers and sleepwalkers: the question of pleasure has an important place in Book II of *Utopia*. So this is an old idea, but also a new one, since in 1516 Magellan proposed his voyage, which would be the first circumnavigation of the world. At the moment when More is writing, the notion of Antipodes is becoming a *geographical* one. Everything is indeed upside-down in *Utopia*: iron is worth more than gold; the River Anider's name means 'waterless'; eggs are not incubated; future spouses show themselves naked to one another; Utopians take pride in buying their enemies rather than fighting them; burials are an entertainment; there is tolerance; goods are held in common.

I draw together here a set of disparate elements, so as to correct the meaning of each term through that of the others. If one mentioned only tolerance, one might valorize Utopia as morally and politically preferable. If one took only the unincubated eggs or the River Anider, one might put them under the heading of humour and work up a reading like Louis Marin's.[2] If one stresses the fact that Utopian gold is used only for making chamber-pots, one is not far from recollecting that Lenin said the same, and hence inferring a sort of constant of socialist imagery. But bringing all these elements together, one obtains an image of antipodeity. This, at any rate, is a possible reading.

The religious and mystical commentaries are too well known to need further coverage here. The point is, in short, that if *Utopia* had consisted only of its second part, a *de facto* plurality of readings would be possible. But Book I establishes a canonical reading and privileges the political meaning of Book II at the expense of the others: as Book I is *essentially* a critique of the social and political organization of England, a denunciation of private property and the English penal system, Book II is taken as being *essentially* a description of the best possible Republic. By writing Book I, More himself provides a principle for decoding his initial text. Or rather three principles: the code of politics; the code of humorous fiction (indicated by the hero's name, Hythloday, meaning teller of idle tales – a hero who declares his own discourse vain); and lastly the code of religion (the hero's first name, Raphael, alludes to the angel in the Book of Tobit, the guide for a journey after recovered sight; one may likewise note the presence of the Cardinal, and the ample theological discussions in Book I).

On this basis a law of genre is created. In Book II, a multiplicity of codes interweave. But Book I imposes three principles: this is a matter of politics; all this is just a far-fetched tale; religion is involved in the affair. After More, it will suffice to amalgamate these three series to make a utopia, for a text to be recognizable in status and immediately readable according to its genre: there will be no need, in future, for an explanatory note or instructions for use. *The City of the Sun* will be an immediately readable text: the tradition will have been established – which is not to say that Campanella did not copiously gloss his own text.

But if this double writing has the effect of forging a tradition such that it will no longer be necessary to write texts twice, this mode of writing must itself be questioned. More and Mandeville are not isolated examples. There are others, though they are sometimes harder to spot. I have already cited Plato. Beginning with Aristotle (*Politics*, VIII), commentators remark on the differences between the *Republic* and the *Laws*, something which amounts to treating these as comparable texts, two projects for a political constitution. And then surprise is expressed that Plato had two different programmes. Yet they are superimposable only on the express supposition that the *Republic* is wholly orientated towards this constitutional project, that the text is truly a Republic: something which is far from certain. It is because of the *Laws* that the *Republic* is read in this way, disregarding the difference in status and function of the political discourse in the *Republic* from that in the *Laws*. All the same, one can recognize the allusive intercommunication of the two texts.

The opening of the *Laws* tells us that the scene is set in Crete, and that the old men are walking towards the cave of Zeus. These two points allude to Book VII of the *Republic*: the Cretan – that is to say, insular specification of place, reinforced by the mention of Minos and Rhadamanthus, judges of the Underworld – evokes the island of the Blessed where, after death, Minos and Rhadamanthus despatch the heroes and sages. Now in the *Republic*, when the philosopher, saved from the cave, has come to the mountain-top, it is said of him that he believes himself transported within his lifetime to the islands of the Blessed (519c). As to the cave of Zeus, there is nothing original in remarking that it evokes the cave of this same passage in Book VII. There is communication between the two texts at the level of their imagery, but this communication only entitles one to see the *Laws* as a partial reprise of questions raised in the *Republic*, a prolongation of Book VII – a laboured reprise, moreover, since the *Laws* themselves turn out to be a double text, a reprise containing a reprise.

I have already mentioned, within this tradition of double texts, the *Social Contract* and the *Projet de constitution pour la Corse*; these two texts communicate historically, since it was the reference to Corsica in Book II of the *Contract* which prompted the commission from Buttafoco for the *Projet*. Lastly, there is a work which has no concern with questions of philosophical politics, but is identical in form to the others: Kepler's *Somnium*,[3] a science-fiction story which the author subsequently 'translated' by fixing its discursive code as that of physics (thus making it into a novelistic version of his *Astronomia Nova*) so as to combat interpretations of this tale as a text on sorcery.

So Plato, More, Kepler, Mandeville and Rousseau[4] are all contributors to a corpus of double texts, each having written a first text, then effected a reprise, writing another text *alongside* the first: the outcome of this reprise, which is not a rewriting, being a double work. One may note that the necessity of this reprise is always masked by anecdote. Thus at the end of Book III of the *Laws* there breaks in, like a *deus ex machina*, the windfall opportunity of the city which is to be founded. If we read *Utopia* in the order it offers itself to be read, then it is only the movement of the narration which carries us over into the second panel of the diptych. Mandeville plays on the anecdote of the pirated edition and Rousseau makes use of the outward circumstance of the commission from Buttafoco. Always an external necessity is invoked, never a recognition of some incompleteness of one or other panel. I shall try, however, to show – though this showing will be no more than a sketch – that there is an incompleteness of meaning in both panels. For convenience, I shall refer to texts which can roughly be distinguished as theoretical, reflexive or general, and whose object is the real, as 'Panel 1', and to texts which deal with some particular matter situated in a spatial or temporal elsewhere, and are more or less fictional in character, as 'Panel 2'. The reprise will be considered as mutual, a reprise of Panel 2 by Panel 1 and of Panel 1 by Panel 2.

Let us look first at the reprise of Panel 2 by Panel 1, which may be called that of the letter by the spirit – to choose, deliberately, categories which are already dubious in their original, juridical usage.

The description (not the theory) of a political system considered the best possible, which I term Panel 2, is never sufficient. Take a city which is to be founded, or an island lost in the unknown. The description of its constitution and social organization corresponds to what jurists call the letter of the law. 'In the senate of Amaurot three representatives of each town meet each year' (More), or 'The judges will be State officials' (Plato) are propositions formally identical to 'Each condemned person shall have their head cut off in a public place'. But legislators are not generally content with these codified measures. The text of every law is preceded by a preamble: a discourse which claims to expound its motives and purposes: 'In the legislator's spirit . . .' This model provides me with a different approach to the question of polysemy. I had initially taken this in its broad sense as meaning a plurality of possible readings of a single text, or even more roughly as a polysemy of the status of the text: political treatise, badinage, caprice on the theme of antipodeity. I find the question posed now in a more precise sense: within the political code itself every measure is polysemic, and this is as much true of More's fictive politics as of the actual politics of a real law. Every legislative utterance is polysemic – that is, from the legislator's point of view, liable to be misapplied. The spirit of the law (the meaning the legislator gives it) does not emerge from its letter. Hence the necessity for an explanatory reprise to state the assigned meaning of the letter.

Take the fact that the Utopians practise the common ownership of goods: not only is this not necessarily a political thesis (it might refer to a Christian tradition drawn from the Acts of the Apostles, or a Pythagorean tradition of friendship: everything should be in common between friends); not only can it be regarded as central only when taken in conjunction with Book I, but furthermore its political meaning is itself made explicit only in Book I, by an argument *a contrario*: when there is no community of goods, there is no equal distribution of wealth, and thus we ourselves produce the robbers whom we will afterwards hang. The political meaning of the community of goods is thus, for More,[5] to suppress the contradictions of ills of social life. This is an incompleteness of the letter, then; it is polysemic, or rather asemic: it has no *one* immediately readable sense; it demands commentary and explanation.

Should one also speak, inversely, of an incompleteness of the spirit or principle delineated by theory? Why is there a reprise of Panel 1 by Panel 2; why must theory be reworked by the image of a fictive application? It transpires that, in the same way as for the letter, there is a polysemy of the principle. At the end of Book I, Raphael presents the community of goods as the only possible remedy: 'I am persuaded that till property is taken away, there can be no equality or just distribution of things, nor can the world be happily governed.' And More, cast in his own person in the dialogue, answers with a series of objections: 'On the contrary, it seems to me . . .' and predicts that the effects of the suppression of private property will be idleness, sedition and murder. Hence the principle is incomplete; it can have effects contrary to the legislator's intention. What particular measures must be taken for it to have precisely the effect expected of it? What particular decrees must be adjoined to it? And, more simply, what are the possibility conditions for the application of a principle such that its effect shall actually be the one intended?

Each panel needs the other to express its own meaning. One must have seen Utopia to be convinced of the possibility of a good usage, a faithful and conformable usage of the community of goods. And one must have seen England to measure the exact scope of this principle, of its precise meaning as an absolute necessity.[6]

But why this dual division, rather than an integration of the two texts? Why is there a separate reprise rather than a revision?

One can read this separation as answering to a pedagogical concern, a concern whose extent will be revealed later. In this respect, Panel 1 serves as a propaedeutic. One might indeed object, against what has been said here, that Panel 2 is not pure letter, since in fact More provides us with the Utopians' commentaries on certain of their own institutions. But apart from the fact that these do not contain a single word about the community of goods – which is described only in its workings (the organization of production and consumption) – any discourse which the Utopians might utter on this would be inaudible for a European. It needs the previous mediation of the critical analysis of English society to lead someone 'who has only false representations of reality' to the right conception of the spirit of the best possible constitution. Panel 2 can only ever preach to the converted. And in any event, the Utopians cannot perceive the indispensable value of the principle which founds their constitution, since they have not suffered under another regime.[7]

But there is a more essential reason. Instead of asking why a propaedeutic is needed for the description of the best possible constitution, let us ask, on the contrary, why, at the moment when the principle is formulated, the question of concrete application is postponed. Panel 1, which declares the spirit of the political project, states the conditions for its necessity. The quasi-apocalyptic description of England matches, on this point, the beginning of Book I, Chapter 6 of the *Social Contract*:

> I assume that men reach a point where the obstacles to their preservation in a state of nature prevail . . . beyond this point, the primitive condition cannot endure, for then the human race will perish if it does not change its mode of existence.

Panel 1 says that a critical point has been reached. Panel 2 gives the possibility conditions for the proper working of the principle. But it then transpires that the philosopher fixes exorbitant conditions to this possibility. In the *Laws*, the Athenian is informed of the plan to found a city; a question immediately arises: where? The only constraint imposed on him, the only limit to his power, is that of the geographical site – and this is already too much. When the site has been described, the Athenian exclaims: 'Alas, what are you saying!'[8]

As though to anticipate Spinoza's criticism,[9] More has taken care to make Utopia an infertile island with difficult natural conditions. But if, as the location for the best possible constitution, one has to have an invulnerable island, providentially colonized by a hero who combines military prowess and wisdom, the necessity conditions (the English contradictions) in no way match these possibility conditions. The same is true for the *Contract*. What makes the social contract necessary is the fact that a critical point has been reached. But what makes its legislation possible is a condition of quite another order – the fact of being situated at an optimum point: being a people who are *already* linked by some union of origin, but have *not yet* borne the yoke of laws; a people who *combine* the simplicity of nature and the needs of society.[10] One is a long way here from the critical point of the social pact.

This disjunction of necessity and possibility makes every atopia a source of unhappy consciousness. It is also what differentiates it from Marxist thought, provided that one reserves the latter epithet for works which deduce possibility conditions dialectically from necessity conditions: for one ought to count among the texts of disjunction such works as Lafargue's *Le droit à la paresse*, for example. By now we are not far from repeating platitudes, such as that Utopia is a chimera located in the break between the ought-to-be and the possible. But what interests me is to correlate this truism of the utopian character of Utopia and the question of its dual character. I have tried to link this latter factor to the polysemy of each panel. But the question then becomes: how is the retroactively corrected polysemy – either of a critique of what is, or of the description of a perfect constitution – characteristic of a whole series of philosophical products relating to politics?

Polysemy is perceived only when no *one* immediate meaning prevails. It is related to a fundamental asemy. Several possible meanings and no definite, precise meaning amount to the same thing, if one accepts the findings of experiments conducted on the perception of blurred images and ink blots. Hence the word 'atopia', which I have ventured to introduce here. *Atopos* means that which has no place, but also that which is bizarre, extravagant, strange. An atopia is a text which cannot immediately be given one single correct meaning by its reader. To return to the juridical comparison: if the promulgation of a law corresponded exactly to a precise demand by the governed, that law would need no preamble, for its *letter* would immediately find its *spirit* in the spirits of the governed; or again, the formal measures would find a content in the desire which had invoked them. Conversely, the polysemic–asemic trait which we have been observing betrays the fact that the text is not directly receivable in its intended univocity.[11]

The thesis of the community of goods necessitates a dual text, calling for commentaries and explanations, because at the beginning of the sixteenth century it has no political meaning. It belongs to a register other than the political (hence the contention that its meaning is mystical); and above all, *in the sense More gives to it* (the suppression of poverty and hence of crime; the possibility of a state organization of production and consumption), it corresponds to no political discourse actually current outside the philosophical sphere. It is atopian relative to actual political discourses, like the heliocentrism of Kepler's

Astronomia Nova, and hence of his *Somnium*, faced with the usual representation of the universe. Hence the necessity for Kepler to explain himself.

A work is atopian if it finds no circle of witnesses or readers already able to receive it. This is to say, also, that it manifests its author's singularity. The text is his own (and he further asserts his mastery of the work by retreiving it into univocity, by operating a reprise of his text) and is shareable only at the cost of a series of mediations. Hence the revealing character of the necessity, which I have called peda-gogical, for an introduction: Marx and Engels do not have to provide instructions for the use of the *Communist Manifesto*. Its political meaning is clear: that is to say, already shared by the group it addresses, the activists of the Communist League. Moreover Marx and Engels do not present themselves in it as authors, but as spokesmen. All these factors go together.

But it is time to say where philosophy has its part in this question. I ask to be granted here that philosophy is a discourse which is con-stantly asserting its own power. It follows from this that in matters of politics, philosophy is the prisoner of a personage, that of the providential and philosophical legislator. The politics of the philosophers is the paternalism of reason. Paternalism expresses the hiatus between governors and governed – something which is revealed also by the preambles of laws. And paternalism is always needing to explain itself. In the story which shows the possible right application of the principle, the legislator is always a foreigner, a fact which reveals the philosopher's aspirations to colonize and become regent of a world of politics which he considers exterior to himself. But when one is a foreigner, one needs an interpreter.

I remarked at the start that we lack criteria for what is properly to be called a utopia, if indeed such a classificatory project is of any interest. By this reflection on the mode of writing of what I call an atopia, I hope to have shifted the problem. Among the host of descriptions of marvellous or ideal cities, some are atopian and others not: for the latter, the question of their meaning does not arise, since there is fantastic or ideological material ready and waiting to invest itself in their images. This is true, for instance, of the Eldorado in *Candide*, or *The Mysterious Island*, where the myth of technological efficiency and the ideology of progress can find ample nourishment. But no one would dream of speaking of the critical value of these texts. Glaucon[12] would have towards them none of that feeling of strangeness which prompts the call for explanation – that secondary explanation which then becomes the site for the critical force of atopia.

5

Red Ink in the Margin

The Invention of 'Descartes's Morality' and the
Metaphors of Cartesian Discourse

I am obliged . . . to beg my readers never to attribute an opinion to me
which they do not find expressly stated in my writings, and to take none,
either in my writings or elsewhere, as true if they do not very clearly see
them deduced from true principles.

(Descartes, Prefatory Letter to the *Principles*)

Is a text wholly innocent of the blunders which commentators, both
artless and eminent, are capable of making about it? There are in the
textual corpus of the history of philosophy a number of remarkable
cases of abduction or misappropriation of meaning whose operation
can be traced and located in the very textuality of the texts. The clue is
always a lexical mutation, whereby commentary ceases to use an
author's own words in order to formulate a concept of his. Thus where
Descartes writes 'I formed for myself a morality *par provision*', later
tradition converts this into 'Descartes's provisional morality' (*morale
provisoire*).

It is a teacher's tic to insist on systematically correcting these
infidelities, castigating the language of the student who talks of the
'world of ideas' in Plato by writing in red in the margin: '*topos!*'.
Similarly when anyone uses the terms 'thesis, antithesis, synthesis' in
talking about Hegel. But the student is not the author of this lexical
abuse. A whole academic tradition has heard the one notion in Plato,
and repeated the other about Hegel. Hence there comes a time when
the question of these mishearings needs to be raised; a time when we
should also question the irritation they provoke in those of us who take
exception to them.

One thing has been said and another heard. Now there are two possible sources of what has been heard, even though the distinction between 'text' and 'reader' may be suspect from the outset. Let us still pose the problem in terms of 'either' and 'or', although the radical form of the disjunction may need to be corrected later: either there is a prejudice in the hearer's mind, a discourse already there, which obstructs consideration of the actual utterance and causes its deformation – in which case we need a Bachelardian reading of the commentary to locate the obstacle which leads to the misappropriation – or it turns out that this is a case of the grandchild betraying its grandparentage, the absent-minded commentator revealing a latent meaning of the text, which the text itself had more or less cleverly occluded. This would mean that a meticulous and diligent reading might not necessarily be the right one, while some more hasty readings might bring to light an interpretation which is doubtless open to refutation but still worthy of consideration.

I take the example of Descartes here as a way of looking at this more general question, which needs to be raised about other authors as well. I shall proceed as follows: after trying to show how what I consider to be a meticulous reading can show the impropriety of the expression 'provisional morality', I shall try to probe the reasons for this misappropriation by the commentators, relating the date of this occurrence to a historical context of ideological conflicts. This has the effect of limiting from the start the tenor of my reference to Bachelard: it is not so much a matter here of the psychoanalysis of an error, as of the philosophico-historical analysis of a conflict. After this, a second reading of Descartes, more global in scope because it takes into account marginalized elements of his discourse (its evasions and images), will seek to show that Descartes is not himself a wholly innocent party to the misappropriation commited on his text. This will make it possible first to situate Descartes's discourse as a double one, open to a double reading because traversed by indecision and slippage; and secondly to situate the diligent and faithful reading, the demand for loyalty to the letter of the text: for if the erroneous meaning is itself latent in the work, this reading repeats the same move made by the writing, occluding once more what is said in the marginalized elements, which is that something is causing problems.

This illustrative study ought further to open up a general reflection: what is the status of rereadings? In the massive output of the history of philosophy, in recent decades a number of rectificatory interpretations have appeared which, grounded in a critique of previous readings, make (or purport to make) visible the truth of the text in the difference, the rectification of commentary's first efforts. These rereadings are generally justified as 'returns to the text': to the letter of the text. One may wonder if this slogan 'back to the text' does not cover a deep ambiguity, so long as the mode and purpose of this return are not spelt out.[1]

One could not look for a better example through which to raise the problem of the history of readings of a text or a work than that of *morale par provision*, since here the lexical slippage towards 'provisional morality' occurs only at a late date; consequently our study will not risk leading us to a banal stereotype of sure progress in the history of philosophy, or 'who reads last reads best'. This is something I wish to demonstrate before embarking on a reading of Descartes which will enable us to identify the misappropriation as such.

No one can claim to have made an exhaustive study of the commentaries on and annotated editions of Descartes's works. One can at most make a few forays into this vast literature. I have consulted the following texts:

The *Recueil de pièces curieuses concernant la philosophie de Descartes*, published by Bayle (Amsterdam, 1684).

The *Éloge de Réné Descartes* by Thomas, a prize-winning discourse for the Academy (1765).

D'Alembert's article 'Cartesianism' in the *Encyclopédie*.

The anonymous collection *Pensées de Descartes sur la religion et la morale*, published by Adrien Le Clere, printer to the Archbishop of Paris (1811).

The Garnier edition of the works of Descartes (Paris, 1835).

The articles on 'Cartesianism' and 'Descartes' in the *Dictionnaire des sciences philosophiques*, published under the direction of A. Franck, 1843 (second edition, 1875).

Victor Cousin's *Histoire générale de la philosophie* (1863).

Bouillier's *Histoire de la philosophie cartésienne* (third edition, 1868).

V. Brochard, 'Descartes stoicien', in *Revue philosophique* (1880).

Boutroux, *Questions de Morale et d'Éducation* (1895).

Hamelin, *Le système de Descartes* (a lecture course given in 1903–4).

A. Espinas, *Descartes et la morale* (1925).

Henri Gouhier, 'Descartes et la vie morale', *Revue de Métaphysique et de Morale* (1937).

There are some large gaps in this list, among them the names of historians commonly consulted as aids to understanding Descartes's philosophy. I was looking for documents, not instruments. But even with regard to documents my method of enquiry involves a very selective sampling. Having observed on the one hand that d'Alembert says: 'he believed it was prudent to prescribe for himself *par provision* this rule . . .'[2] and, on the other, that Hamelin writes: 'the Third Part of the *Discourse* contains, *as is well known*, only a provisional morality',[3] I set out to locate the initial date of the error, by searching forwards from the point where it has not yet been made, and backwards from the point where it has become common currency; and this led me to the last quarter of the nineteenth century. In 1868 Bouillier still speaks of morality *par provision*; in 1880 Brochard speaks of provisional morality. So the result of my study is a picture in two parts, one extending up to 1868, the other from 1880; except for one nuance. After 1880, the terms 'provisional' and 'definitive' are seen as opposites, and thus as posing a problem. Does Descartes let us down? Why did he not write a definitive morality? Why does he finally offer us only, by way of a definitive morality, the rules of his provisional morality? The nuance I mention is exemplified in the 1835 Garnier edition of Descartes's works, which does employ the terms 'provisional' and 'definitive' without, however, opposing them and making a problem of them, since 'provisional morality' is taken here as meaning the germ, the basis of definitive morality.[4]

Apart from this nuance, one can divide the history of the problem into two periods: a first phase up to the last quarter of the nineteenth century, where:

(1) Descartes's few reflections on ethics interest the commentators very little. In the *Pièces curieuses* the concern is chiefly with physics and the problems posed for the theory of the Eucharist by the Cartesian definition of matter. The *Éloge de René Descartes*, despite its conclusion ('I have tried to follow Descartes in all his works'), does not say a word

about morality. Nor, for all its two long articles, does Franck's *Dictionary*. The most paradoxical example is the anonymous collected volume of 1811: its copious introduction deals extensively with the theory of vortices but says nothing at all about morality, which is a good indication of the influence of a certain viewpoint on Descartes, effective even in a preface to a collection of thoughts concerning morality.[5]

(2) When mention happens to be made of the Third Part of the *Discourse*, the summary given of it is in line with my thesis, not only because the expression '*par provision*' is used but because it is indicated that Descartes placed to one side the maxims of morality *together with the truths of faith*, an important detail since, in order to speak of a provisional morality, one must forget that the fate of the maxims is linked to that of the truths of faith – given that no one would dare to speak of a provisional religion.

This first phase is followed by a quite spectacular change of viewpoint: Brochard inaugurates not only the provisional–definitive distinction understood as an *opposition*, but also an extraordinary level of interest among historians of philosophy in this aspect of Descartes's work. Fifty years later Gouhier can give a long bibliography on the question, which even then is not quite complete. For Gouhier covers essentially only publications which specialize in this aspect; but one should add that after the onset of this mutation, all general works on Descartes devote a chapter to this question: to claim completeness, a general study of Descartes *must* henceforth proceed via the Third Part of the *Discourse* and the other ethical texts.

In short, when the question arouses no interest, the texts are rendered with fair accuracy; when it becomes interesting, the errors multiply and soon take hold: there are only twenty years between Brochard and Hamelin, but the thing is already common knowledge: 'the Third Part of the *Discourse* contains, *as is well known*, only a provisional morality'. But if the misappropriation is prompted by the new interest, what is this interest? But first one must show what makes the term 'misappropriation' legitimate.

J'avais déjà fait provision d'un garçon qui sût faire la cuisine à la mode de France . . . (I had already provided myself with a lad who knew how to cook in the French way)[6]

When one asks if an author is innocent of the blunders commentators are apt to make about him, a first rule is to avoid appealing to all the texts at once. My aim is to show that nothing *explicit* in the *Discourse on Method* entitles one to speak of a provisional morality; I shall on occasion juxtapose a few of the other texts with that of the *Discourse*, but not all of them, so as not to force into coherence utterances which one may suspect to be heterogeneous. This will thus be, provisionally of course, a philosophically blinkered reading.

The expression 'morality *par provision*' appears in the *Discourse*. One can establish from a seventeenth-century dictionary that '*par provision*' does not mean 'provisional'. It is a juridical term meaning 'what a judgement awards in advance to a party'; thus one can award *par provision* a sum of a thousand *livres* damages to a plaintiff suing for assault. The *provision* is not liable to be put in question by the final judgement;[7] it is a first instalment. One of Madame de Sévigné's letters (10 July 1675) illustrates this meaning well:

> Feeling a little more oppressed, I judged that I should have myself bled before departing, so as to put this bleeding *par provision* among my baggage.

Obviously it would be absurd to speak of a 'provisional bleeding'. The difference of meaning between 'morality *par provision*' and 'provisional morality' works on two levels:

The expression 'provisional morality' is a devaluing one; it designates something which is destined to be replaced, something probably inadequate, to be invalidated once something better is found: something which awaits its own rejection. Whereas the word *provision* signifies the validity of this morality. There is in this term a positive notion of consumption ('It was ordered *par provision* that he should enjoy such and such a piece of land'; '*provision*: furnishment of things ordinarily consumed in a household, or which are necessarily in a place for the defence or maintenance of a garrison'). *Provision* is that which is, at most, capable of completion, but not withdrawal. Thus there is here a difference of meaning regarding the value of this morality.

There is a difference also in that 'provisional' belongs to the qualitative register, and '*par provision*' to the quantitative. The provisional is replaced by something else; the *provision*, where necessary, augmented.

The morality Descartes prescribes for himself is not provisional; it forms, with the truths of faith, a baggage, a vital minimum stock, at once necessary ('so that I might not fail thereafter to live as happily as I could'[8]) and, if one adjoins to the *Discourse* a passage from the prefatory letter of the *Principles*, sufficient:

> . . . a man who as yet has only vulgar knowledge . . . must, before all else, strive to form for himself a morality sufficient to rule the actions of his life, since this may suffer no delay, and since we must strive always to live well.

As to the value of this morality, Descartes's testimony in the *Discourse* is very clear: the prescription of this morality has two ends, and it attains both of them. Descartes expects two things from it: to live as happily as he can, and to be able to continue to instruct himself: 'The three preceding maxims were grounded only on the design which I had to continue instructing myself.'

The first form of validity of this morality is that it permits one to live in contentment (and the letter of 4 August 1645 to Elizabeth of Prussia says that *each person* may make himself content provided he observes it), and the second that it permits one 'to employ all my life in cultivating my reason and advancing as much as I may in the knowledge of the truth'.

In short, in the *Discourse* Descartes is satisfied, '*content*', with the line of conduct defined by the three or four maxims, inasmuch as to this advance portion of happiness ('to live thereafter as happily as I could') is added the satisfaction given by knowledge of truth acquired thanks to this method:

> I had felt such extreme contentments since I had begun to use this method, that I believed one could have no sweeter or more innocent ones in this life; and discovering every day, through its means, some truths which seemed to me quite important, and commonly unknown by other men, the satisfaction I had of it so filled my spirit, that all else touched me not at all.

The quantitative model explains, in my view, the somewhat particular location of this passage: it is not truly a maxim of the morality *par provision* (hence the Cartesian hesitation: 'three or four maxims'); it is its '*conclusio*': the end, the completion which assures fullness of contentment.

Thus nothing in the *Discourse*, at least in its explicit content (I will return below to the implicit sense conveyed by its metaphors) justifies the devaluation of this morality, or its characterization as a makeshift, a short-term expedient which will have to be reconsidered later on; what Descartes says is not that he will content himself with it for the time being, but that he is content with it.

But one can already notice here two unsettling points. The converse relationship is not theorized: Descartes tells how study and the discovery of the truth bring him extreme contentments, but he does not theorize the value of knowledge as happiness. Further, this Third Part of the *Discourse* effects a striking historical reversal. In classical culture theories of wisdom are, to put it briefly and schematically, discourses on the value of philosophy, based on the idea that the ethics is dependent on theory. One must seek to know because the good life depends on knowledge. But although ethics is dependent on theory, if ethics is the end of speculation then theory is nevertheless itself ruled by its orientation towards ethics. Not only does Descartes separate practice from theory, excluding morality from the enterprise of the Method, but he also inverts the ancient schema of wisdom: to adopt a morality for the purpose of continued learning is to relativize ethics with respect to theory; Descartes adopts a rule of life such as will enable the speculative enterprise to be carried forward.

Here, then, is a first set of reasons, apart from the argument based on the linkage of these maxims to the truths of faith, which casts in question the commentators' use of the term 'provisional'. Let us consider some further reasons.

The habitual sequel to this mistake is a quest elsewhere in Descartes's work for a *definitive morality*: elsewhere and later, at the stage when the method of doubt has done its work. The Prefatory Letter in the *Principles* is often cited on this. Let us continue here our blinkered reading, leaving aside what may be conveyed through imagery. For the imagery here is liable to obscure things: the famous tree (which we will be discussing later on) overshadows the rest of the passage, and it is very often overlooked that this Letter follows exactly the same order as the *Discourse*:

Firstly, a man who as yet has only vulgar knowledge . . . must, before all else, try to form himself a morality sufficient to rule the actions of his life, since this will bear no delay, and we must above all try to live well.

The ordering proposed by the *Discourse*, 'life first, philosophizing afterwards', or rather, 'first live, and live well, so as then to pursue learning at leisure', reappears here. Morality (this time called not *'par provision'*, but necessary and sufficient) is still placed outside of the speculative enterprise but, again as in the *Discourse*, it is made the indispensable condition of that same enterprise.

Further light is thrown on the *Discourse* by the letter to Elizabeth of 4 August 1645. Descartes here refers without hesitation to the *Discourse*.

> Now it seems to me that each person may attain contentment with himself and need nothing else, provided only that he attend to three things which are covered by the three rules of morality I put in the *Discourse on Method*.

Not only is the validity of the morality in the *Discourse* reaffirmed and generalized (*'each person'*), but Descartes does this without the least abashment. If the *Discourse* had contained a provisional morality, and so promised another, definitive and certain one, Descartes ought to have felt the need to excuse himself for finding nothing better after eight years of work. This is why I cannot agree with Geneviève Rodis-Lewis when she writes:

> Even in 1645, returning to the 'three rules of morality . . . given in the *Discourse on Method*', he seemed still to remain at the provisional stage where knowledge is by no means certain.[9]

Certainly Descartes keeps to the morality of the *Discourse*, a morality established outside the domain of the certain, but in this same letter he explicitly sets the question of truth aside from the search for contentment:

> It is not also necessary that our reason should never err; it suffices that our conscience should testify that we have never been lacking in resolution and virtue, to execute all the things which we have judged the best, and thus virtue alone is sufficient to make us content in this life.

Virtue alone suffices, truth is not necessary: one could hardly be more categorical.

Here are some factual arguments for our rectification, but the most convincing such argument seems to me to be one derivable from d'Alembert's words: 'He believed it prudent to prescribe himself *par provision* this rule . . .'[10]

What seems important to me is the order of these words; if someone who spoke a language closer to ours than that of Deseartes could write this, one can conjecture that Descartes could equally well have written: 'I formed myself *par provision* a morality which . . .' , or '*par provision* I formed myself a morality which . . .': this is to say that the expression '*par provision*' does not qualify the morality in question; it is a relatively independent segment of meaning not grammatically tied to the word 'morality'. In the last analysis one should no more say 'morality *par provision*' than 'provisional morality' but rather, like Descartes in the letter of 4 August 1645, 'the morality of the *Discourse*'.

So much for the factual arguments. Now let us try to see whether a concept of 'provisional morality' – that is, a promise of a certain morality – was possible within the Cartesian system.

> For the rest, I pray you to remember that, touching on the things which the will may embrace, I have always set a great distinction between the usage of life and the contemplation of truth.[11]

For the morality of the *Discourse* to be provisional, the disjunction between theory and practice would need to mark only one stage in the Cartesian journey. In that case, it would be necessary that finally constituted knowledge should have a power over conduct and happiness. Now the Cartesian text invites us to think that if there is a knowledge capable of affecting conduct and happiness, this will not be a purportedly certain morality but rather a medicine finally worthy of its name:

> . . . if it is possible to find some means to make men commonly wiser and more skilful than they have been up to now, then I believe that it is in medicine that this must be sought.[12]

The reason given for this is that the mind depends heavily on the temperament and disposition of the body. This entitles us to suppose that behind the whole problem which is occupying us there is the question of the separation of soul and body, and the epistemological status of their substantive unity. The separation of soul and body produces the impossibility conditions of the classical concept of wisdom: in order for the practice of philosophy to be capable of totally regulating conduct and happiness, assuring by itself the good life, it is indeed necessary, as Montaigne puts it, for the sage not to be at the mercy of a maddening toothache. Now the substantial unity is not conceived by Descartes in a hegemonic mode; hence there emerges a whole domain of pleasures and pains which escape the control of thought:

> There are two things in the human soul, one of which is that it thinks, the other that being united to the body it can act and suffer with it. (21 May 1643)

> There are contentments which depend on the body and others which depend on the mind. (18 August 1645)

> There are two sorts of pleasures: the ones which belong to the mind alone, and the others which belong to man, that is to say to the mind inasmuch as it is joined to the body. (1 September 1645)

Descartes thus reiterates these discriminations, which draw a limit to the existential power of philosophy. One should even add that it is philosophy which depends on the state of the body, and not the body which perfectly follows philosophy:

> . . . there are maladies which, removing the power to reason, remove also that of enjoying the satisfaction of a reasonable mind; . . . and often the indisposition which is in the body, prevents the will from being free. (1 September 1645)

One can approach the question from another angle by considering the separation of soul and body from an epistemological point of view, drawing on the famous letter to Elizabeth of 28 July 1643. The soul is conceived only by the pure understanding; it belongs among the 'metaphysical thoughts'. The body can be known by the understanding alone, but much better so by the understanding aided by imagination; and it is the study of mathematics which accustoms us to form really distinct notions of the body. But 'the things which belong to the union of the soul and the body are *known* only obscurely by the understanding alone, or even by the understanding aided by imagination'; they may be conceived simply through life and ordinary conversations.

I have emphasized the word 'known': it is not only a matter of conceiving the union, but of knowing the things which belong to the union. Let us also emphasize the difference between metaphysical thoughts and mathematics on the one side, and ordinary conversations on the other. This is the difference between a philosophical and a vulgar knowledge.

If substantial union, which is to say man, falls within the sphere of ordinary conversations, it is perfectly vain to look for a morality founded on certain knowledge. Even Cartesian medicine will respect the separation of soul and body (*Discourse*, Sixth Part).

So, if there were a promise in Descartes of a certain morality, there would be an incoherence between this promise and the rest of the system. There would be an incoherence in its vocabulary also. For this would be the dream of a morality endowed with a 'more than moral' certainty, which would be a paradox. In the *Principles*[13] Descartes uses the notion of moral certainty as a foil for defining more than moral certainty, the only true certainty which is founded on a metaphysical principle:

> . . . I shall distinguish here two sorts of certainty. The first is called moral, which is to say sufficient for regulating our behaviour, or as great as that of those things we have no habit of doubting touching on the conduct of life, even though we know that, abstractly speaking, it is possible that they may be false.

Descartes thus abandons the question of morality to an extra-philosophical style of approach, and this is a necessity of his system. But the fact that morality is not produced by philosophy does not make it valueless. The certainty which it carries is *sufficient*.

> Philosophers should treat questions of morality most succinctly, and always as philosophers, not theologians. In former times one spent no more than three weeks or a month on a treatise of morality.[14]

I have tried to show above how the history of this problem can be divided into two large periods: over two centuries of general disinterest and a half-century marked, on the contrary, by an abundance of works on the question. Let us add a point of clarification: when, before the late nineteenth century, Cartesian texts on morality are quoted, the commentators do not really discuss them: they are content to summarize them, which is something very different. No one takes these texts as an object of philosophical study.

Why is there such a change in the later nineteenth century? Before reaching what seems to me the major reason, a few auxiliary remarks should be made.

The appearance of works on Descartes's moral thought coincides with the historical emergence of a certain style in the historiography of philosophy. This is the epoch when great scholars compile collections of fragments, where effort is made to reassemble what had been dispersed and to elicit a thought from the evidence of bits and pieces. This phenomenon had begun earlier in Germany, but the style gained sway in France only towards the end of the nineteenth century. Previously one either practised rhetoric and summarized a doctrine, if necessary using philosophical categories foreign to the author; or one made a study of the value of some philosophy, so much so that certain studies read like settlings of accounts; or one sought to provide a general panorama of the history of philosophy in its different moments: these three possibilities being, naturally, far from mutually exclusive.

I am not claiming that the work of bringing together disparate fragments marked a break which inaugurated a scientific era of work on texts. Rigorous work on documents does not suffice to make out of a discipline, the history of philosophy, a science. It seems to me even highly contestable whether one should *wish* it to be one.

The fact remains that the way the history of philosophy is conceived changes in the later nineteenth century, and this change is pertinent to our concern: since Descartes's ethical reflections are dispersed through his whole *œuvre* – arising, incidentally, in relation to something else – it required, for them to be discussed, a generation habituated to making card-indexes, joining together fragments and reconstructing a thought. This legitimates Henri Gouhier's choice of word: 'the *historians* have sought to use familiar adjectives' . . .[15] It was indeed the historians who forged these words 'provisional' and 'definitive' for speaking of Cartesian morality, since they were the only ones concerned with speaking of it. But this possibility which they opened up for speaking of

Cartesian morality seems to me to have been a perversion belonging to the style of work they promoted: legitimate as it may be to seek to reconstruct a thought lost over the centuries but which one is sure existed, it is equally questionable to try to constitute a never-written treatise, to cast together vestigial fragments and marginal elements within an individual's thought.

Elsewhere, this late nineteenth century sees the emergence of the first works of sociology (Durkheim, Lévy-Bruhl), works concerned with moral systems from the point of view of their historical and social insertion, something which does not make morality fashionable but justifies the fissuring of moral philosophy into monographs on this or that moral system.

Finally – although this takes us into what is said about Descartes, whereas my concern in this section is, rather, to see why there was an interest in Cartesian morality – this is an epoch which reads Auguste Comte. Even when he is not read, a certain number of Comtean philosophemes are diffused in the university – one which, under Victor Cousin, had been strongly hostile to this thought. They are diffused via the output of Taine, Littré, and Clemenceau,[16] to mention but a few. This is why a publisher of the *Discours sur l'esprit positif* can write in 1898:

> The name of Auguste Comte has become popular. This great philosopher is more and more seen as the master of modern thought; *he inspires even those who believe they do not follow him.*[17]

This throws some light on the commentators' vocabulary. As far as I know, the couplet provisional–definitive has had a philosophical pertinence only within the system of Auguste Comte. I doubt whether he ever applied it to morality. But on the other hand, morality figures within the series of the positive sciences right at the very end; and in the *Discours sur l'esprit positif* Comte affirms the possibility of a positive theory of rules of conduct, a theory encompassing 'conclusions just as certain as those of geometry itself'.[18]

This does not directly explain the interest in Descartes's morality. But there is an indirect relationship: I have been seeking to show that for more than two centuries no one *speaks* of Cartesian morality; at most, it is summarized. And one is justified in suggesting that if commentators say nothing about it this is, also, because they have nothing to say. On the contrary, once the pairing of provisional and definitive has been applied to Descartes's work and the Comtean dream of a theory of morality with 'conclusions as certain as those of geometry' have been lent, as a major concern, to Descartes, at a stroke a problem is encountered, and so there is something to be said; just as it is possible to discuss (an issue I have left aside in this study) Descartes's supposed Stoicism from the moment when this Stoicism is perceived as a bizarre anachronism: that is, from the moment when moral systems are inserted into a history.

These points needed to be noted in order to avoid assigning a single cause or historical condition of emergence to the spectacular phenomenon of change analysed here. Like every historical phenomenon, this one is caught in a complex web of *possibilities* and *necessities*, a web whose analysis this study does not claim to exhaust.

The humble and sure region of usual morality.[19]

Let us now turn to what I consider the major reason both for this mutation of the centre of Cartesian commentators' interests and for the misappropriation of the Cartesian text. Why the sudden interest in a morality which, though issuing from a philosopher's pen, is grounded, as our reading above has argued, on its exclusion from philosophical research? What was going on in this period around 1880? It was a time of teaching morality to schoolchildren. The connection may not spring to mind at once, the more so since the violence of the debates aroused by Jules Ferry's educational policies was soon forgotten.[20]

In the years before 1880, Jules Ferry, Ferdinand Buisson and the pedagogues of their circle provoked great argument over their proposal to teach morality to children; to support this project, they produced a large body of speeches and texts; to direct its execution, they drew up a large number of official circulars. And this was not a narrow issue confined within the Ministry of Public Education: the affair was a noisy one. The discourse of the ministerial participants presents a number of aspects; I shall deal here with only one of these, the exclusion of metaphysics or philosophy. For this I shall use chiefly the texts of F. Buisson's *Dictionary of Pedagogy*, a more accessible document than the others; these texts date from two or three months *after* the article by Brochard, but they can be taken as the formal version of the hurried theorizations already diffused by parliamentary speeches, harangues to teachers (for example, on the occasion of the Universal Exhibition of 1878), not to speak of ministerial circulars and newspaper articles. Let us add that the affair excited the passions of partisans and adversaries of the regime down to the 1914–18 War, and echoes of it can still be found in the secularizing literature of the Liberation.

The issue, then, was teaching morality to schoolchildren, and the project was not free of difficulties: it was the point where the ideology of secular neutrality was at its most vulnerable; the adversaries of secularization were themselves prepared to declare that there are several moralities and that every morality involves principles which are not neutral. Hence the necessity for Ferry's party to promote the idea of a common morality: that is to say, a morality which is at once ordinary, usual and held in common, and thus certain or assured; to affirm that there exists a 'humble and firm region of usual morality' within which teaching can and must dutifully [*sic*] confine itself. So a theme runs through the official discourse: the exclusion of philosophy, often pejoratively designated as 'metaphysical', for two reasons which perhaps amount to one: because philosophy is the place where opinions diverge, hence the state can have no doctrine on it; and because, further, the age of primary-school pupils does not allow – or, rather, forbids – a philosophical treatment of the moral curriculum:

> All theological and philosophical discussion is manifestly forbidden to [the teacher] by the very nature of his task, the age of his pupils, and by the trust placed in him by families and the state.[21]

No doubt the idea that there is an age of ripeness for philosophy, imported from the doctrine of Cousin, ought not to be separated from the argument for the necessity of a shared morality. Unity must come *before* difference; divergences can occur only on the basis of a common foundation, for it matters to the unity of the state that divergences should never be fundamental – that is to say, by way of a simplistic conceptual slide: never chronologically earliest.

Here, then, is the leitmotiv for the exclusion of philosophy:

> The teaching of morality to trainee primary-school teachers must have a philosophical foundation . . . In the primary school, the character of moral education is no longer like this . . . one condition is indispensable: that this teaching reach the living part of the soul

. . . Let him [the teacher] limit himself to the essential points, remain elementary, but be at once clear, simple, imperative, persuasive. He must leave aside developments which would have their place in a higher stage of education.

The article 'Morality' in Buisson's *Dictionary* from which these lines are drawn goes on to quote a letter written by Ferry:

. . . to convey, along with scholastic knowledge properly speaking, the very principles of morality, I mean simply that good and ancient morality which we received from our fathers and do honour to ourselves by following in the relations of life without labouring to discuss its philosophical basis. . . . Others will charge themselves later with completing the work you begin in the child and adding to the primary teaching of morality a complement of philosophical or religious culture. As for you, limit yourselves to the office society assigns you.[22]

The article 'Secularity' takes up the same themes:

'What morality?' he [Ferry] was endlessly asked. And he tirelessly replied: 'Simply the good old morality of our fathers, ours and yours, for we have only the one. We have various theories about morality, but in practice it is the one and the same morality which we received from our parents and hand on to our children . . . Yes, school-teachers can teach morality without the need to enter into metaphysical research.

These two texts are complementary, the article 'Morality' showing, with remarkable lack of shame, how the exclusion of philosophy is the condition for a process of indoctrination ('reaching the living part of the soul', 'imperative and persuasive'), while the article 'Secularity' shows how this process of indoctrination can be argued from the distinction between theory and practice. A common morality ('we have only the one') which leaves a place for some other morality, defined either as philosophical or as higher relative to what is graspable by children or ordinary men; but this opposition is limited, for in practice 'it is the same thing': between humble morality and the morality of the hero or the sage there is a difference either only of degree, or only of vocabulary:

On a humbler stage, in less tragic circumstances, each of us, more than once in his life, faces the same choice as that of Regulus.

The noble adage: do what you must, come what may, expresses in a popular and arresting way what Kant renders as the two words 'categorical imperative'.[23]

Thus the exclusion of philosophy from the teaching of morality to children produces a dualism regarding morality. To examine this doctrine of the politico-pedagogues, we have had to lose sight of Descartes. Let us now return to him. In the commentaries on Descartes contemporary with this debate on primary schooling there is also a dualism at work, since the historians of philosophy read Descartes through the opposition between the provisional and the definitive. It would be all the more tempting to think that the duality created by these historians is modelled on the duality present in the texts of Ferry and Buisson, because the so-called provisional morality is anterior to methodical doubt, and thus non-metaphysical, and the so-called definitive is, on the contrary, grounded in philosophy. But the affair is much more complex, because the duality of shared morality and higher morality does not tally with the duality of provisional and definitive morality. In fact the pedagogues' dualism is seldom expressed in temporal terms. The idea that one must provide children and the people, because of their immaturity, with a pre-rational morality to be going on with is not one which occurs in strictly pedagogical texts – although it might have been expected, such an idea being wholly serviceable for Ferry's programme. It is barely to be found except in the writing of Parodi, in (and this is not without significance) an article in the *Revue de Métaphysique et de Morale*:[24]

We place all our trust in reason, but we know also that for almost a century we have been pursuing what is doubtless the first ever experiment in founding the whole of society on the exercise of reason.

Now is the average humanity of our Europe, our contemporary France, ripe for this experiment? Can it take on, without aid or safeguard, its full charge and responsibility? Is it right precipitately to hasten the experiment and to make it even yet more radical and total? Is it not ill-considered and foolhardy to refuse from one day to the next the aid of all the traditional brakes which have the accumulated strength and prestige of centuries? Shall we confer the entire direction of himself on the workman or peasant who is barely sentient to the life of the mind? Are we to believe in the sufficient volition, the rational autonomy, of the alcoholic or the alcoholic's son?

What, on the other hand, does operate on a massive scale is the concept of provisional morality, the image of provision, stock, baggage. In ministerial circulars, texts of the moral teaching programme and works of pedagogical theory, one often finds such expressions as 'procure a provision of justice', 'that his heart provide itself in some sense for life', 'that the child take from school, with his little patrimony of elementary knowledge, a yet more precious treasure, an upright conscience', etc.

And even when a *'later'* appears, which is rare, this is designated as a *complement*:

> Others will charge themselves later with completing the work you begin in the child and adding to the primary teaching of morality a complement of philosophical or religious culture.[25]

This *'later'* is rare, and features here more for the sake of religious than of philosophical culture, for good reason: the pupils of the free, secular and compulsory school will not go to the *lycée*, nor therefore into its philosophy class. To gain access to secondary schooling, one had at this time to pass through the *'petites classes'* of the *lycée* (these still existed until a few years ago), which fall outside of Ferry's legislation on the matter which concerns us. This means that the duality of philosophical and common morality cannot be a temporal duality, but must rather be a socially determinable one. The provision of morality given by the primary school, the protection against dishonesty and alcoholism, is designed for the future proletarians: Compayré's 'common run of men', Parodi's 'average humanity'. As for philosophical morality, this remains the appanage of a cultivated class.

Thus, so far as I can ascertain, the concept of 'provisional morality' was not, despite Ferry's affiliation to positivism, coined by the pedagogues of elementary schooling. Since there is an accordance of dates between the debate on moral education and the misappropriation which interests us, this must be explained otherwise than through a direct causal link, a mechanical transposition of the politico-pedagogues' ideology into the domain of the history of philosophy. Besides, a pure and simple contagion of the latter by the former would have been surprising, given that Ferry and Buisson belonged neither to the same social caste nor to the same political milieu as Brochard, and that the whole 'primary world' which Ferry has bequeathed us was constituted by a break with the university: the training of school-teachers in primary *écoles normales*, not *lycées*, the training of professors for the primary *écoles normales* at the schools of Fontenay and Saint-Cloud, not in the university faculty, specialized diplomas at all levels, etc.

This was not a simple effect of contagion, then. However, since the debate was a national one, the theoretical products of the politico-pedagogues pose a problem for university philosophy. The former deal harshly by philosophy; they restrict it to the role of a complement; they reiterate that so far as practice is concerned, one can and must dispense with it; they allow it only the domain of 'theories about morality' – which, of course, have no claim to legislate over their object. One cannot appreciate the scandalous character of such views unless one remembers that university philosophy had, under the post-Commune presidency of MacMahon, put itself forward as the best qualified artificer for the reconstruction of moral order. It is worth quoting in full here the conclusion of the article 'Philosophy' in the 1875 edition of Franck's *Dictionary*, a work which in its time was as much consulted as our Lalande but is hard to come by today:

> After all it has achieved already, what is there left for philosophy to do? . . . Pure speculation has, as we have already shown elsewhere, almost run its course . . . But nowhere is philosophy called upon to play so useful and glorious a role as in the institutions, education and government of society, or in the field of political and moral applications. Indeed, the principle is now rooted in men's minds and nothing can henceforth shake it. Society is, like science, enfranchised: like science, it now has reason as its sole foundation. It is in the name of reason that one must address it to discipline, govern and convince it. Every authority, legislation and education not recognizable by reason is condemned in future to an irremediable impotence. Philosophy, therefore – that is to say, reason raised to the level of a science – must intervene in all these high questions, if it does not wish to leave the field to empiricism and anarchy. The task which

it began in the last century with the demolition of all outdated institutions must be continued in our century to further organization and discipline, through the slow and considered creation of new institutions. To define more precisely than hitherto the duties and rights of man in general; to prove that the latter cannot exist without the former, and that each alike has its common basis in the spiritual part of our being – that is, in our intellectual and moral faculties; to trace the development – or, if one prefers to put it thus, the successive realization – of these duties and rights first in the family, then in the state, and finally in the universal society of the human race; to restore esteem for the sanctity of marriage, an object of such vehement and persistent attacks; to defend, along with marriage, the right of property, without which no family is possible; to ascertain how far the family and the individual, without sacrificing any of the conditions of their existence and dignity, must both be subordinated to the unity of the state; to show that this unity has as its indispensable condition that of education; lastly to show what the state is in itself, what is its end and its principle of existence; what the elements are which necessarily compose it, what degree of authority belongs to it over the diverse forms of association which it encompasses, what its obligations and rights are towards foreign states, and what natural principles must preside over international relations: such is, in large part, the task which philosophy must undertake today. We know of none which it might accomplish that is more noble, useful and suited to elevate its standing in the spirit of our time. It will find there the means to secure for itself in the *moral order* a power and consideration analogous to that of the natural sciences in the sphere of material interests. Still sustained by speculation, by the most significant findings of pyschology and metaphysics, there is no ground to fear that it will lower itself to the level of party-political discussion; it is the parties, on the contrary, who will be forced to raise themselves to the level of its principles; it will restore to them the dignity, authority and conviction which they have lost, or at least gravely compromised.

Since this was the official doctrine (the institutional positions occupied by Franck and his collaborators allow no doubt on this), one can imagine the welcome these academics would accord to the exclusion of philosophy pronounced by Ferry. Hence it became an urgent philosophical task for these same academics to declare that no morality not established by philosophy could in any way be held worthy of consideration. To call Descartes's morality 'provisional' was to rule it invalid. To speak of the Cartesian project of a 'definitive morality' was to reinstate the idea that philosophy must legislate over morals, and to affirm that no philosopher has ever disavowed or abandoned the claim of philosophy to constitute morality and thereby handed morality over to an extra-philosophical mode of treatment. For the risk was precisely that the politico-pedagogues might seize on Descartes to justify their position.

So, as these politico-pedagogues had created a dualism between common and philosophical morality, the academic philosophers seized on this dualism and radicalized it: the politico-pedagogues made it a quantitative duality (common morality is the precepts without the foundations, the basis, or the theory; higher morality is the same precepts together with their foundations, philosophical basis and/or theory), the academic philosophers established a qualitative one (provisional versus definitive), thus introducing a difference in nature between the two moralities; otherwise they would hardly have been astonished to see Descartes retaining his maxims ten years after the *Discourse*. If Brochard disquietedly wonders how it can be that the provisional morality has become definitive, it is because he would have expected Descartes, on the contrary, to have rejected and abjured his provisional view and undergone an ethical conversion.[26] He did not give us the promised morality – so much the worse; let us content ourselves with ruling invalid the morality of the *Discourse*. The most exaggerated form of this devaluation, extended to every morality not founded in metaphysics, is found in Espinas's book:

> This morality is above all utilitarian, but it is not coherent. It is visibly an expedient . . . The provisional, almost fictive character of these rules is not in doubt. It is not without irony that Descartes offers his reader this morality in which there figures no duty worthy of the name; as he says in his notes, *personam induit*: he puts on a mask.[27]

Every morality not ordered by a metaphysical system is a mere expedient. This was to be the line of argument mobilized against the politico-pedagogues and at the same time alongside them, through the mediation of the dualistic conception they had created in the sphere of morals. We have seen university philosophy's claims to construct the moral order. The discourse of Ferry and Buisson could accordingly be perceived only as an attack on philosophy.[28]

Yet so far as I know, there was no open quarrel. For the *content* of the morality which Ferry wanted to instil in children hardly differed from the one the university philosophers wanted to establish, and the two participant clans agreed on the necessity of promoting and institutionalizing morality; in the last resort they could have come to an agreement by dividing their object, leaving the teaching of precepts to primary-school educators and reflection on foundations or the search for a more precise determination of duties to the philosophers. Although the philosophers had a few years earlier laid claim to the object in its totality (including the power to determine elementary precepts), they could have yielded to the politico-pedagogues the right to devise a morality for children or the people; we shall, moreover, see later on that there are circumstances where they abandon this very willingly.

There was no open quarrel, because the underlying political project on either hand was the same – or almost. But there was nevertheless a conflict, because it is philosophy itself which is at issue here. For the duality proposed by the politico-pedagogues presented philosophy as a luxury, a complement, a non-essential. Hence the need to mobilize, within the philosophical field, an argument in self defence. The misappropriation we are examining can be taken as a theoretical counter-move to the danger posed for philosophy by the discourse of Ferry's camp. How, when this discourse placed morality in the extra-philosophical domain, could the historians have accepted that a philosopher had done the same?

THE PLACE OF PHILOSOPHY

One can thus put forward the hypothesis that there is a historical link of both contagion and opposition between the politico-pedagogues' philosophy and the investment (in the mode of miscomprehension) by the historians of philosophy of a hitherto neglected aspect of Descartes's philosophy. But this would remain only a hypothesis if we did not have texts available to verify it. Now there are two texts by the same university philosopher, two contemporary texts which harbour contradictory evaluations of Descartes's thought, and in especially revealing circumstances: Boutroux, Professor of History of Philosophy at the Sorbonne, says two different things: one in 1895 when addressing an audience of primary-school pedagogues; the other in 1896 before an audience of the *Revue de Métaphysique et Morale*.

In 1895 Boutroux published with Delgrave a book called *Questions de morale et d'éducation*, which is a reprinting of lectures given at the École Normale de Fontenay-aux-Roses in 1888, 1891, 1892 and 1894 and published in these same years by the *Revue Pédagogique*.[29] The 1895 reprinting is of interest because it is preceded by a preface where Boutroux asks in what spirit the teaching of morality in primary schools should be envisaged; and where it is precisely Descartes who is discussed. But let us first give an idea of this text's tone. The first two pages of this foreword indicate quite clearly Boutroux's opinion of his Fontenay lectures: something marginal to his habitual university practice, a journey into the exotic, indubitably a *displacement*: 'These lectures were, to tell the truth, intimate chats, by no means intended for publication.' They had an educative purpose ('cultivating in them [the trainee teachers] the spirit of reflection and moral conduct'), not one of academic instruction. Boutroux opposes intellectual skill (which this audience does not have) to 'what in conscience one regards as true', this conscience being something he is willing to attribute to these girls; the whole being crowned by a wholly candid denial of adaptation (read vulgarization): 'While I prepared these talks with a view to their destined audience, I did not think of subjecting my thought to any kind of adaptation.' Thus Boutroux did not go to the École Normale de Fontenay-aux-Roses to give courses, to do his technical work as a historian of philosophy; a vaguely Molièresque ideology appears in his foreword, privileging general instruction and moral and spiritual elevation over claims to knowledge.

After these two pages presenting his chats at Fontenay, Boutroux asks in what spirit one should envisage the teaching of morality in the primary school; and here, quite naturally, he falls into the groove of the politico-pedagogues' discourse: above all, no philosophy (philosophy being here identified with philosophical systems); and this rejection is argued, first of all, in a manner made familiar by Ferry; in the name of the distinction between life and thought, of the plurality of philosophies, the refusal of dogmatism, which is doubtless related to the demand for neutrality, but whose 'truth' will be apparent in a moment:

> But what ought this teaching of morality to consist in? Should it aim to inculcate a dogmatic system in the pupils, one which is considered the most perfect expression of the truth in this matter? Far be it from me to depreciate the magnificent speculations of an Aristotle or a Kant! But it is a question here of life, and not only of thought. Now, without speaking of the difficulty, for intelligences as yet little exercised, of understanding these learned systems, who would dare attribute to one of them a certainty permitting its teaching to be made obligatory? To be sure, one can give them the deductive form of mathematics: that will not change the nature of the principle on which they rest. It is an undeniable fact that these principles: duty, happiness, dignity, right, liberty, pleasure, interest, solidarity, struggle for life, social existence, equality, national existence are all more or less devoid of the evident and exact character of mathematical notions. Thus they remain standing in confrontation with one another, without any of them being assured of a definitive victory. A teaching given over to system would be obscure, pretentious, abstract, and subject to individual caprice or dogmatism.[30]

As we nevertheless meet the idea of duty again a few pages further on, let us point out here, concerning this enumeration of 'principles' which are 'more or less devoid of evidence' and 'standing in confrontation with one another', that if it leads Boutroux to the rejection of philosophy, this is all the better to prepare the path for *a* philosophy or morality, which is naturally that of duty.

Having begun by caricaturing philosophy, Boutroux does not wait long before invoking Descartes. As far as I know, Ferry and Buisson had not thought of using the *Discourse on Method* to justify their distinction between theory and practice or their separation of morality and philosophy. They may indeed have had no interest in doing so, because it might have been retorted that their exclusion of philosophy was grounded on *one* particular philosophy; though they were not people to recoil before an incoherence, since they rejected all philosophy but invoked where expedient the authority of Kant or Kantian modes of argument – only, on the same page, to criticize Kantian 'rigidity'.

In any case, Boutroux sees the possibility of exploiting Descartes (and Kant) within an apologia for common morality, morality without a metaphysical system. The passage is quite long but, given its documentary value, I quote it in full:

> Descartes, who nevertheless dreamed of constituting a truly scientific morality, has already said this: morality thus understood can come only as a sequel to all other sciences. Its object is the most complex of all. So long as the other sciences are imperfect, it is premature to enter upon this one. One risks being mistaken in everything by proceeding rigorously from principles which are incomplete or erroneous. Yet one must live, and action will not wait. We must needs look elsewhere for the maxims which science, even at its boldest, cannot offer us hope for except in a far distant age, and we must compensate our lack of formal proofs with practical sense.
>
> How, indeed, does each of us proceed in determining the moral maxims by which he will rule his conduct? It seems to me that we arrive in the end at this question, and that it is spurious and illegitimate to imagine a method for the school other than the one which, in real life, is followed by decent people.
>
> Now we do not ordinarily rule our conduct according to a metaphysical system; above all, we do not confine ourselves within a single system. Even less do we pride ourselves on scientific rigour; for in that case, just as we turn to an engineer to solve a problem of practical mechanics, so we would have even better reason for consulting a professional deontologist to obtain the solution to a moral problem. But our reflection – prompted by life, by observations, conversation, readings, knowledge – attaches itself to certain ideas which seem to us more important, more true, more beautiful, more inviolable than others; and from these ideas we compose for ourselves a sort of code which we think it wrong to break. Further, the more our knowledge and intelligence develop, the wider the basis of our morality, the greater our effort to give it harmony and unity. But maxims borrowed directly from tradition and life remain the essential part, and we are not wrong to depart from some system which we have drawn up in our head when it seems to us that some contrary maxim, examined by a careful conscience, has a higher value. It is all the more necessary to stick to this method and prefer it to the dogmatic teaching of some philosophical system or other,

because these very systems are, like those which each of us forms for himself, in fact only the reflection of great minds on the moral notions humanity lives by. Kant, whom one would be tempted to cite as the archetype of the pure speculative mind, recognizes this. He begins, he tells us, from common moral notions. The existence of morality, like that of science, is for him a fact. His philosophy can no more envisage constructing morality than it can the laws of nature. In the *Critique of Pure Reason*, he explains how science is possible – that is to say, intelligible; in the *Critique of Practical Reason*, he reflects likewise on morality as it is given to us; and he elicits from it, in the manner of a chemist, the essential elements, determined in their nature and role. The greatest minds have thus not proceeded, in the formation of their moral systems, otherwise than the vulgar.

Without pausing to dwell on the philosophical vulgarity of the psychologism (and the psychology) at work in this passage, let us look at the use it makes of Descartes. The word 'provisional' does not appear here; it will appear in the article for the *Revue de Métaphysique et de Morale*. This is to be expected: as it is a matter of justifying the morality of the decent man untutored in metaphysics, this is not the place to depreciate the morality of the *Discourse* as merely provisional; it is the other morality which is to be repudiated. Here the word 'dream' appears: Descartes dreamed of a scientific morality. And Boutroux pronounces that the time has not yet come (it is 'premature'), so that the goal of morality founded in proof is postponed indefinitely ('a far distant age'). And Descartes is implicitly praised for not having proceeded 'otherwise than the vulgar'.

All of this validates 'the humble and sure region of usual morality', to borrow the ministerial expression; and all this dictates the line of conduct pedagogues must take: teach the result of your 'meditations in real life' (p. xii) and remember that if the method of authority 'has no use in science', 'which of us does without it in life?'

The opposition between life and thought, life and science, life and system, life and dogmatic rigour, life and magnificent speculations, life and dogmatic system structures this whole text; it is refracted in the opposition between scholar and man of action, the former being required to establish 'a principle pure of all inner contradiction'; the second needing, 'on the contrary, most often to reconcile views which, logically, appear contradictory'; it is refracted also in the opposition between great thinkers and little children, except that the greatest geniuses intended only to 'organize common moral notions', although this is no reason for forgetting that 'one does not raise children by teaching them to chop logic about duty' (p. xv), which is to repeat the already-cited ministerial prohibition to schoolteachers: 'all theological and philosophical discussion is plainly forbidden for him'. On the one hand, the Minister forbids *discussion*; on the other Boutroux, despite his severity towards '*dogmatism*', sings the praise of pedagogical dogmatism:

> To the question: why must one do this or refrain from that? the master knows only one answer, the only one which humanity ultimately possesses: this is good, that is bad. (p. xv)

So much for the rejection of philosophical dogmatism. But the point is that 'given over to system, teaching would be . . . subject to *individual* dogmatism', whereas it must rather be made subject to collective (read state) dogmatism; the schoolteacher 'will speak with the windows wide open, so as not to say anything but what can be heard by the whole of society'.

This then is the context and the set of purposes which accompany Boutroux's description of Descartes's morality through proofs as impossible and his assertion that Descartes supplemented the deficit of proof by 'practical sense' and proceeded 'not otherwise than the vulgar'. This was to an audience of pedagogues.

The tone changes when Boutroux writes in the *Revue de Métaphysique et de Morale*.

In 1896, what had in the 1895 text been the laudatory conclusion (Descartes appealed to practical sense, not to philosophy) recurs, subject to an important modification at which we shall look shortly, in the form of a problem, not to say a scandal:

> The part of Descartes's writings dealing with morality is not inextensive; but it seems neither by its nature or content to belong, properly speaking, within his philosophical *œuvre* . . . It is true that a sketch of practical morality figures in the *Discourse on Method*. But, according to a document recently published by Monsieur Charles Adam, Descartes may have added these rules only against his own inclination, because of the pedagogues and suchlike people who

would otherwise have accused him of lacking faith and religion and wanting to overturn both with his method. As for its content, it is certainly elevated in thought and admirable in form, but it seems little alongside the philosopher's real doctrine.[31]

The first important change in this text is that Descartes's morality is no longer dictated by 'practical sense' but 'marked by Stoicism'. It is no longer a 'not otherwise than the vulgar' which is counterposed to philosophical demonstration, but a philosophy (Stoicism) counterposed to another (Cartesianism), 'two rivers which flow in parallel without mingling their waters'.[32]

The second modification is that the fact that Descartes did not produce a morality as a part of his system may be only an *appearance*.

'It *seems* not to belong within his philosophical *œuvre*.'
'Descartes *may* have added these rules only . . .'
'The content of these writings *seems* little alongside the doctrine.'
'It *seems* particularly marked . . .'
'It *seems* then' [that Descartes was uninterested in moral enquiries].
'In themselves they *seem* hardly linked to his philosophy.'

Whereas the separation of morality and metaphysics was presented in the text of 1895 as both certain and highly positive, in the *Revue de Métaphysique* it becomes a mere – and scandalous – appearance; for if it were true, then:
– this would be a cowardly concession to pedagogues and suchlike people;
– it would be a contradiction in the Cartesian discourse, 'wholly out of keeping with the philosopher's ceaseless declarations about the object of philosophy': namely that Descartes's eager desire to learn to distinguish true from false was governed by his knowledge that this was the way to see clearly in his actions;
– lastly, Descartes would be a liar or a hypocrite: 'No doubt Descartes gives us the rules of his provisional morality as rules of his method. But what is this affirmation worth, if he introduced these rules only to sidetrack the pedagogues?'

One can guess, then, the article's purpose: to show that this was only an appearance. Certainly Descartes never wrote a properly Cartesian morality, but this was because he died too young; but as one can find in his work the seeds of a morality, one can be sure that he never abandoned the project of constituting a definitive morality.

> It would be illegitimate to judge Descartes solely on what a life prematurely cut short permitted him to finish. In works of thought, the inner tendency, the living principle of development often matters more than immediately observable results. The reality of a Cartesian morality would be sufficiently demonstrated, if one proved that Descartes's philosophy contains the seeds of a morality.[33]

A morality which – the term occurs twice – will come to *replace* the provisional morality. And the opposition provisional–definitive does not work only in the reading of Descartes, it allows a rethinking of the whole history of humanity: Socrates, the Stoics, the Ancients in general 'knew only how to contemplate or acquiesce, to turn inward on themselves'; with Descartes,

> Man is no longer crushed by nature: he uses it. The soul is no longer the prisoner of the body: it leads it. Morality is no longer the art of self-sufficiency and self-isolation from things: it is the command to make of reason, which is our essence, a living and sovereign reality, the queen of nature.

Without forcing the text, one is entitled to say that the Ancients produced only humanity's provisional morality and that Descartes laid the foundations of a definitive morality which Boutroux divines in the 'Promethean' ideology of this *fin de siècle* which sees the *Académie Française* honouring the works of Jules Verne.

But it is not only a question of man's power over nature which is at issue here; it is also the question of the place of philosophy in conduct. A comparative diagram may help to show this (see facing page).

In the 1895 text the whole objective is to reduce the place of philosophy. In the 1896 text the whole aim is to enlarge it.

It is hard to imagine that one and the same man could unconsciously change his discourse in this way within a few months, adapting so obligingly to his audience's expectations; but the confrontation of these two texts proves, in my view, that there were indeed two different publics: one ministerially non-philosophical, to whom one had to say

The morality of the *Discourse*		The other morality
1895	Not metaphysical Produced by practical sense That of honest people Not otherwise than the vulgar GOOD	A dream A far distant age
1896	Provisional Stoic *Apparently* not related to *Cartesian* philosophy *DECEPTION?*	A seed . . . his life prematurely cut short . . .

that philosophy could be dispensed with; the other institutionally philosophical, before whom it was necessary to defend with eloquence the place of philosophy, and defend it just at that point where its position was most at risk. The proliferation during the Third Republic of works on Descartes's morality looks less like a harvest than a mobilization.

The irony in this affair is that it was possible for the pedagogical and university publics, so opposed theoretically and politically, to be served by one and the same man. It matters little how such a duplicity is possible psychologically. What it serves to indicate is that the *object* of this discourse is undetermined, or non-existent enough to permit such contradictory utilizations (for to talk of interpretations would be euphemistic here). There is no constituted moral philosophy in Descartes, only a few passages here, a few lines there, which are always marginal and cannot be assumed to compose a homogeneous sum. Contradictory utilizations are possible either because the commentaries' object does not exist, or because these scattered lines and passages themselves participate in the very duplicity which we might over-hastily be tempted to blame on Boutroux. We had to read the Cartesian texts with blinkers to defend the literal sense of the *Discourse on Method*. This tends to show only that a single thread can serve to join together some of the texts, but not all. It is time to reconsider the passages that we have so far set aside, and to reread those we have cited. But before looking at those which makes Descartes himself less than innocent of the misappropriation denounced above, let us try to identify some evidences of malaise in Descartes's discourse.

Larvatus prodeo, larvatus pro deo:* Cartesian Denegations and Evasions

If one confines oneself to the *Discourse on Method* and leaves aside what is conveyed through the slant of its metaphors, nothing entitles one to disvalue the morality one finds there – nothing, that is, except the rumour that Descartes wrote it only for reasons of pure opportunism, to keep himself out of trouble. This is what one must have in mind when reading the prefatory letter to the *Principles*. I leave on one side, provisionally, the image of the tree, to consider only the explicit content of the text, which says:

> The first part of these essays was a discourse touching on the method to conduct one's reason well and seek truth in the sciences, where I placed in summary form the rules of logic and of an imperfect morality.

Certainly nothing in the *Discourse* entitles one to disvalue the morality *par provision*; but if in the *Principles* Descartes himself calls it *imperfect*, must one not by a retroactive reading consider, against the actual letter of the *Discourse*, that he never thought that those three or four maxims were worth much? What place should one give this late (1644) statement of depreciation, given that later still (1645) a letter to Elizabeth of Prussia will vaunt afresh the merits of this morality?

I propose reading this judgement of imperfection as an element in a series of Cartesian utterances: a series of what I will call his evasions.

The first term in this series is the Third Part of the *Discourse* itself. Descartes presents himself in the *Discourse* as a reformer; but it was vital for him to *localize* his will to reform, and to state clearly that even if he will doubt everything in order to restore everything, he will touch neither religion nor morals. For every reform project is liable to find itself being given a capital 'R' in this century so prone to alarm and censure.

*'I advance masked, masked for God.'

Writing a morality which affirmed by its content the will to conform and which, by its place outside the methodical enterprise, proclaimed the will not to subject maxims of conduct to philosophical examination, amounted already to offering guarantees to Church and state, and to a Church which wanted philosophers (cf. the passage excerpted by Bayle and cited above) not to delay for more than three weeks over moral questions.

The judgement of imperfection is directly in line with this prudence (but is it only a matter of prudence?). Not only do I not claim, as philosopher, to produce a reconstructed (reformed) morality by methodical doubt, but I am moreover aware that the one I have made for myself is far from being remarkable or worthy of interest. Though one should perhaps allow this word 'imperfection' to have a more technical meaning.

The series can be continued; the letter to Chanut of 1 November 1646, where Descartes says that he has never discussed morality, can be read as a link in this curious chain of denegations: a privileged link because it gives the reason – or at least *a* reason – for the series: the Regents would otherwise have left him no peace.[34]

Another reason, advanced on the occasion of another evasion: morality is the business of politicians, not philosophers:

> It is true that my custom is to refuse to write my thoughts on morals, and this is for two reasons: one, that there is no subject where the malicious can as easily find pretext to calumny me; the other, that I believe it belongs only to sovereigns, or those authorized by them, to regulate the behaviour of others. (Letter to Chanut, 20 November 1647)

One can range in the same class of statements Descartes's clarification regarding his treatise on the *Passions of the Soul* (Adam and Tannéry, XI, 326), saying that he dealt there with the passions as a physician and not as a moralist. Likewise his evasiveness towards Elizabeth: since she insists that they talk about morals, Descartes proposes to her that they read Seneca together (21 July 1645).

Lastly, to return to the prefatory letter to the *Principles*, let us note the singular trick which Descartes allows himself here regarding morality: the one he made for the *Discourse* is called imperfect from the viewpoint of another morality, supposed to be perfect or exact; but the indication of this perfect morality is there only to be immediately *repudiated*; it is a better which serves as argument against a good but which, the instant it has achieved this function, fades into renunciation:

> But in order to carry this design to its end, I would need . . .; and then lastly to treat exactly of medicine, morality and mechanics. This is what I would need to do to give men a complete body of philosophy; and I do not yet feel so old, I am not so mistrustful of my powers, and I do not feel so far removed from the knowledge of what remains, that I would not dare to undertake the completion of this design, had I the means to make all the experiments I would need to support and justify my reasonings. But seeing that this would entail great expense which a private individual like myself cannot bear without public aid, and being unable to expect such aid, I believe that I must henceforward content myself with studying for my own instruction, and that posterity will excuse me if I fail henceforth to work on its behalf.

So there was once a philosopher who refused to deal exactly with morals, for lack of public funding.

If one takes all these evasions (I give myself a morality anterior to my methodical doubt; it is imperfect; I have never spoken of morality in my writings; there is a perfect morality that is possible in principle but materially unrealizable for me; in any case it is the politicians' affair), one finds something formally assimilable to the argument of the kettle recorded by Freud at the end of the analysis of the dream of Irma's injection:

> The whole plea – for the dream was nothing else – reminded one vividly of the defence put forward by the man who was charged by one of his neighbours with having given him back a borrowed kettle in a damaged condition. The defendant asserted first, that he had given it back undamaged; secondly, that the kettle had a hole in it when he borrowed it; and thirdly, that he had never borrowed a kettle from his neighbour at all. So much the better: if only a single one of these lines of defence were to be accepted as valid, the man would have to be acquitted.[35]

But why this series of evasions and denegations? On a first analysis, one can put forward the hypothesis of external necessities: each time

Descartes writes a line concerning morality, this discourse, far from being his own, is commanded from without by a complex system of prohibitions and demands: prohibitions emanating from politico-religious power, demands by his public and by his circle of friends. It is Elizabeth, or Christina via Chanut, who makes him keep taking up his work again. But this demand does not fall from the sky, nor is it explainable merely through the contingencies of Elizabeth's life. It issues from a dissatisfaction left behind by the *Discourse on Method*. The absence of an ethical discourse is detected by these correspondents, just as it will be regretted by d'Alembert.[36] But this dissatisfaction is reiterated by Descartes's answers. There will never be anything but more or less contradictory evasions: as witness still this letter to Chanut of 20 November 1647 where, even though elsewhere Descartes had said that the *Passions of the Soul* were a physician's work, this time, as he is insistently required to give means to attain the Highest Good, he sends his *Treatise on the Passions*. Which is another way of not answering the question.

But if none but circumstantial answers are ever to be had from Descartes, is this not a sign that his correspondents' dissatisfaction is based not only on a contingent actual lack, but in the perception of a lack which is radical and definitive? Descartes can say nothing on morals because his system excludes any possibility of an ethics in the traditional sense of the term. This is why it seems to me that the explanation of certain passages in terms of Descartes's prudence is at once right and insufficient. Certainly he is torn between the needs of his tranquillity and the demands of his friends, but the evasions and circumstantial answers which he then offers are all the easier because they take the place of no other discourse. He does not speak against his own thought here, but in the place of a void; if there had not been all these outside pressures, he might perhaps have said nothing at all.

If, that is, it is really possible for a philosopher to resign himself to leaving 'void of mark and trace'[37] a place formerly invested by philosophy.

THE QUESTION OF LODGING

We have so far traced two threads in the Cartesian discourse: one, running through the explicit content of the *Discourse* and some letters, which enables us to reject the translation of '*par provision*' into 'provisional'; the other, linking the preface to the *Principles* and some other letters, which allows us to discern the floating character of Descartes's discourse. But all this is possible only on the express condition that one brackets off the images in the Cartesian text. Now it is these, and these only, which lead to talk of a '*provisional*' morality. I am alluding, of course, to the image of the dwelling in the *Discourse* and that of the tree in the *Principles*.

Commenting on the images which run through philosophical texts, even deciding what is an image, is an enterprise which seems simple only from a naïve viewpoint. This is not the place to enter on all the problems posed by this question, nor is it the place to discuss the mode of approach which is often currrent today and which, borrowing its means from Jung or from a banalizing reading of *The Interpretation of Dreams* or Bachelard, aims to decode or 'translate' images. I ask to be granted, without proof, that to deal only with the symbolic, imaginary or affective value of images is far from sufficient when these images appear in a philosophical text. The reading I propose is relatively abstract in that it leaves aside the meaning that can be conferred on the image of the house or the tree. Two things interested me here: how can a metaphoric mode undergo transformation while on the road, even in the course of a single text, and what does this transformation indicate? Next, from what language is it borrowed? What I am looking for is a migration, but a migration from text to text; for, most often, philosophical images have this remarkable property of being adopted, in an obvious manner, from precise sources.

To utilize an image already invested by an earlier philosophy is to give a nod of acknowledgement, for reasons to be examined, to something of that philosophy; it means to continue a philosopheme which the philosophy that borrows the image cannot produce of itself. One can imagine a plurality of functions for this borrowing: the mask of a lack or a transgression, the recurrence of a past blind spot, itself already given in an image (when an image has become classic one no longer sees that its reason was to soften an aporia); the repetition of a wish or a desire regarding philosophy; a process or attempt at validating an enterprise by placing it under the 'patronage' of an already recognized authority . . .

Thus it transpires, most often, that when a philosopher uses an image he is speaking another's tongue, but only then to rework the garment, to transform the given image in its passage through one's text; and if I have chosen these two axes for studying images, this is in accordance with a sole principle of reading: the image, far from being a more or less pedagogical 'illustration' of an abstract thesis contained elsewhere in the system, is always the mark of a tension, a signification incompatible with the rest of the work. Speaking the other's language and having additionally each time to transform his metaphoric mode, seem to me indications of the impossibility of formulating, in the system's own language, a meaning which, in spite of everything, demands to be given its place.

And so we have a problem of lodging in the *Discourse* and a tree in the *Principles*: two images which respond to one another, since the lodging is designated as provisional ('before beginning to rebuild the dwelling . . . one must have provided oneself with some other where one may be suitably housed during the time of one's work'), while the tree promises a morality produced out of the totality of knowledge. The imagery plainly suggests a duality concerning morality, and it alone suggests this. Let us mention in passing a singular phenomenon: although it is the imagery which carries the opposition between provisional and perfect, the late-nineteenth-century commentators who took this question as their object never mention it; at most, certain words (fruits, trunk) appear in an incidental way. It is the imagery which suggests the davalorization of the morality of the *Discourse*, in a way which is operative yet unspoken. The provisional character of the morality in question is given as self-evident and known to all; it is never formally established. There is, in this absence of explicit reference to images, matter for reflection.

Taken together, these two images convey the same conception of the relations of philosophy to ethics; the image of the dwelling designates the morality of the *Discourse* as provisional because other (some *other* one where one may be lodged during the time . . .), a morality which is outside philosophy but only for a time, and only for a time because outside philosophy. The image of the tree renews the idea that philosophy can produce a morality, that only constituted knowledge can produce a perfect morality.

One could almost content oneself with this superficial approach, if one were prepared to affirm dogmatically that the fact that this classic representation of the dependence of morality on philosophy is given through imagery indeed proves that this dependence is not theorizable within the system; that the fact that there is metaphor is the mark of nostalgia for another philosophy which guaranteed philosophy itself a greater power. It is this very nostalgia which, in my eyes, prompts these images, but I would like to show in more detail what makes it incongruous – that is to say, precisely a nostalgia, a lost dream, a dream prompted by a loss. To do that we must trace the unease, the tension in the discourse which marks the incongruity of the meaning produced.

I spoke earlier of the modification, within the text, of metaphoric material; I shall now try to show the difference between the general metaphor of the tree or building (when these images refer to Descartes's general speculative enterprise, and not to the precise point which concerns us) and the same metaphor when it refers particularly to morals; I would like to show how the surfacing of the ethical question produces a traceable distortion within the metaphor itself.

But before looking at this I must say a word or two about the general metaphor. Metaphors of building and tree-husbandry occur at a number of places in the Cartesian texts. For someone aiming to decode or interpret them from a symbolic or psychoanalytic viewpoint, these images would seem very different; from my point of view, as this is not my concern, they are mutually assimilable. This is primarily because they seem interchangeable in Descartes's text; Descartes says indiscriminately 'knock down' or 'uproot', 'build' or 'cultivate'. In the *Discourse*, where the vocabulary of the building predominates, one nevertheless finds many gardening terms;[38] in the *Principles*, where the metaphor of the tree is fully developed, one still meets the vocabulary of architecture.[39] A second and more telling reason is that these two metaphors both gesture towards one and the same text, where they assume parallel functions of discrimination. This is the Gospel according to Saint Matthew, Chapter 7, verse 15 and after:

> Beware of false prophets, men who come to you dressed up as sheep while underneath they are savage wolves. You will recognize them by the fruits they bear. Can grapes be plucked from briars, or figs from thistles? In the same way, a good tree always yields good fruit, and a poor tree bad fruit. A good tree cannot yield bad fruit, or a poor tree good fruit. And when a tree does not yield good fruit it is cut down and burnt. That is why I say you will recognize them by their fruits . . .

What then of the man who hears these words and acts upon them? He is like a man who had the sense to build his house on rock. The rain came down, the floods rose, the wind blew, and beat upon that house; but it did not fall, because its foundations were on rock. But what of the man who hears these words of mine and does not act upon them? He is like a man who was foolish enough to build his house on sand. The rain came down, the floods rose, the wind blew, and beat upon that house; down it fell with a great crash.

These are metaphors of discrimination, then; and Descartes's allusion to this passage is all the clearer because the rock and the sand appear several times in the work. It is not a matter of indifference that this image-material (like, also, the metaphor of the way, which appears in Matthew immediately before the passage quoted) should have been borrowed from the Gospel; this heavily accented allusion can be interpreted as an act of redemption intended to annul a transgression. Descartes speaks the language that his work excludes ('natural reason without the light of faith' . . . 'I set no store here by divine revelation',[40] etc.).

These two images are not called upon only when the ethical question appears; they are already being used in regard to knowledge, before the moral question arises; but the appearance of that question induces, in the *Discourse* as in the *Principles*, a distortion of the imagery. In the *Discourse* (and elsewhere), so long as only knowledge is at issue, the image of the building reduces to the problem of foundations (firm or otherwise) and to a binary schema: that which is built on the rock, that which is built on sand. Even Descartes's critique of the moralists of Antiquity falls into this pattern.

But when the question of extra-philosophical morality appears in the Third Part, one can observe two modifications: on the level of vocabulary, the words 'build' and 'building', with their associations with the question of solidity, yield to those of 'lodging' and 'being lodged', associated rather with the question of commodity: the use-value of the house, perhaps the affective value of the word 'lodging', but above all the lexical juxtaposition of this morality with the body, for lodging is one of the modes of relation of the soul to the body: 'I am not only lodged in my body . . .'[41] But above all, the binary schema which was the point of the metaphor of the building loses all meaning here, since the provisional lodging is strictly undetermined with respect to the opposition of sand and rock, of weak and solid foundations; and this is because this neutral third term is not founded on a (sure or doubtful) *principle*, but on a *design*: 'the three preceding maxims were founded only on the design which I had . . .' In short, the question of morality introduces a disorder into the metaphorical system itself; this is the sign of the interpolation of an element heterogeneous to the global project.

The same thing may be observed in the *Principles*: so long as it is only a matter of metaphysics, physics, mechanics and medicine, a certain coherence of imagery is sustained. Trivially this means that the tree is one that can be drawn. But morality introduces a total confusion into the design since it is simultaneously one of the branches among others, joined directly to the trunk, and '*presupposes an entire knowledge of the other sciences*', in which sense it is no longer a branch among others but a result of all the branches – something which it is strictly impossible to represent within the image, unless one supposes that the tree completes itself by confluence; there is an incompatibility between the representation of a totalizing result and the already-given representation of a process of distinction.

In short, there is indeed a devalorization in Descartes of the morality sited outside knowledge, and a dream of a morality produced by philosophy. But that is realized at the price of a passage into the metaphoric mode, and of internal displacements within a general imagery. The nostalgia for wisdom – that is, for a knowledge which makes possible the Good – is thus a pure nostalgia, the mask of an irredeemable loss. It is the conflict between the possibilities of the system and the philosopher's wish concerning the power of philosophy which summons up the images, and draws them from a place whose recollection carries a great power to reassure. I return to my question: 'What other's language speaks in the image?' Certainly the tree is an evangelical parable; but there is another, much more powerful evocation here in this passage of the prefatory letter to the *Principles*: comparing philosophy point by point with a natural being is a typically Stoic metaphoric mode:

They compare philosophy to a living being: the bones and nerves are logic; the flesh is morals; the soul is physics. They compare it also to an egg: the shell is logic, the white morals, the yolk, at the very centre, is physics. Or again to a piece of fertile land: the hedge which surrounds it is logic, the fruits are morals, the earth and the tree are physics.[42]

Adopting a Stoic metaphoric mode amounts to renewing the theme of the interpenetration of the theoretical and the practical in and through philosophy. Brochard had seen Stoicism in the *Discourse*, but this seems to me highly questionable; it is the Descartes of the *Principles* who is Stoic, not provisionally but for the occasion, so as to hide the fact that the new light produced by the system casts a new shadow: there can no longer be any question of philosophy by itself and as such assuring the conduct of life and access to happiness. One can, on this point, follow Henri Gouhier's conclusion: with Descartes there is something which 'reason resigns itself to leave outside of truth'. But this should be rectified: the problem is not posed in terms of resignation but of nostalgia: that is, of a conflict which produces images.

I opposed at the beginning of this study two types of reading: one which misappropriates the literal sense of the discourse commented on, and one characterized on the contrary by a certain fidelity to the text: schematically, that of Brochard and late-nineteenth-century commentators, and that of a good number of philosophy teachers today. How are these two modes to be located relative to one another?

Brochard's is in a certain way a mystifying one in that it holds out an untenable promise while occluding its strict impossibility. But it reveals how far the morality of the *Discourse* is unsatisfactory for a philosopher, how shocking it is for philosophy's practitioners.

The reading which, conversely, displays lexical precision and rejects the expression 'provisional morality' as contrary to sense, in that it evacuates all the underlying unease and tension of this thought, finally seems to us, at the end of this analysis, no more faithful than the first. It fails to take into consideration the fact that Descartes, in his imagery, insinuates the contrary of what he performs and validates in the Third Part of the *Discourse*; it refuses to consider Descartes's own attempts to nullify his discourse.

From a logical point of view, the failure of these two readings signals perhaps our common incapacity to handle the category of contradiction in what relates to the history of philosophy.

But from a theoretical point of view, the error, which is not a neutral one, of these two readings is to 'forget' that when a philosopher touches in his discourse, even indirectly, on the question of the power of philosophy, the question of the range of validity of philosophical reflection, his discourse can never be a simple and univocal one and can by no means be free of influence by unanalysed exigencies. And the discourse of commentators can no more be so than that of producers of philosophical texts.

So it is hardly surprising, in my view, that the object 'Descartes's morality' was exhumed and exorbitantly invested with meaning in the later nineteenth century, and that the commentaries written on it sprang up as a reaction to a questioning of the necessity of philosophy. I asked whether the origin of a deformation of meaning should be sought in a prejudice or projection on the part of the hearer, or if the misunderstanding might not have its origin in a marginal meaning of the text itself. But in both hypotheses, the same issue is at work: a certain idea of philosophy, contradicted for Descartes by his particular philosophy, contradicted for the nineteenth-century historians by the philosophical discourse of the politico-pedagogues; a certain idea of philosophy which needed – against the tide of events and even against a certain practice of philosophy – to be restored.

Lastly there is the pedagogical place where this question is implicit even today, in a contradictory manner. In nearly all the manuals and collections of selected excerpts (the 'Little Classics'), the expression 'provisional morality' appears, and there is nothing astonishing about this. We have read in this lexical misappropriation an excessive valuation of philosophy: that the teaching of philosophy should involve a kind of apologia for Philosophy[43] as saviour is a matter of course in several ways, including a sociopolitical one: to have received a philosophical education works as a symbol of demarcation from the 'common run of men', a sublimated way of marking the hiatus between the 'ruling élite' and the 'people', to use the terms of the Third Republic theorists.

But in that case how is one to interpret the red marks on the students' essays, and the irate '*par provision*' in the margin? Unjustified (and even catastrophic) as it is relative to the defence and celebration of philosophy, the claimed demand of fidelity to the letter would be incomprehensible if we did not take account of the inscription, in the output of schools and universities (the essays and their 'correction'), of the (pedagogical) place and relation which engender them. The rectification functions, on this hypothesis, as a mark of the peda-gogical.[44]

It would be oversimple to add; pedagogical in so far as pedagogy is not unrelated to sadism. For the point of this correction is, rather, for the master to confirm his mastery – that is, in the first place, his difference relative to the pupil, who lives only off a philosophical subculture, whereas the master 'knows his texts' otherwise than through second-hand sources. If this otherness (between him and the student) is the teacher's wish, this wish finds in the difference of cultural capital a source of not insignificant satisfaction – together, doubtless, with the discreet gratification of the depositary and proprietor of 'great texts', the legate of 'great authors'. This does not happen only in the pedagogical relation between teachers and their students; it operates also, in brutal manner, in examinations. The charge of 'hearsay knowledge of the great philosophical texts', of 'vague knowledge of the most classical works', is too insistent in the examiners' reports to be ignored. I would gladly wager that what is called 'vague' is not always devoid of sense, and that one might learn a good deal by giving a hearing to the failed scripts. At any rate, the incapacity which we perhaps all share to handle the category of contradiction in what pertains to the history of philosophy is not a result of simple logical infirmity: having once recognized the non-univocal nature of philosophical texts, how can one correct an essay, mark a commentary? The maintenance of a hierarchy of readings is a necessary corollary of the use of texts in school and university. What are the implicit criteria of this hierarchization? Their exploration remains to be undertaken.

6

Long Hair, Short Ideas

Let us avoid getting caught up in a mere lament about the fact that 'woman', as well as having been from time immemorial alienated, beaten and deprived of political, sexual and social rights and legal identity, last and least of all found herself forbidden all access to philosophy. So far as a classification of the rights denied to women is concerned, it is clear that there is a disproportion between the right to have one's own salary or to decide one's sexual destiny, and the right to philosophize, and that this disproportion can only leave the right to philosophize foundering in the anecdotal. Moreover, such a conception runs up against 'facts': certain periods have allowed some women to approach philosophy. Very few, you may say. Certainly, but how many men were there? Up to and including today, philosophy has concerned only a fringe – minimal, indeed evanescent in certain periods – of what was itself a minority class. Sexist segregation seems of slight importance compared with the massive exclusion that has caused philosophy to remain the prerogative of a handful of the learned.

And we have every reason to be suspicious of such a lament, since it can lead to (at least) two so-called feminist positions with which we should have nothing to do. One, shamelessly exploited by the apologists of the 'advanced liberal society', consists in stating that the old times are changing and that we can enter into a contract of progress which will nullify and obliterate this long oppression. This kind of discourse, which from obvious electoral motives contrasts the past with the immediate future (already half present), can be maintained only by recourse to the ploy of abstraction, avoiding analysis of the concrete modalities of oppression, in support of a so-called 'established' fact of massive alienation, a fact which contrasts mystifyingly with once again abstract promises: this simplification plays into the hands of immediate ideologico-electoral exploitation. The other position which we have equally good reasons to avoid adopting is dominated by a feminism of difference which is apparently unaware of how much it owes to Auguste Comte. Some women say:

> We have been forbidden access to the philosophic realm; rightly understood, this is something positive, and we do not demand any such access; this discourse is riddled with masculine values, and women should not be concerned with it; they must seek their specificity, their own discourse, instead of wanting to share masculine privileges.

We need not always and completely reject a feminism of difference. But when we can see in it the echo of a philosophy – namely Comte's positivism – of the discourse on women produced by a masculine philosophy, we must recognize that this kind of feminism may do the opposite of what it claims, that it may be misled by schemas produced by the very structures against which it is protesting. I shall oppose this mystification by the paradox that a practical application of philosophy is necessary in order to oust and unmask the alienating schemas which philosophy has produced.[1] For, whether we like it or not, we are within philosophy, surrounded by masculine–feminine divisions that philosophy has helped to articulate and refine. The problem is to know whether we want to remain there and be dominated by them, or whether we can take up in relation to them a critical position, a position which will necessarily involve the deciphering of the basic philosophical assumptions latent in discourses about women.

In order to try to get away from abstract lamentation, which is a major obstacle to answering the question 'what is to be done?', I shall begin by recalling a few women who have achieved some kind of approach towards philosophy. Their very existence shows that the relative non-exclusion of women is nothing new, thus making it possible to ask whether anything has really changed – whether women are not admitted to philosophy today in ways which reiterate an archaic permissiveness (and restriction).

WOMEN PHILOSOPHERS IN THE PAST

Some women, then, have had access to philosophical theorizing; and let us add that the philosophical was not so forbidden to them that they had to pay for their transgression by losing their female 'nature' in the eyes of observers. The woman who philosophizes has not always or necessarily been seen as a monstrosity. Indeed, this is what makes one suspicious, permissiveness often providing a more revealing indicator than the crude practice of exclusion. For example, Diogenes Laertius has left us a portrayal of Hipparchia which betrays some esteem for her. Certainly, it seemed to him quite a feat (and so it was) that a woman should calmly adopt the Cynic's way of life, but no trace of mockery sullies his chapter on her. He relates the gibes to which Hipparchia (like all the Cynics) was subjected but dissociates himself from them, describing them as vulgar and stupid, and recounting with a certain admiration the *bons mots* with which this 'woman philosopher' replied to tasteless sallies. In the eyes of Diogenes Laertius, it is not femininity that Hipparchia renounced (the expression 'woman philosopher' prevents one thinking that) but, as indeed she said herself, the loss of self implied in the female condition ('I devoted to study all the time which, on account of my sex, I should have wasted at the spinning-wheel').

Similarly, the access to the philosophical of Héloïse or Elizabeth (Descartes's correspondent, who is recorded in history under that one Christian name) has never been characterized as a loss of the mythical advantages of femininity: the antagonism between 'being a woman' and 'being an *honnête homme*' seems to have come later, and I believe it is not until Rousseau (*Émile*, Part V) and Comte that access to philosophy is described in terms of danger, of mutilation, even of degradation. So let us take care not to project historically specific schemas on to the whole of history; for a woman to approach philosophical study is not such an outrage as one might suppose from reading *Les Femmes savantes*. In the same period Madame de Sévigné gently teased her Cartesian daughter about vortices, without appearing to think that reading Descartes was leading her daughter away from 'her true character', from a 'feminine nature' in danger of 'fatal degradation' (all these words are from Comte). A century later Rousseau wrote: 'Believe me, wise mother, do not make an *honnête homme* of your daughter.'

However, both Theodorus (the malicious joker who attacked Hipparchia) and Molière are very useful witnesses; for by suggesting a different reaction from that of Diogenes Laertius or Descartes, they enable one to evaluate or interpret the attitude of these last. There seem to be two points of view, that of the semi-clever and that of the more cunning. The semi-clever argue that there really is a prohibition. As for the clever, they have a more subtle relationship with the prohibition: a relationship which can be described as permissive, as long as it is understood that permissiveness is a sly form of prohibition, and just the opposite of anything that might count as transgression or subversion.

For at first an explicit prohibition was not necessary: at the moment in history where the discourse called philosophy arose, a sexual division in education and instruction was already well established. 'Girls learned only to spin, weave and sew, and at most to read and write a little' (Engels, *Origins of the Family, Private Property and the State*). Imposing limits on the culture of women is quite sufficient to bar them from the philosophical, and their (unspoken) exclusion[2] from philosophy is an epiphenomenon, at least at first sight, of the distinction between what it is appropriate to teach a girl and what a cultivated man needs to know. Similarly, the education of the daughters of the aristocracy in the seventeenth century is essentially linked to the idea of 'social graces': what is important is to give them an attractive wit, pleasant conversation, and to teach them Italian and singing. And when Hegel writes that 'women have culture, ideas, taste, and elegance, but they cannot attain to the ideal', he is repeating on a theoretical level a division already inscribed in actual 'masculine' and 'feminine' forms of education.

At this point there arises a question that I shall only mention: is there a historical change in the relationship of philosophers to women towards the middle of the eighteenth century? Plato had not felt the need to theorize about the sexual distinction of education in his day, and he did not propose to maintain it in the just city. Twenty centuries later Thomas More was equally 'egalitarian', not only in his Utopia but also in the education he gave to the boys and girls who lived in his house. On the other hand, it seems that references to women's incapacity for theory begin to proliferate from the eighteenth century onwards.[3] The whole period establishes and re-establishes divisions and distinctions: divisions between literature and philosophy, techniques of the attractive and art, ideas and ideals, culture and knowledge. A sexual division of faculties, aptitudes, and intellectual destinies was connected with these different distinctions, and this was a considerable change in anthropological theory. This connection, strongly emphasized at the time, continues today as an ideological 'accepted fact', an *idée reçue*.

So let us return to the permissiveness shown to those few women who did (but how, and to what extent?) approach philosophy. First let us note that although they lived in very different times, these women had one thing in common: they all experienced great passions, and their relationship with philosophy existed only through their love for a man, a particular philosopher: 'Hipparchia fell so passionately in love with the doctrine and way of life of Crates that no suitor, however rich, noble or handsome, could turn her from him. She went so far as to tell her parents she would kill herself if she could not have her Crates.' And Héloïse experienced an analogous confusion of amorous and didactic relationships, a confusion which can well be described by the concept of transference. The relationship of Elizabeth to Descartes, though more discreet, seems to me to be of a similar nature. Descartes was 'the one who knows', the one who is asked for knowledge (and not just any knowledge: you who know everything, tell me how to be happy despite all my troubles) and of whom one wants to be a favourable disciple, an intelligent reader, a 'good pupil'.

An unimportant psychological matter? That is not so clear. It can already be noticed that this erotico-theoretical transference (one might as well simply say: this transference) is equivalent to an absence of any direct relationship of women to philosophy. Only through the mediation of a man could women gain access to theoretical discourse. Here we find a predicament common to the feminine condition: that of not being able to do without a protector and mediator in any part of life defined as social. Moreover, the necessity of this mediation seems to me to be inscribed not so much in a prohibition which would directly affect philosophy for women, but in a much simpler prohibition and a much more radical exclusion. Until the Third Republic women did not have access to institutions which taught philosophy. What 'well-bred', 'respectable' Greek woman could have registered at a school, and attended the lectures of Plato or Aristotle? Before even requesting admission, they would have had to be able to leave the gynaeceum: access to philosophy as it was dispensed institutionally would have meant a break with the customary, material framework of the feminine condition. Diogenes Laertius does in fact mention a woman, Themista, in his list of Epicurus's disciples; but she had followed her husband Leontyas of Lampasque to Epicurus's garden. In the Middle Ages women left the home more, but universities were closed to them, even to those who were destined to be abbesses. As for Moslem universities, the question does not even arise.

This is the starting-point for the story of Peter Abelard and Héloïse: it was out of the question for Héloïse to mingle with the audience of five thousand at Abelard's lectures at the École du Cloître de Notre-Dame. So Abelard gave her private lessons in grammar and dialectic. Such 'private' teaching is obviously much more likely than the public lecture to go beyond the didactic sphere. Francine Descartes would not have been admitted to the college of La Flèche, where her father was educated. It is rather comic to see Hegel writing that 'women are educated – who knows how? – as it were by breathing in ideas'; and above all attributing this to the feminine nature (a plant-like, botanical nature bathed in the spirit of the times), whilst the 'who knows how?' is merely the result of the impossibility of entering colleges and universities, where presumably it is known (or is it?) how knowledge is transmitted.

L'ÉCOLE DES FEMMES?

This curious form of transference seems to me to be basically the price women pay for the amateur position to which they are condemned. Only an institutional relationship, with a place and meaning in an organized framework, can avoid the hypertrophy of the personal relationship between master and disciple. But why does philosophical didactics have such a tendency to become erotic? Why does it tend to inscribe itself, without disguise, in the field of the instinctual, to such an extent that only recourse to a third element (let us call it 'school') can enable it to remain within the didactic sphere? I believe that philosophical didactics itself tends to take the form of a dual trans-ference relationship, and that it is obviously not women who pervert this relationship and divert it towards the instinctive realm.

For having once taken note of this singular relationship of women to philosophy one might feel inclined, after going on to look at men, to abandon the assumption of its singularity. In fact, you – Tom, Dick and

Harry – who were at the Sorbonne or prepared the *agrégation* with me, did you really act any differently from Hipparchia?[4] Was it not only too easy sometimes to sense – in the knotting of a tie, in a hairstyle or some such fad – the symbol of allegiance to some cult figure? One could even tell, just by hearing you talk about your student career, that there was always – at the *lycée*, the university or, most commonly, at the preparatory courses for the *Écoles Normales Supérieures* – some teacher around whom there crystallized something similar to the theoretico-amorous admiration which we have been discussing here.[5] Not only women experience it, then. One thing I am sure of is that this privileged teacher was the one who finally seduced you to philosophy, who captured your desire and turned it into a desire for philosophy.

But there is a considerable difference between these student companions and Elizabeth or Sophie Volland.[6] In general, the 'god-father' relationship has opened up the whole field of philosophy to the disciple's desire, whilst women's transference relationships to the theoretical have opened up to them only the field of their idol's own philosophy. I say 'in general' because there are also 'failures' with men, and disciples may remain philosophers of particular schools (read 'cliques'), and never get beyond a repetitious discourse. This repetition, far from being a monstrosity come from God knows where, is only a special form of a general situation. And the particular image of philosophizing women is particular only because certain modalities of philosophical didactics are kept hidden and Plato's *Phaedrus* is either never understood or regularly half-rejected: it was the Greeks, it was the peculiarity of the Platonic doctrine . . . when perhaps one should take it seriously, as a general characteristic of the philosophic journey, without however taking it literally or word for word. *Phaedrus* is a text which has yet to be unravelled and deciphered and, first of all, rescued from the university tradition's strategies of asepticizing, neutralizing and euphemizing it.

The reason why men (both now and in the past) can go beyond initial transference, and why the love component of their transference is sublimated or inflected from the very beginning, so that it can return to the theoretical, is that the institutional framework in which the relationship is played out provides the third factor which is always necessary for the breaking of the personal relationship; the women amateurs, however, have been bound to the dual relationship, because a dual relationship does not produce the dynamics that enable one to leave it. The result of the imprisonment in such a relationship is that philosophizing women have not had access to philosophy but to a particular philosophy, which, it seems to me, is something very different. Their relationship to the philosophical is limited, from outside the theoretical field, by the relationship from which they could not possibly detach themselves. A definitive fealty to one particular form of thought seems to me to be a negation of the philosophical enterprise. To say with Rousseau: 'Woman should have no other religion than her husband's' does not mean that her religion cannot still be a true religion – quite the contrary. On the other hand, if a woman has to have a philosophy of her tutor-lover, she is no longer within the philosophical enterprise, because she is spared (that is to say pro-hibited) a certain relationship with lack, with that particular experience of lack, a radical lack which the Other cannot complete. And this, to my mind, forms the true starting-point of philosophy.

Let us recall, for example, the *Phaedo* or the *Discourse on Method*. In both cases we are given the account of a disappointment and a frustra-tion in teaching: 'I imagined I had found the man who would teach me . . . but he disappointed me.' (97c–99d.) The disappointment begins the story of 'all the trouble I went to' in trying to fill the lack. There is nothing like this in the relationship of women of the past to their master's philosophy: he knows all, his philosophy has an answer to everything. It was not the philosophical lack that Hipparchia, Héloïse and Elizabeth experienced, but 'ordinary', 'classic', 'psychological' lack, the lack which the Other is seen as capable of meeting. No room, then, for 'all the trouble'; these women were not condemned to philosophize, nor to write – not to say 'I'.

Thus we begin to understand the permissiveness of the really cunning, of those who understood what philosophizing means. We are beginning to understand why these women were necessary to their masters (although the men's need for them could produce some ambivalent feelings; this is particularly true of Crates). The theoretical devotion of a woman is very comforting for someone experiencing his own lack; for it is not only the teachings of Anaxagoras or of the Jesuits that are objects of disappointment: the discourse of Socrates or of Descartes reiterates the lack in knowledge. How can it not be gratifying to be seen as a plenitude when one is oneself caught in incompleteness and disappointment? We still smile at the court of women who flocked round Bergson, but we systematically forget to wonder whether this court was not in fact satisfying (or inspired by) Bergson's own desire. The fact that this court was composed of women who were following the Collège de France lectures in an amateur capacity (without expecting qualifications, cashable university diplomas, from them) seems to me significant.

Hipparchia and her great-nieces would be of no interest to us if these women could not provide us with a negative of the actual situation, or of what the actual situation might be. Looking at history mechanically, one might think that now that women have institutional access to philosophy, the block in transferential limitation no longer has a *raison d'être* and therefore no longer exists. But this is not so. The danger of amateurism and the particular position it implies is still there, the only difference being that our female predecessors were condemned to it, while we are merely exposed to it. Virginia Woolf said that in order to write a woman needed at least a room of her own and a private income of five hundred pounds. I would say that in order to philosophize a woman needs both a room of her own and the necessity of earning her living by philosophizing (she must not have avoided this possibility). Today a system of real constraints is needed to counterbalance another subtle system of prohibitions and discouragements. A woman who was not forced to adapt to academic professional constraints would be all too liable to find herself trapped in a typecast role.

YOUR ATROPHY, MY FULLNESS

This system of discouragements is linked first of all to philosophical anti-feminism. It would be all too easy to compile a large book based on the horrors voiced by philosophers, notably from the eighteenth century onwards, on the subject of women. Here I shall quote only three texts:

> The search for abstract and speculative truths, for principles and axioms in the sciences, for all that tends to wide generalization, is beyond the grasp of women; their studies should be thoroughly practical. It is their business to apply the principles discovered by men, it is their place to make the observations which lead men to discover those principles . . . Men have a better philosophy of the human heart, but she reads more accurately the heart of men.

Woman should discover, so to speak, an experimental morality, man should reduce it to a system. Woman has more wit, man more genius; woman observes, man reasons. (Rousseau, *Émile*, Everyman translation, p. 350)

Women may be capable of education, but they are not made for the more advanced sciences, for philosophy and certain forms of artistic production which require universality. Women may have ideas, taste, and elegance, but they do not have the ideal. The difference between men and women is like that between animals and plants; men correspond to animals, while women correspond to plants because their life is more a placid unfolding, the principle of which is the undetermined unity of feeling. When women hold the helm of government, the state is at once in jeopardy, because women regulate their actions not by the demands of universality, but by arbitrary inclinations and opinions. Women are educated – who knows how? – as it were by breathing in ideas, by living rather than by acquiring knowledge, while man attains his position only by the conquest of thought and by much technical exertion. (Hegel, *Philosophy of Right*, para. 166, Zusatz, trans. Knox, modified by the author, pp. 263–4)

And finally Auguste Comte, whom certain people are valiantly trying to bring into fashion today – which is paradoxical, for whether one reads him or not, he is the unconscious inspiration of numerous discourses, and not only on women:

It is in order better to develop her moral superiority that woman must gratefully accept the rightful practical domination of man . . . First as a mother, and later as a sister, then above all as a wife, finally as a daughter, and possibly as a maidservant: in these four natural roles woman is destined to preserve man from the corruption inherent in his practical and theoretical existence. Her affective superiority spontaneously confers on her this fundamental office, which social economy develops increasingly by releasing the loving sex from all disturbing cares, active or speculative. (*Système de politique positive*, vol. II)[7]

This anti-feminism can be analysed in various ways. If we emphasize the date of these texts, we can see in them the affirmation of bourgeois values against the entirely relative permissiveness of the aristocracy with respect to feminine culture in the eighteenth century. It would still remain to be explained why it was the bourgeoisie who were anxious to confine woman to the sphere of *feelings* ('love is an episode in men's lives and the whole story of women's') when the psychology of the royal age (Racine) had not laid down any fundamental inequality between man and woman with respect to *passion* (in the *Traité des passions* Descartes does not refer to sexual differences). Nevertheless it can be noted that this restriction to the emotional is correlative to the expression of a speculative and philosophical incapacity; in which respect this pseudoanthropology needs also to be interpreted not only as a phenomenon of social history, but additionally in terms of philosophy's implication in the matter. It may be that before the eighteenth century it was not necessary to develop a defence of philosophy against women (it is not Molière's problem, for example); but the philosophical salons, and then someone like Madame de Staël, perhaps went too far for the liking of the philosophers of the time; these men could easily have afforded to be permissive to the point of allowing an Héloïse-like relationship to philosophy (as with Rousseau's Julie, and even she repents in time). But because of the relatively determined incursions by women into philosophy at this time, they were driven to adopt a much more clear-cut position: to cling to the trenchant standpoint and flippant sarcasms of Theodorus and make themselves clowns and dogmatists of prohibition; something which was to be all the more advantageous for their male successors today in that the latter would be able to seem like enlightened liberals at a very small cost.

But what were they worried about? Where is the threat to philosophy in women being capable of it? It might be suggested that the so-called sovereignty of philosophy is at stake here. Philosophy, queen of the sciences . . . When a respected activity admits women it loses value: this is not a finding proven by some rigorous, scientific sociology, merely a theorem of intuitive commonplace 'sociology' ('consider what happened to medicine in the USSR! Since women have been practising, doctors have lost their prestige, the profession no longer has any social standing!'). It may be the great dignity of philosophy that keeps women away from it; conversely, for this great dignity to be maintained, women must be kept away. But Bachelard's ectoplasm whispers to me that philosophy reigns today merely in the fashion of the Queen of England, and one can envisage repealing the Salic Law. In this respect, Hegel's comparison between women's incapacity to govern and their unsuitability for philosophizing may be significant, in that political power, whether exercised by a man or a woman, remains power because it is based on real means of coercion, whereas the hegemony of the philosophical is more fragile and therefore has to defend its 'ascendancy' more forcefully; and it is significant that the few women who have ruled – Christina of Sweden and Catherine II – did insist on having access to philosophy.

It might also be suggested that the lack from which the philosophical enterprise stems is, in a man's eyes, inadmissible in a woman. It must not be forgotten that phallocentrism also contains the theory of a phallopanacea. It is well known that all a woman needs to fulfil her every desire is a good husband. In fact it is woman's desire that has always been minimized, since it is often thought that babies' rattles are enough for them. What! Is a man not sufficient to make them feel complete? Is there still a lack, the recognition of which creates the desire to philosophize? And there we have Madame de Staël regarded as a castrating female and vilified by generations of critics. Look at what the typical textbook says of this 'female reasoner', this 'formidable schemer' who attempted to 'play a prominent role' despite her 'superficial views', her 'lack of art' and her 'ugliness'. Rereading *Les Femmes savantes*, one might think that Clitandre is making a rather similar reproach to Armande: 'But your eyes did not consider their conquest fine enough.'

But all these explanations remain inadequate. The exclusion of 'woman' is perhaps more consubstantial with the philosophical, and less historically definable than our quotations from the eighteenth and nineteenth centuries might lead us to believe. The eighteenth century had women to exclude – real, concrete women who had reached the limits of the permissible. But this historically specific struggle reactivated some much older themes and motifs which until then could afford to remain implicit. Plato's *Phaedrus* does not say that women must be excluded from the dialectical enterprise, but with Zeus in love with Ganymede serving as an example, it is clear that this is not women's business. Moreover, the story of the little Thracian servant-girl in the *Theatetus* (a juvenile version of Xantippe?) shows a feminine vulgarity which is obviously far removed from disinterested research.

These older topics, revived in the late eighteenth century, could be seen as an attempt to mask the nature of the philosophical, or as an effort to reassure its always problematic positivity. 'Woman' was to be invoked here in a strictly fantasy-orientated sense, as a purely negative otherness, as an atrophy which, by contrast, guarantees a philosophical completeness. I say atrophy, not negativity, because in the Hegelian perspective it is, in a way, women's lack of negativity that is in question. 'Woman is woman through a certain lack of qualities' (Aristotle): the Hegelian perspective is not far from this definition in that it is the passage through the negative that has become the missing quality. And woman's placid botanical unfolding, falling short of anguish, serves as a foil to the real and substantial completeness of the philosophical, which, having striven through work, effort, suffering and thought, has transcended all inward fracture and is then beyond torment. Here women pay the cost of a defence as, elsewhere, do children, the people, the common man, or the 'primitive' (whose image has not been entirely formed by ethnologists; it owes a lot to what the historians of philosophy have said about the 'debility of reason' among the 'pre-Socratics').

But what, then, is the defence really against? Perhaps it is against the reality of remaining indefinitely in the condition of inner division and torment, of never being able to produce any knowledge equal to one's standard of validation: 'We have an incapacity for proof, insurmountable by all dogmatism' (Pascal, *Pensées*, no. 395). The incapacity of philosophical speculation, the fragility of all metaphysical constructions, the lack, the anguish that torments every 'world system', are not things the philosopher is unacquainted with. The reference to women (or to any other subject deemed 'unfit' for philosophy) allows this powerlessness to be overlooked, for there it is projected, in a radicalized form, on to a subject who is even situated on this side of the search for speculative truths. Or again, the fact that there is someone incapable of philosophizing is comforting because it shows that philosophy is capable of something. It is perhaps this relationship of philosophy to woman that we encounter in the transferences described above. The theoretical devotion of a woman is the distorting mirror which transforms bitterness into satisfaction, but in that case prohibition and permissiveness play the same role. To say that women are incapable of philosophical knowledge, or to be a Diderot and benefit from Sophie Volland's listening in admiration, is one and the same thing.

IN VINO VERITAS

So it is perhaps the distribution of roles effected by philosophy, and required for its reassurance, which forms the first barrier to women's effective access to the philosophical; and if this barrier still exists, the (only very relative) progress represented by women's access to the institutional teaching of philosophy is all for nothing. Not to mention the imaginary portrait of 'woman': a power of disorder, a being of night, a twilight beauty, a dark continent, a sphinx of dissolution, an abyss of the unintelligible, a voice of underworld gods, an inner enemy who alters and perverts without visible sign of combat, a place where all forms dissolve. This portrait has connections with the most ancient metaphysics. In the list of Pythagorian oppositions (given in Hegel's *Lectures on the History of Philosophy*, vol. I) one finds the following:

    limit and infinity
    unity and multiplicity
    masculine and feminine
    light and dark
    good and evil

This list (and the associations which it suggests) is probably not out of date. There is undoubtedly in many men an unconscious, almost superstitious feeling of repugnance at the sight of women approaching philosophy. They could sour the wine in the precious barrels of Plato's *Gorgias*.

But where does this imagery come from? It would be much too convenient to explain it in terms of archaic 'immediate experiences' or of an unconscious constituted *prior* to metaphysics which, like a 'primeval soul', comes and expresses itself, to our regret, where it shouldn't. This would mean treating metaphysics as the innocent party, something which seems hardly possible. When one is in the presence of an 'unconscious' which is structured like a metaphysic, and whose schemas are congruent with this metaphysic, it is not possible either to think that one is dealing with an unconscious or, consequently, to fail to recognize that one is confronting an element of this metaphysic. As for the possibilities of such as element having progressively become absorbed into a more collective imaginary, that is another story. The sphere of influence of the gender-dichotomies created by philosophy is actually very limited. This notion of woman as sphinx and chaos is surely current today only among certain factions of the ruling class. Lower down the social scale, woman is more thought of as a power of order, as a 'sensible' – that is, killjoy – influence, whereas the pole of fantasy and insouciance is seen instead as being occupied by the masculine. A detailed sociological study of masculine and feminine roles might help to explain not only the problems of identity which affect women who change their social milieu, but also the difficulties of communication, at the level of the imaginary, between us – I mean within the women's movement.

Let us limit ourselves, however, to imputing to metaphysics the notion of a 'dark continent' of womanhood – of a femininity of chaos. And perhaps one should, with certain modifications, take this passage from Hegel's *Phenomenology of Mind* seriously:

> Since the community gets itself subsistence only by breaking in upon family happiness and dissolving self-consciousness into the universal, *it creates itself in what it represses* and what is at the same time essential to it – womankind in general, its inner enemy. Womankind – the eternal irony of the community – alters by intrigue the universal purpose of government into a private end . . . (Baillie translation, modified by the author, p. 496)

This text about the state may be transposed into the question of philosophy, though we must add that the philosophical creates that which it represses. This is first because the discourse which we call 'philosophical' produces itself through the fact that it represses, excludes and dissolves, or claims to dissolve, another discourse, other forms of knowledge, even though this other discourse or forms of knowledge may not have existed as such prior to this operation. For philosophical discourse is a discipline, that is to say a discourse obeying (or claiming to obey) a finite number of rules, procedures or operations, and as such it represents a closure, a delimitation which denies the (actually or potentially) indefinite character of modes of thought; it is a barrage restraining the number of possible (acceptable) statements. The simple fact that philosophical discourse is a discipline is sufficient to show that something is repressed within it. But what is repressed? The reply is either too easy or too delicate. Too easy if one is content to quote the list of philosophy's historically varying exclusions: rhetoric, seductive discourse, inconclusive syllogisms, recourse to final causes or occult forms, analogical reasoning, arguments from authority, and so forth. These are mere anecdotes. I would suggest, rather, that this something that philosophy labours to keep at bay cannot be properly defined. It is not and cannot be defined, perhaps because it is precisely the indefinite, or alternatively because philosophy is just the formal idea that discourse must involve exclusion or discipline, that admissible modes of thought cannot be undefined. It is perhaps a general form of exclusion, capable of being given a variety of different contents without itself being essentially allied to any of them. This is why the object of exclusion is not properly definable.

But then this nameless, undefined object, this indeterminable otherness, can only be described metaphorically: I mean by making use of an available signifier, seized upon by philosophical discourse to pinpoint a difference. A signifier is, of course, a term expressing some discrimination. And the man/woman difference is invoked or conscripted to signify the general opposition between definite and indefinite, that is to say validated/excluded, an opposition of which the *logos/mythos* couple represents one form, for the *mythos* is 'an old wives' tale', or at best the inspiration of a Diotima. But in so far as the activity of separation, of division, is philosophically creative (the field is created by its exclusions), philosophy creates itself in what it represses and, this object of repression being essential to it, is endlessly engaged in separating, enclosing and insularizing itself. And the old wives' tales and nannies' lore are always 'obscuring' the clear light of the concept – not because the repressed in general might be overwhelming by nature, but because the finite stock of admissible procedures is never sufficient. All thought presupposes an undefined area, a certain play of structures, a certain margin of free-floating around the codified procedures. Thus shadow is within the very field of light and woman is an internal enemy. For in defining itself through negation, the philosophical creates its Other: it engenders an opposite which, from now on, will play the role of the hostile principle, the more hostile because there is no question of dispensing with it. Femininity as an inner enemy? Or rather the feminine, a support and signifier of something that, having been engendered by philosophy whilst being rejected by it, operates within it as an indispensable dead weight which cannot be dialectically absorbed.

This is, in other words, to say bluntly that women (real women) have no reason to be concerned by that femininity; we are constantly being *confronted* with that image, but we do not have to recognize ourselves in it. I stress that in order to prevent the repetition, in our topic, of the 'paradoxes' which are current today about madness: that reason first excludes unreason and that it is again reason which proceeds to speak of unreason. In the same way it would be too easy to say that my present discourse is being conducted from the standpoint of philosophy, that it is yet another colonizing discourse, and that femininity is no more allowed to express itself here than in the texts of Hegel. As soon as we regard this femininity as a fantasy-product of conflicts within a field of reason that has been assimilated to masculinity, we can no longer set any store by liberating its voice. We will not talk pidgin to please the colonialists.

However, that is exactly what is expected of us. Apparently writing under the heading 'the best soup is made in old pots', Lardreau and Jambet in *L'Ange*, for instance, argue as follows:[8]

> It is time we return to the frankness of the Greeks, to say that in fact the slave and the woman lack reason; that when a slave, as slave, or a woman, as woman, reason about slaves and women, their utterance can only be that of unreason. My wager against Freud – that there is an autonomous discourse of rebellion – can be won only if today an unprecedented, although always existing, discourse irrupts: the discourse of those who lack reason. I know this, but I can only announce it rationally. (Lardreau, p. 37, note 1)

This is incredible: I, who am neither slave nor woman, know, however (and doubtless I am the only one to know; slaves and women don't), what the nature of your discourse should be, slave and woman. Knowledge about women has always been masculine property (in which case *L'Ange* is not *announcing* anything).

It is time to return, not to Greek frankness, but to elementary historical materialism, to recall that it is slave-owning societies which say that a slave is a being without reason; that patriarchal societies are fond of tenderly repeating that *woman* is a dear being without reason; and that colonialist societies proclaim that the Negro, or the savage, is a being without reason. And it is being a little too generous always to credit power with the privilege of reason – just as it shows a somewhat unwarranted complacency to announce 'rationally' a claim exclusively based on the pleasure it yields. Men are held to have a reasoned or rational discourse about woman, whilst woman *qua* woman (here Monsieur Lardreau seems to make epistemo-ontological cuts in the dark continent so that we end up as schizoids without our consent) can only utter nonsense! I will content myself with contrasting this old division with the fact that it is enough for one question concerning the feminine condition to be raised at the National Assembly for all the debates to be transformed into a psychodrama where fantasies unfold which it never occurs to their 'authors' to censure. The debate on contraception in 1967 was a prime example of this. Is it necessary to recall that it was men who talked and raved with total assurance, without the slightest self-control or any hint of *reasoning?* It is probably always the same when anti-feminist men talk about women: they project their desires and anxieties, and attempt to pass off this discourse of desire and defence as a rational theoretical discourse. Luce Irigaray (in *Speculum of the Other Woman*) has provided an exemplary demonstration of this in the case of Freud.

INCOMPLETENESS OR TUTELAGE

From which position, then, do we speak? Not from that other position produced by philosophy as a preserve of purely negative otherness. Nor from within metaphysics, since this founds the duality of masculine rationality and feminine disorder. But there are other possibilities, for logocentrism is not the ineluctable presupposition (or hypothesis) of any rational position. By this I mean (and I am not the first to say it) that up to now logocentrism has left its mark on the entire history of philosophy, separating this history from the possible domain of a 'history of ideas' and turning it into the reiteration of a 'fundamental' thesis, that of the power of true discourse. A discourse is philosophical if it expresses the power of philosophy, identified with the possession of true *knowledge*. This can be seen, for example, in the domains of ethics and politics: look at the concept of wisdom or the figure of the philosophical and providential legislator. Even the materialists of Antiquity do not escape this apologia for true knowledge, this being indeed precisely what marked them out as philosophers and cut short their efforts at materialism. Today it is possible to think of rationality otherwise than in a hegemonic mode – possible, but not easy or straightforward. It is what we struggle for, not a historical gain already at our disposal. This struggle was begun by historical materialism, in so far as this is a rationalism which renounces the idea of the omnipotence of knowledge. From here on one can trace a new form of philosophy, as a fellow-traveller of conflicts which arise outside its realm and which, similarly, will be resolved (if at all) outside it, by means which do not rely on its inherent power. Even so, this is not to pronounce the extinction of the philosophical enterprise but rather to evoke a mediation which still remains difficult to conceptualize.

The fact remains that this change is likely to alter the interlocking of the 'philosophical' and the 'feminine', for it is now possible to cease wishing to mask the incomplete nature of all theorization. That knowledge is always defective, but nevertheless still a necessity ('ignorance has never done anyone any good', Marx once said), enables us to dispense with the logocentric-phallocratic phantasmagoria. But this new relationship to knowledge is still far from being established. Since for the last twenty-five centuries philosophers have been comparing the world to a theatre and philosophy to a tragedy, relating this metaphor to the close of the performance that makes a well-finished whole of the play, I would say that the future of a philosophy that is no longer anti-feminist is being performed somewhere in the region of Brechtian drama, which (again I am not the first to say it) produces unfinished plays which always have a missing act and are consequently left wide open to history. Insisting on philosophy's lack, while making of this lack the condition of its insertion into historical reality, allows philosophy to be moved towards a position where the alternative between a hegemonic reason and a revolt of unreason can be seen as mythical, a connivance or complicity between forms which present themselves as opposites.

Pending the time when such a stance concerning knowledge can gain more than a marginal place in philosophical practice, there persists the discourse, still dominant today, of a philosophical science which is above suspicion. And for women the game is far from being won. The fact that the archaic permissiveness continues seems to me to indicate this. Bergson is dead, but the need for theoretical adulation has not been buried with him: the mandarins still need to be transference objects and, moreover, they are not the only ones.

This will not be news to women who have studied philosophy; they will surely recall the male fellow-students who tried to take them under their wing. And the less need we have for this kind of support, the more we try to get by without masters, the more insistently we find this tutelage being pressed on us. Faced with a woman, a male philosophy student often attempts to adopt the stance of 'the one who knows': knows which books to read, what to think about this commentator on that philosopher, what lectures are worth going to, etc. These aspiring protectors find it difficult to imagine a woman relating directly to philosophy (or even to the teaching of philosophy). Such an attitude can be seen as the reproduction of the relationship they had with their favourite master, or as an attempt to become masters in their turn, as if becoming the object of a transference were the only way of resolving one's own transference. In this way, many young women definitively abdicate all conceptual self-determination in the course of their studies and allow themselves to be guided by a male fellow-student who is supposed to be more brilliant than they are. I hope I am right when I add that this seems to happen less today than ten years ago. Perhaps women have got better at resisting the annexation attempts to which they are subjected. If this is true, then it must be attributed to the growth of the women's movement. But before these dead-end transference relationships can disappear, we must change the very conception of philosophy – this 'we' referring here not only to women, but to all those who are ready to accept the implications of modernity *completely*, including among them the loss of certain narcissistic satisfactions.

It may be said that I am inventing this survival of the Héloïse-like relationship to philosophy. '"From now on I will take you in hand," he said when he told me I had passed the *agrégation*.' How many Jean-Pauls who never became Sartres have said this to Simones who never became feminists? The outrageousness of this conclusion of the first volume of Simone de Beauvoir's autobiography, *Memoirs of a Dutiful Daughter*, often goes unnoticed. It is considered normal. To me, this theoretical 'taking in hand' (and its correlative: the fact that Simone de Beauvoir was confined to the feminine condition, that is to say accepted a ready-made philosophy; or that, in accepting existentialism as a constituted doctrine, she was excluded from the philosophical enterprise) does indeed seem 'normal': that is to say, overdetermined by philosophical and historical conditions. What I find very difficult to understand is that Simone de Beauvoir relates this episode years later without any hint of critical hindsight, even after writing *The Second Sex*.

Before leaving the problem of transference I should like to add that it is perhaps the danger of subjugation as the ransom of amateurism which explains why certain women take such a conformist attitude to university diplomas. This conformity (concern about obtaining academic status, preference for formalized forms of working, for doctoral theses rather than less conventional research) is perhaps unconsciously conceived of as a convenient antidote to, or as a means of resisting, the pressures to make us into great readers or precious admirers. Investing as much as possible in the institution can also appear as a conquest, when an institutional relationship to philosophy has been forbidden for so long. The irony is that the creative areas in philosophy today do not lie in the region of academic work, so that this conquest is perhaps actually a relegation, but it takes more confidence to offer a manuscript to a publisher than to submit a thesis proposal. Having been trapped in dual relationships, women are now in danger of burying themselves in a relationship to narrowly university-defined institutions. Besides, the value of the institutional relationship as an antidote is very problematic. Is it a denial or a sublimation of the transference relationship?

ANTI-FEMINISM IN THE EXAMINATION SYSTEM

At all events, it cannot be said that the institution welcomes women with open arms (except in the Héloïse-role described above) – that is to say, recognizes their philosophical capacities. For example, one often sees the 'masters' (teaching either in a preparatory class or in a university) choosing 'followers' – that is, transmitting a flattering image of themselves to some of their pupils. This attitude is part of an important process of overstimulations which organize the future succession and designate, often from the earliest stage, those who are going to feel 'called' (and in fact are) to play a so-called leading role in the philosophical enterprise. The teachers' sexist and sociocultural prejudices take on a considerable importance in this period of philosophical apprenticeship. Many women are aware of the un- conscious injustice of numerous teachers: young men are selected 'followers' – often, moreover, for obscure reasons – while women constantly have to fight for recognition. Incidentally, the personal involvement of teachers in this search for an heir apparent needs to be analysed. Perhaps this too is a question of an avatar, this time 'from man to man', of the lack which torments the master and which in the 'man to woman' case leads to a search for female admirers. The sexist distribution of these favours needs to be denounced, but first of all one should object to the very existence of this type of behaviour. Besides, it would be useful to investigate the precise moment in the school or university course at which the teachers' sexist prejudices are most fully operative as an instrument of selection. My impression is that it occurs later than the selection based on sociocultural criteria.

However, this fundamental aspect of philosophical studies remains unofficial and the system of exclusion which it operates in itself calls for a real effort at establishing the facts. On the other hand, the results of the selective examinations for teaching jobs, while they too need to be subjected to analysis, yield some extremely cruel 'findings'; since 1974, when the *Capès* and *agrégation* in philosophy became mixed, the number of women who pass has been very small.[9] The anti-feminists may well proclaim that now the examinations are mixed, one can see what should have been clear all along – the distinct inferiority of women compared to their masculine counterparts.

Even if one tries, as some do, to explain this theoretical inferiority either in material terms (a poor female candidate has a double job, her phallocrat of a husband or lover letting her deal with all the domestic chores) or (quite acceptably) in terms of some neuro-endocrinological fantasy, the disparity between men's and women's results remains a problem. I will not cite the evidence of teachers who prepare candidates for these examinations, teachers who have never during the year of preparation had occasion to note this so-called inequality of 'standards' and are always surprised by the results; this kind of evidence would surely not be considered proof. I shall just refer to the report on the 1971 *agrégation*. That year the exam was not mixed, and the Minister had designated two sets of teaching jobs, one for men, the other for women; but the two boards had amalgamated so that through an interchange of posts there was in fact only one board. To its credit, the board noted so great a disparity in favour of the women between the 'standard' of the men and women at the bottom of the list that they thought it their duty to take some posts from the men to award them to the women. That was in 1971.

In 1974, for the first time, the examination was mixed, and the proportion of women absurdly low. What hormonal (or conjugal) change had occurred during these three years? Had the education of girls born after 1950 been so different from that of girls born immediately after the war? I doubt whether any satisfactory explanation is to be found by looking at the candidates. Equally questionable would be any attempt to account for the present disparity in terms of the inveterate and more or less unconscious anti-feminist prejudices of the boards; for in that case, how could the 1971 boards have escaped the effects of this phallocratic unconscious? I prefer to say that the historical and social context has altered slightly in three years, and that this alteration has reinforced a virilophile preference (which in 1971 had reached exhaustion point). An examiner is first and foremost a social agent like everybody else: he fulfils historical options which may well escape his conscious mind.

The point here is not to seek to put certain individuals on trial for their conduct, but rather to try to establish the kinds of circumstances in which anti-feminism is liable to revive. What was it, then, that really happened between 1971 and 1974? In the years up to 1971, the numbers of posts available seem to have followed an upward curve. I wonder – although perhaps historians will smile at this kind of hypothesis – whether those mini-periods which encourage a belief in the positive movement of time are not apt to induce a kind of mild future-euphoria which gives historical agents, at least in those sectors where such a belief can have effect, a tendency to behave in a relatively progressive manner – and, conversely, whether periods of regression where the fear of dislocation prevails do not lead social agents (those, at least, who occupy positions of power) to become more reactionary, more fiercely hostile to all opening towards the new, more anxious to protect a tradition and its exclusivities.

A strange idea, perhaps, but have there ever been so many diatribes against everything philosophically or pedagogically modern as since the teaching of philosophy has come explicitly under threat? 'Go back to *cours magistraux* [formal lectures], have the courage to speak with authority, and above all do not talk of Freud.' This is the kind of conservative directive that we now increasingly hear. The gap between philosophical research and university power did not exist, at least in this form, ten years ago.[10] Georges Canguilhem, at that time an inspector and president of the *agrégation* examination board, concretely backed the research of Lacan and Foucault. Today, however, there is a dream of returning to a golden age (the age of Alain?) which expresses itself in terms both of theory (Descartes, not Freud) and pedagogy (the authoritative teaching style). In such a situation anti-feminism has a twofold position: if philosophy teachers are to wield more authority today than they did previously, then it is obvious that more trust will be placed in men than in women teachers. And doesn't one see well enough that the examination papers of male candidates can be identified as such by their authoritative tone? And there is anyway, in the current policy, a general desire – not confined to philosophy – to defeminize teaching. And then philosophical anti-feminism is linked, as I have tried to show, to philosophy's claim to present itself as a form of knowledge which places its holder in a position of strength. So it is not surprising that the return to philosophical dogmatism (and any anxious return to a former position is a kind of dogmatism) should accompany a wave of anti-feminism. Certain questions about philosophy's status, about the gaps opened up within philosophy by a certain effect of modernity, are closed off, and at the same time the feminine is foreclosed and confined to femininity.

Finally, there is now in France a philosophy made popular by the media (of which the *nouveaux philosophes* are a prime example): a philosophy which is apt to propagate ideas half-baked but carefully chosen for their rather facile shock value. These writers are not ashamed of saying all kinds of things about the inabilities of women. Unfortunately, these books have an impact and may cause certain women to lose some of their philosophical zeal and so to co-operate with this historical tendency, a tendency which works against them.

Let us be fair: these virilophile preferences do not themselves explain the change. The 1971 candidates had taken an '*ancien régime*' degree (*licence*), with a standard syllabus, the same for everyone, and this syllabus was supposed to cover in three years the whole field of philosophy. The 1974 candidates took a degree based on 'options' with sometimes extremely narrow subjects. The new system gives the students a 'choice', which means above all that it gives free scope for self-assessment by students in their choice of options. As such, it represents a covert form of social and sexual selection. I should like to see statistics on men's and women's choices. I would strongly suspect that they are different, and that women tend to choose the options which are considered easy, whilst men opt for the 'noble' ones – those which are 'difficult', but supposed to 'train the mind'. For men overevaluate their capabilities, whilst women underestimate theirs.

None the less we can be fair without needing to be taken in: it is above all in the written examinations that women are eliminated. Since there are no little pink or blue stickers on the papers to compensate for anonymity, some people might argue that it is impossible for sexist preferences to operate here. But anyone who has corrected student papers will know that it is possible to distinguish two types of philosophical writing, one masculine and the other feminine, and that these two types usually tally with the sex of the candidate.

I remember marking commentaries: a paper can be identified as masculine by its authoritative tone, by the way interpretation dominates over receptivity to the text, resulting in a decisive and profound reading or in fantastic misinterpretation. Women, on the other hand, are all receptivity, and their papers are characterized by a kind of polite respect for the fragmentation of the other's discourse (this is called 'acuteness in detailed commentary but lack of overview'), by a great timidity (it is as though they left it to the text to explain itself), and also by a talent for what one might call the 'flattering comparison'. A particular passage in Rousseau's *Discourse on the Origins of Inequality* may remind them of a letter in the *Nouvelle Héloïse*, a rather curious form of recall. It is like a salon where a guest alludes to one of his claims to fame: the good hostess picks up the allusion immediately and recalls it in a few flattering terms, so offering the guest the pleasure of feeling he is being asked about himself.

Men treat the text familiarly and knock it about happily; women treat it with a politeness for which girls' education has its share of responsibility. If the timidity and the desire to flatter are not too strong this form of reading can, I think, produce great successes, a distanced kind of reading which enables one to see what is implicit in the text or to pick out the 'gaps' in a theorization. The question is whether it is because this kind of reading is not highly valued that the women fail, or whether it is not highly valued just because it is evidently feminine. I prefer the second hypothesis, and would add that the feminine is excluded because it is associated with the idea of lack of authority. In any case, if a text is immediately identifiable as masculine or feminine, the anonymity is a mere joke – and this identification is in danger of being the more efficient for not always being conscious.

VESTALS AND AFTER

I would have liked to consider women's relationship to philosophical writing, and how people respond to philosophical books by the dozen or so women who have succeeded in getting their work published, and sometimes even read. But this would be the subject of another paper.[11] Here I shall confine myself to one point: there is one area where women today have completely free access – that of classic works on the history of philosophy. No one considers studies by Marie Delcourt, Geneviève Rodis-Lewis, or Cornelia de Vogel as 'women's books' to be read with indulgence and condescension. Is this because these women impose on themselves the 'austere necessity of a discipline', so finding the 'third factor' needed in order to direct the desire to philosophize towards the theoretical field? How is one to interpret the fact that our elders succeeded in getting themselves respected and recognized for commentaries or editions, whilst none of them produced such texts as *The Phenomenology of Perception* or *The Critique of Dialectical Reason*? That women should be admitted to the commemorative history of philosophy seems to me to be primarily a reflection of what is generally held to constitute a commentary. Who better than a woman to show fidelity, respect and remembrance? A woman can be trusted to perpetuate the words of the Great Discourse: she will add none of her own.

Everyone knows that the more of a philosopher one is, the more distorted one's reading of other philosophers. Think of Leibniz's reading of Malebranche, or Hegel's reading of Kant! They cannot respect the thought of the other: they are too engrossed in their own. Nietzsche said that a scientist's objectivity indicated his lack of instinct. How could a woman manhandle a text, or violate a discourse? The vestal of a discourse which time threatens to eclipse, the nurse of dismembered texts, the healer of works battered by false editions, the housewife whom one hopes will dust off the grey film that successive readings have left on the fine object, she takes on the upkeep of the monuments, the forms which the mind has deserted. A god's priestess, dedicated to a great dead man. This phantasmagoria of the commentary has to some extent enabled women to find a place for themselves in philosophical work. A minor one, however: as in cooking, so in commentary – the high-class works are always reserved for a Hyppolite or a Bocuse. It is true that Hyppolite did not confine himself to 'explaining' Hegel, but from Hipparchia to the women historians of philosophy, there has been little progress in emancipation.

At the moment all of us remain more or less imprisoned in this phantasmagoria of the commentary – the commentary trapped between the alternatives of violation and fidelity. When what bears the name of commentary has been decoded, and the phantasmagorical representation of the activity has been dismantled, it will perhaps be possible to stop assigning such a 'subordinate' position to women in the distribution of theoretical tasks.

Whether forbidden to enter the area of philosophizing, or 'benefiting' from a more or less cunning permissiveness, women have not yet won the battle that would give them a right to philosophy. For the moment it is important to know against whom – and with whom – this struggle can be fought. We must test out the following two propositions:

1. Is it possible to make philosophy, or philosophical work, abandon its wish to be a speculation which leaves no room for lack of knowledge, to make it accept its intrinsic incompleteness and create a non-hegemonic rationalism, so that philosophy will no longer need a defence mechanism involving the exclusion of women – and children? Alain Delorme's account of an experiment of philosophical teaching to twelve-year-olds could well point in a similar direction. Two, probably interconnected, points become apparent in his account: first, proof of children's capacity to philosophize, and then the idea of an unfinished philosophical discourse, never closed and never concluded, and hence the abandonment of any totalizing aim. It may be that only a form of philosophy that no longer considers its incompleteness a tragedy would be able to avoid projecting a theoretical incapacity on to children, women . . . or the Pre-Socratics. This hypothesis is certainly too schematic to be accepted as it stands; but it is important to work on it.

2. Is it possible to transform the relationship of the subject to the philosophical enterprise? For until today, the subject of philosophical research has always presented itself as a person: Aristotle, Spinoza or Hegel. And philosophical dialectics has likewise operated between two personal poles: the master 'who knows' and the pupil 'who does not yet know'. This connection between the subject of philosophical knowledge and the individual person (a highly complex association, for the idea of a bearer of philosophical knowledge has contributed to the historical produc-tion of the idea of person) has numerous theoretical and pedagogical effects. Since at this point my ideas get muddled, I open a work by Hegel or Leibniz, and I catch myself thinking: 'What a cheek, all the same! You must have an incredible nerve to claim intellectual

mastery of all that is in heaven and earth – and in human practice. A woman would never dare.' But this nerve, if it has strongly masculine connotations, is even more marked by a necessity: since the subject of knowledge is the person, what 'I know' (or claim to know) gets confused with what 'is known' – indeed, with what it is possible to know. The metaphysical (and logocentric) nerve of such and such a 'great philosopher' is what supports the idea of the existence of a form of knowledge. If the philosopher vanishes there will be no one left to know, and there will be no more knowledge. But if the subject of the enterprise is no longer a person – or, better still, if each person involved in the enterprise is no longer in the position of being the subject of the enterprise but in that of being a worker, engaged in and committed to an enterprise which is seen from the outset as collective – it seems to me that the relationship to knowledge – and to gaps in knowledge – can be transformed. Here again, it is hard to describe the revolution that would be effected by a collective form of philosophical work *and* by a recognition of the fact that, in any case, the enterprise cannot be reduced to personal initiatives.

Still confused, I now open Pascal – and I suddenly see why, however foreign the religious concepts of this work are to me, I feel more 'at home' in the *Pensées* than in any of the other classic texts. It is because the religious perspective hints at this penumbra of unknowledge (a penumbra which has nothing to do with the limits of reason), which metaphysics has denied. Here is a form of writing which does not claim to reconstruct and explain everything, which slides along the verge of the unthought, develops only by grafting itself on to another discourse, and consents to be its tributary. Perhaps it will be said that it is outrageous to envisage a 'different kind of writing' for the future (one in which women will be able to be reintegrated) in a work that wraps up its meanderings and 'blanks' in dogma and mystery.

But replace obedience to these dogmas (or to another discourse already commenced) by the recognition that 'I do not do everything on my own', that I am a tributary to a collective discourse and knowledge, which have done more towards producing me than I shall contribute in continuing to produce them; and replace the mystery with a recognition of the necessarily incomplete character of all theorization. What will we have then, if not today's only correct representation of the relationship between the subject and knowledge? And also the only psychotheoretical attitude which makes collective work possible and necessary – a 'collectivity' whose scope obviously extends beyond the 'group' of people working together. The refusal to lay claim to an inaugural discourse, such as one finds in Foucault's *L'Ordre du discours*, may serve to indicate the position that is trying to emerge today, and if the reference to Pascal bothers readers, let them replace it by a reference to Foucault – though this is a more dangerous reference, since it threatens to reorganize the transference which we ought to be denouncing.

The belief which has emerged from my still very recent experience of collective work is that the future of women's struggle for access to the philosophical will be played out somewhere in the field of plural work. More especially as working groups are likely to acquire a structuring power (of acting as a 'third factor' and as the system of constraint needed to counteract the discouragement resulting from negative narcissism) analogous or equivalent to that of the institution: they enable one to avoid both the Héloïse position, probably through a transference on to a peer group – hence the need to clarify further the notion of transference which has been used here – and its equally undesirable opposite, which is the overinvestment of the desire to philosophize in the 'academic' or the 'institutional'. In this kind of practice, at every moment I encounter the fact that the others' discourse being the origin of mine, as well as an unforeseeable future, gives it a continuing sense of its own limits. Here, one has the impression of experiencing a new rationality, in which a relationship to the unknown and to the unthought is at every moment reintroduced.

7

Philosophy in the Larynx

Philosophical texts which deal with the voice cannot be treated as a unified theoretical ensemble. It is therefore not possible to achieve an exhaustive treatment of their topic simply by surveying a discourse which, one supposes, remains one and the same throughout the history of philosophy.

Rather than attempting to summarize an entire corpus of philosophical opinions, pronouncements and systems, I have chosen here to look in detail at just one of its aspects, one that can be taken as an inversion of the myth of the Sirens, and to follow through the issues it involves. 'They charm all mortals who approach them. But mad indeed is he who yields to listen to their songs, for the fresh voices of the Sirens bewitch him : . . .' There is no worse Siren, the philosopher will say, than the one who does not sing.

> I would think that the true distinctive character of the singing voice is to form appreciable sounds whose unison can be grasped or felt, and to pass from one to the other by harmonic and commensurable intervals, whereas, in the speaking voice, the sounds are not sufficiently sustained or (so to speak) unified to be appreciated; the intervals which separate them are far from harmonic enough, their relations far from simple enough.

There is, then, according to the article 'Voice' in Rousseau's *Dictionary of Music*, something troubled and troubling in a voice which might have been thought of as banality itself: the voice which speaks. Appreciable, commensurable, made of calculable intervals, the singing voice promises an ordered and reassuring world, cleared and colonized by measure and numbers. The speaking voice, on the other hand, is disquieting because of its 'insufficiency'; it is a place of pure multiplicity, incommensurability, inappreciable deficit. This sense of trouble is scarcely theorized as such in the remainder of Rousseau's system, since most often he works by setting up a tripartite distinction (the speaking or articulated voice/the singing or melodious voice/the pathetic or accented voice) and the speaking voice is commonly dis-valued there by reason of its monotony, its fading accents, its merging qualities, its coldness. Associating pathos with vocal accent serves to exclude from consideration the troubling dimension of the spoken voice and its uncertain timbre.

The binary division in the *Dictionary of Music* might well, for its part, tend to work in favour of the speaking voice, the place of irrationals: the disorder of the passions might well find a privileged mode of expression in its inappreciable medium – the more so because the indefinite and complicated nature of the speaking voice's timbre opens the possibility of an infinite variety, and hence of an individualization of voices, whereas singing voices subdivide into a total of six or eight classes. A woman and a castrato can sing the same melody; speaking voices cannot be interchanged. Hence Rousseau hastens to annul the effect of this binary distinction by adding the further specification that some languages (Italian and Ancient Greek) are more harmonious than others, in that the spoken voice there comes nearer to the singing voice. Again, Strabo is cited here ('speech and song were once one and the same'). But the heart has gone out of this theme. It is now three years since *La Nouvelle Héloïse*, and Jean-Jacques must force himself to follow the opposite path to that taken in his novel: the *Dictionary of Music* will speak only of the singing voice ('the only one which relates to my subject'; 'I return to the singing voice and shall confine myself to it'); but this very effort betrays the will to dam up another speech, and a malaise which *La Nouvelle Héloïse* may help us to understand.

Italian song – alone worthy of Julie's voice – in which 'the exact measure and choice of accords', 'the just and equal tones' have 'so complete a rapport with the tone of the language' that Julie, who reads Italian poetry, begins singing it without realizing she is doing so – this all-too-celebrated Italian song forms the culminating motif of the novel's first part, and nothing more. This is the youthful euphoria of two lovers who have not yet encountered that tragic negativity and dissociation which, according to the novel's logic, open up the depths of unavowed abandon to the irreducible, a passion which has no common measure with beauty, goodness, truth or knowledge of self. For the first half of the novel Julie and Saint-Preux indeed play and live out a possible commensurability between love and virtue, beautiful music, and reasoning sincerity. But this defensive formation breaks down at the end of Part Three and a shattering force is unloosed: the force of the uttering voice.

Thus in this letter where Saint-Preux strives to persuade Julie not to reveal her past loves to Wolmar, a letter closing with a last resort: 'Finally when all these reasons, solid as they are, fail to persuade you, do not shut your ear to the voice which expounds them to you.' Thus also the notes in Part Four on Julie's 'tone', that 'voice sound' which makes Saint-Preux start, the 'she spoke to me', 'she continued speaking to me in the same tone', and the numerous remarks by Julie about the transformations in Saint-Preux's tone of voice. But no one sings any more. Is this because Julie's conjugal fidelity and Saint-Preux's plans to reform are a sufficient concession to censure and ideals? The lovers hardly now exchange any but decorous words, but the timbre of their voices maintains the love relationship, an element still untamed by Clarens's order; and the vocal relation is all the more an amorous one because everything else, everything which is text, is subject to censorship. Giving over all text to the law leaves timbre free to speak.

The dissociation between the relation to the materiality of the other's voice and the content of what is said doubtless corresponds to the mental contradiction described by Wolmar (they are completely cured; they have never been so much in love; these two contradictory propositions are true at one and the same time). This dissociation will be suspended only for a moment, in a silence, that of the walk by the lake. The distance has grown so great that a compromise can be reached only by the annulment of one of its poles.

Julie dies. And Claire, the inseparable cousin, can no longer eat or speak. A formidable cathartic scene is now staged. Little Henriette used to look so much like Julie that she was often dressed in clothes identical to her aunt's. So Wolmar disguises her 'in as complete imitation of Julie as possible', and asks her to take Julie's role at table. The sight of this *representation* only touches and moves Claire. But then Henriette takes it into her head to copy Julie's tone of voice, and say: 'Claire, will you have some of this?' Whereupon everything explodes,

Claire starts, bursts out laughing, begins to eat avidly, and goes mad. The everyday voice of Julie, the tone of her words at table – this is all that is necessary to provoke an illness or produce hallucinations. 'At each instant of the day,' writes Claire – and this is on the novel's last page – 'I hear the accents of her voice' – and, near her tomb, 'I seem to feel her heartbeat, I hear a plaintive voice's murmur.' The novel has unmade the compromise formation, the sublimity of the singing voice which remained just and beautiful and measured even while depicting the passions' disorder, opening itself to the great unrecognized perturbation, seduction without an alibi, the theme which takes the speaking voice as its emblem. One can understand from this why Rousseau, in the *Dictionary*, has such difficulty in 'returning to the singing voice' and 'confining himself to [his] subject'.

A pacified, secure world, the space of the singing voice and, somewhere in the picture, the indication of another voice vested with disquieting values – such a model can be read as a Platonic resurgence.

> 'In so far as the voice is used in music,' says the *Timaeus*, it has been given us for the sake of harmony. The revolution of the soul in us is, of itself, inharmonic. Song sets it in order and accord with itself. And if we ordinarily lack measure, the gods have given us rhythm as a remedy.

Hence the considerable educative importance accorded by the *Laws* to songs, which are naturally made subject to a minute legislation. The inscription of law in affectivity features in the programme of the ideal Cretan city: the end of education is that the child should become accustomed to having neither pleasures nor pains which are counter to law. It is with this motive that songs are required to act as incantations on souls. They produce (II, 659) a concerted harmony in the soul – an order with evident political virtues. The state can annex the singing voice and charge it with making citizens, from their youth, love that which is well ordered. To be sure, song can disappoint this hope – there are soft, slack musics which indulge the taste instead of raising it. Still, music is manageable by the state. Perhaps it is important to note also that this concerns a *practice* of singing, not hearing. This harmonic political education takes effect via the larynx, not the ear.

Yet it is hearing a voice, one which is not singing, that can cause dire risk to the city: the voice of the tragedians: 'Suppose one day these

Strangers ask us for access to our territory. Shall we let them set up their boards here?' The answer to this question centres on considerations regarding the risk to the city resulting from the fact that 'the tragic actors have a fine voice which speaks louder than ours'. A relation of forces which has nothing to do with the meaning or content of discourse makes its appearance here. Faced with an element unrelated to the truth-value of language, the philosopher-legislator admits defeat in advance: 'It would be utter madness on our part' to allow these actors without precaution to 'address themselves to children, women, all the crowd.' Let the choice of vocabulary be taken seriously: the learned construction of the city of the *Laws* is liable to be wrecked by a finer-timbred voice. Such a voice, moreover, cannot be tamed. The singing voice can be regulated; the tragedians' voice can be accepted or excluded only according to whether, in the event, it says or does not say the same thing as the lawmaker, whether the pure pathos of this voice happens to accompany an admissible text.

The voice is stronger than the Law [*phonè nomou*]. How much stronger? Twice, three times? The question has no meaning; if it had one, the problem would be less serious. For the more and the less, the strong and the weak fall, in the terminology of the *Philebus*, into the category of the *apeiron*: they prevent the realization of a definite quantity, dissolve measure, and constantly introduce into all action the opposition of the more violent and the more pacific. This is the genus of the indefinite, the absence of figure and measure, as opposed to the genus of limit, of numbers and harmony, which produces the equal and the double and all the factors which end the opposition of contraries, rendering these commensurable and harmonizing them through the introduction of number.

Should one then read the threat contained in the tragic voice in terms of the ontology of the *Philebus*, and say that it is as a fragment of pure *apeiron* devoid of numeric admixture that the voice acts as troublemaker? Such a step would commit us to recognizing the circularity of the Platonic models. For this ontology is expounded in the *Philebus* through examples, one of which is precisely the human voice as forming an infinite diversity until music determines precise intervals, fixed sounds, relations measured by numbers. Politics, legislation of the voice, ontology, mathematics: each notion relies on the others; and that is not all. The uneasy question of paternity, the difficult encounter of the sexual and the legitimate, can also provide a model for thinking voices, *or* can be ordered and disordered by voices.

Two dangers are to be avoided: illegitimate erotic relations, and sterile legitimate relations. The tragic tone, so pleasing to women and the young, stands on the side of the frenzy of lawless love. Writing stands, for its part, on the side of sterility (*Phaedrus*, 277a). For all to go well, the modes of song suited respectively to men and women must be legally regulated,. and sexual relations strictly monitored. Then 'women will have the affection for men which belongs to their nature'. Thus true, spoken (not written) discourses are 'legitimate sons of their author' (*Phaedrus*, 278a) and 'bear a seed which will give birth in other souls to other discourses', etc.

There remains the risk that some vigorous young man might appear, raise his voice against the city's rules of conduct and fill it with his clamour. Once more all is compromised, the law is impotent to tame this exceptional force. Law must find itself an ally in the public voice and, if need be, in tragedies portraying persons guilty of illicit love who hasten to their own death as punishment. There is no direct way to domesticate or tame the clamorous voice, but one can utilize it against the pathos which inhabits it, by coupling it to something the state can control: the tragic moral *fable*, or a prescribed content for the public voice. This is the final expedient: in order to extend the state-enlistment of the voice, play off ill against ill, employ the unassimilated residue in the voice to liquidate the frenetic residue of the passions.

From this short ramble through Plato I shall retain the motif of circular variation of a problem, considerations on the voice forming one link in a closed metaphoric chain. And the voice functions here less as a model, privileged or otherwise, than as a vulnerable point (like, in this respect, every other link of the chain: thus geometry is the model of justice, but the *Laws* remind us that there are incommensurables): as a result of counting so heavily on it as an intermediary between law and affectivity, the voice has displaced on to it, over and above hopes for the colonization of affectivity, the panic and obsession of the legislator. These anxieties crystallize around the possibility of the voice's loss of musicality – something which the Latin expresses in a single word: *solut…. Sermo solutus* is speech freed of the constraints of rhythm, but *solutus* also means unleashed, unbridled. Thus, 'necessarily', the less music there is in a voice, the more emotional power it will possess.

This is the paradox to which theory leads: consider also what is said about this in the *Letter to d'Alembert*. In the final act, Berenice, in a 'stifled voice', gives 'speech to a cold pain'; and then, but only then, the audience start to weep. It is truly time for Titus to exile her to her distant Palestine if he wants to protect Rome; and time for the republic of Geneva to renew its prohibition of the theatre. Titus dismisses her 'without the farewell of the pit', '*invito spectatore*' – in spite, that is to say, of which spectator? Of a certain Jean-Jacques who has just finished *La Nouvelle Héloïse* and discovered, in so doing, his seduction by a voice improper for use in philosophy, by the inverse of his professional fantasy. This fascination is so dangerous that he makes on the spot, as he declares, the undertaking no longer to write on what does not interest him, or against what he loves. Thus 'I return to my subject which is the singing voice, and shall confine myself to it.' Without this self-censorship, would we have had the *Social Contract*?

Need we raise the question of the truth-value of this binary division? Does it matter to ask whether, in truth, the sounds of the singing voice are 'appreciable', or whether the speaking voice is *really* troubling? All these philosophical discourses probably tell us nothing about the voice or voices. There is no need here to invoke, for example, the Breton tonalities of the Goadec Sisters to contest the banalizing aesthetics of these theories of song. The theories I have mentioned tell us not about the voice but about philosophy. They are blazons and armorial bearings – drafts of specular objects in which the scriptor thinks himself and his relation to the Other. (And the voice is not an ill-chosen 'motive' for this: who would deny that it implicates a relation to the Other?) In the singing voice, with its adjusted and harmonious sounds, a certain philosophy, that which claims to regulate the political, inscribes and contemplates its promises and hopes; the singing voice is indeed 'its subject': it is the emblem of achieved colonization ('being at home in one's Other', as Hegel puts it). The timbre of the speaking voice is the counter-myth, marking the impossible meeting of two scenes, that of the best-possible-form-of-government – elaborated in the non-place of philosophy – and that of real political conflicts.

It is more comfortable for philosophy to think of this non-junction in terms of relations of vocal forces incommensurable with the order of reasons. Painful problems concerning the pertinence and acceptability of the philosopher's political project can thus be reduced to a relatively simple set of terms. Here there is room neither for disavowal of the project itself nor for questioning of the text, since the necessity of failure

has been *situated* beforehand, in an element which is incommensurate
with or heterogeneous to that of the text! This is the way to sidestep
reality's dismissal of the sage who proclaims his own providential
mission: 'I am entirely in the right, but my voice is not loud enough.'
The second proposition sustains the first, and preaching in the desert is
preferable to having one's self-proclamation endangered. This does not
prevent some delightful incursions through the looking-glass: playing
with the seduction previously vested in the other voice, entrusting to a
woman the direction of a philosopher's conscience – in short, writing *La
Nouvelle Héloïse* – amounts to the same thing, bar the difference of a sign,
as enclosing the Territory of reason.

'Though it is a sad thing to acknowledge, it is vocal capacity which
decides in the final instance – and not what is just, or what is said.'
Analysing this mythic statement would offer little interest if such an
idea did not have a currency reaching a little beyond the philosophical
sphere, and if certain circumstances did not give it a mystifying
credibility. The course taken by some of the General Assemblies of
May 1968 might, for instance, have led one to think that an orator's
voice timbre had something to do with the greater or lesser hearing he
or she obtained. The mistake is to make this factor into a 'last instance',
rather than recognizing that vocal timbres are related in turn to the
social place of the speaker, as an index of the social weight objectively
and subjectively assumed by the orator (the same might be said of the
persistent misapprehension which consists in treating qualities of
writing and style as an element *sui generis*).

We women notice that a 'deep' (masculine) voice prevails more
easily than a soprano timbre. But this is because 'deepness' is a sign of
the positively marked social status of the utterer (as also is a voice
which is 'distinguished', 'free of provincial accent', etc.), and an
audience reacts to the materiality of the voice as a sign which is
immediately interpretable within a grid of social positions and
oppositions. The social importance crystallized around the speaker's
name and the social values which govern reaction to the voice's timbre
work together to form an unconscious hearing which hierarchizes
individuals' utterances.

What consequences are to be drawn from this situation? I have no
idea. All I know is that a demi-critique is as mystifying as a non-critical
attitude. Letting oneself be manipulated by what is encoded through
vocal timbre – or the literary qualities of a text – is doubtless a

deplorable thing. But cutting short the analysis halfway, making vocal power into a force *sui generis* which disrupt the conditions of 'fair debate', is to risk retreating into a complacent daydream and the suspect plaints of the voiceless orator, the philosopher who suffers from having, as they say, 'such a nice voice, he'd better write'.

8

Pierre Roussel's Chiasmas:
(From Imaginary Knowledge to the Learned Imagination)

There is no equality between the sexes as to the consequence of sex.[1]

The layer of dust that accumulates on learned books, said Georges
Canguilhem, measures the frivolity of women of letters. But when a
book on 'Woman' written by an eighteenth-century doctor is able,
despite all subsequent·advances in physiology, to escape its deserved
fate as a dust-laden manual of quackery, one may feel like retorting that
the absence of dust covering books about 'Woman' is a measure of the
inertia of everyday – or bookish – sexism.

In what follows I present a reading of the *Système physique et moral de la
femme* (1777) by Pierre Roussel. This book is beginning to become a
familiar one in feminist studies.[2] I am not here exhuming a forgotten
work, still less a baroque relic suitable for a museum of pre-scientific
horrors. Whereas to read (for example) the works of eighteenth-
century chemists demands a considerable imaginative effort on our
part, since we now share with them no common intellectual ground,
one can still follow Roussel's intellectual path with great ease. Even
worse, when I gave a summary of this book to a study group I was
working in, I met with the reaction that, leaving aside a few nowadays
obsolete notions, Roussel's position 'in depth' is still one that can be
defended – or attacked, which comes to the same thing, since to think of
attacking a work is to recognize its continuing relevance.

This was my starting-point. Roussel's book has outlived the science
which it invokes and furthers, a fact which would seem to indicate that
its real meaning and value lie on a different level from one of simple
pronouncements about women's bone structure or nervous constitution. Below or beyond these physiological propositions, one needs to
attend to something else. Closer reading led me partially to modify this

initial view: the book ultimately has so little to do with physiology in any strict sense that the amount which is capable of being made scientifically obsolete is actually very slight, consisting in little more than the bare minimum of 'technical' pronouncements required (mainly) in order to establish that the book is indeed written from a scientific standpoint. The progress of knowledge can falsify only propositions formulated with a certain precision: the progress of knowledge has indeed falsified the falsifiable part of this book, but this in the end amounts to little. One might have thought that, since Roussel explicitly bases his global interpretation of femininity on a few pre-scientific ideas, his entire discourse would fall along with these foundations. The fact that even today the book can be read obliges one to revise this optimistic view.

I was driven to look for an explanation of the scope and meaning of this work in terms of its possible mythical value. But what sort of myth was at work, and what sort of need did it serve to meet? Given the subject of the book, I expected to find some new everyday/literary avatar of sexist (or misogynist) mythology operating here. And of course there was one, but things are not quite that simple. For one thing, one needs to make clear at the outset the 'soft', euphemistic brand of sexism Roussel deploys. It is not medieval phobias which are directly voiced here; these indeed are often rebutted. Moreover, the tenor of Roussel's theses on femininity is peculiar enough, his construction of the feminine image complex enough, to give rise to the suspicion that something other than simple sexism is at work in our author's way of structuring woman's body-space. My attempt here to uncover these other, original components in Roussel may seem laboured. I hope the reader will excuse my inability to simplify the problem further, and be kind enough to persevere until the final section to see why, even today, this book remains such a fascinating document.

We shall not concentrate only, then, on the inane opinions, the picturesquely sexist component in the *Système physique et moral de la femme*, but attend also to the quiet shaping power in Roussel's work, productive of new, abstract intellectual structures which are, perhaps, profound through their very abstraction. The fact, for example, that for Roussel there is just *one* feminine temperament in comparison with the *plurality* of masculine temperaments seems to me something quite as

important as the droller passages which he devotes to feminine
sensibility. While opinions may go out of fashion or be refuted, their
underlying structure is liable to outlive debate as long as it is not itself
clearly established and objectified.

For lack of a better word, I use the rhetorical term *chiasma* here to
describe the general functional principle of the gynaecographia, this
treatise whose author, according to the author of its Preface, deserved
to be crowned by the enchanting sex.[3] I shall define this abstract figure
as follows: the denial of a quality 'X' to an object or place which
common sense holds it actually to possess, with the compensating
attribution of that same quality to everything but that object or place.
Thus, Roussel sees sexual difference in every element of women's lives
and bodies, but holds that there is one bone in the body which admits of
no sexual difference: namely the pubis. Silence as to the literal
meaning, a void at the centre; metonymic proliferation everywhere
else. In my view we have here a function over four terms, not just over
three, as in the figure of 'displacement'. When Roussel treats
menstruation as an acquired characteristic produced by dietary excess,
his denegation of the genital character of this phenomenon is something more than a simple denial.

This figure manifests itself first of all – and not, perhaps, in its most
superficial manner – in the way Roussel plays on the issue of his own
scientific competence. The author of this *Physical and Moral System* is a
doctor, but it is the moral aspect of his theme which occupies the
preponderant space. Shoemaker, stick to your last, railed the poet
anxious about the strict demarcation of competences. Here one would
have to picture a shoemaker who sticks to the shoe only so long as is
necessary to entitle him to hold forth on everything but shoes. Doubtless this is a banal image typical of the ideological utilization of a partial
competence, one which serves to define one half of our chiasma, the
transposition of an authority founded on a competence which – here the
figure becomes less banal – makes it possible to suspend the reign of
authority over the very domain the writer himself is supposed to
master. No one, says Roussel, is entitled to dogmatize concerning the
normal duration of pregnancy: nature sometimes retards delivery even
beyond the tenth month; our knowledge in this domain is only probable
and conjectural. This admission of non-science follows after lengthy
pages in which Roussel has been dogmatically holding forth about
women's 'inaptitude for abstract science', and their 'aptitude for

compassion': all this being argued on the basis of excellent *physiological* reasons.

An imaginary knowledge is elaborated out of a partial science which the author himself labours to render problematic; correlatively, Roussel concentrates in woman's body a number of representations developed in various other sectors of the age's encyclopaedia, within the general space of letters which that period termed philosophy. Roussel *realizes* (in the strongest sense of the word) his century's theoretical creations; he projects on to the female body the Enlightenment's conceptual products, and thereby invents a physiological image, an anatomical compendium of the new normativity which has been (or is still being) constructed in anthropology, aesthetics, the philosophy of history, the theory of morals . . . That is, he transforms a *lettered* imagination (that which belongs to the general culture of the educated) into a *learned* [*savant*] imaginary. One looks in vain to Roussel for an echo of 'popular prejudices' or common mythological notions about women. The virginity-taboo, for instance, hardly sets him a-fantasizing: in this book, the hymen is simply an occasion for some comparative psychology about the men of the North and the men of the South.[4] It is, it seems, easy enough thus to reject a body of fantasy still interwoven with popular superstition (how stupid to imagine that menstrual blood could be venomous!), in favour of an educated imagination (periods are a phenomenon of equilibrium, peculiar to social life; they do not exist in a state of nature).

THE FEMALE SYSTEM

The title and Preface of the work insistently emphasize its acknowledged, or purported project: to systematize. Roussel reproaches his predecessors for having regarded woman as similar to man except in sexual functioning. Wrongly so, he says, since 'the essence of sex is not confined to a single organ, but extends, through more or less perceptible nuances, into every part; so that woman is not woman merely in virtue of one place, but rather is so in every aspect from which she is regarded'. And there follows the paradigm of the hunchback – an old acquaintance: ' . . . as with hunchbacks the curvature of the spine always induces a certain disorder of the other parts, so that all hunchbacks seem to look alike'.[5] During the previous fifteen years or more, this hunchback had haunted Diderot's writings on painting: 'A hunchback is hunchbacked from head to foot. The smallest particular defect has its general influence on the whole. Such an influence may become imperceptible, yet . . .'[6] For Diderot too, the hunchback is the privileged paradigm for 'a system of necessarily connected deformities'.

What consequently needs, in Roussel's opinion, to be developed is not a gynaecology,[7] but a general physiology of woman – woman's bones, muscles, nerves, blood vessels, tissues all thus becoming appropriate objects of 'special' study. For Roussel, this systematizing project prompts a material reverie. The soft, the supple, the elastic, the labile, the mobile work as a system of epithets which gradually make it possible to capture intuitively a kind of 'deep essence' of femininity. As for systematization strictly speaking, none whatever is to be found here.

Roussel's standpoint ought really to have led him to a double physiology of woman and man which would have overturned the species-concept of Man [*homo*]. To convince oneself that this fails to occur, it suffices to compare the book we are looking at here with the *Fragment du système physique et moral de l'homme*. This other work by Roussel, far from treating strictly of male man [*vir*] and studying the more or less insensible consequences of masculine sex for the whole of the body, simply summarizes the epoch's knowledge about the 'human constitution'. And Roussel holds forth here on the stomach, kidneys, suprarenal glands and skin,[8] without a single mention of any possible influence of sex. This asymmetry is congruent with the disparity formulated by Rousseau: there is no parity of the sexes as to the consequence of sex. The idea was new, as Roussel's critique of his predecessors attests. But it was one which was to go far, in medicine and elsewhere.

Moreover, the notion of system used is by no means the same in the two texts. The first chapter of the *Fragment* develops the idea of the organism as an assemblage of organs linked by reciprocal relations, whose actions combine and concur in the maintenance of life. In this text, then, we have an organic totality; in the treatise on woman, we find only an interminable metonymic construction; the sex, as a part of the body (and its primordial function, procreation), is assigned a directing role. By degrees it comes to inform all the other parts and functions of woman's body, as well as her 'moral' and relational existence. The sex is a sort of causal nucleus, from whose functioning one can deduce the configuration of the organs, then woman's temperament, and hence a certain number of psychosocial facts. A deduction, but from a function (procreation); Roussel's method quickly proves to be a logical monstrosity, floating between mechanistic explanations,[9] massively teleological attitudes,[10] analogies and transpositions (from the feeble consistency of muscles to that of ideas, for example), and spectacular deductive short cuts from the quality of 'resilience' [*ressort*] proper to feminine organs to the disastrous effect of any fondness for gambling in women. At times one finds a 'mathematical' ideal of reasoning;[11] almost everywhere recourse is had to a prudent and far-seeing Nature which has taken care to prepare well in advance the instruments appropriate for the execution of its designs.

And so Roussel mobilizes every possible kind of argument[12] to 'deduce' from physiological grounds a range of 'consequences' which have been posited, for other reasons, beforehand. These are, in summary form, as follows. Woman's body is more elastic, more plastic – that is to say, more apt to yield to external impulses. Mucous tissue is present in greater quantity, giving the body its rounded, graceful contours, removing any kind of angularity from its articulations. Nature has done everything in woman to render her graceful and agreeable. Woman's organs have more sensibility than consistency, and woman owes to this disposition that tactile sensitivity which enables her to perceive an infinity of nuances and details in the objects which impinge on her – a vivacity of impressions which, it is true, makes her changeable, the tyranny of her sensations always confining her attention to their immediate cause. This means that she masters nothing, has no gift for the Fine Arts, and is incapable of creativity; and that general notions of politics and the great principles of morals escape her grasp, even though she may possess a very active moral faculty. Her imagination is too mobile for her to devote her study to the abstract sciences, but instead it renders her affectionate and gentle . . . Two points seem to me to merit particular comment here: the question of beauty, and the modelling of the theory–practice distinction on the demarcation of sexual differences.

Nature has done everything in woman to make her graceful. More precisely, nature has essentially concerned itself with the conservation of the species. Womanly curves are a consequence of the demands of maternity. 'Beauty comes from an order which tends towards the

Good' and, 'in only pursuing the useful', nature 'necessarily at the same time creates the pleasing'. Later, Roussel contests certain ideas put forward by the article 'Beau' in the *Encyclopaedia*, and again asserts that the impression made on us by those elements of beauty which seem most to depend on fantasy 'obeys no other fundamental rule than the sense of physical utility'. A beautiful woman is thus one whose elastic, rounded body proclaims her aptitude for maternity 'even without our mind appearing to perceive this'. This calls for a number of comments. As befits Roussel's method of argument, beauty here is no more than the centrifugal sign of fertility. But by reducing visual pleasure to an obscure sense of utility, Roussel masks the fact that the only level on which his notion of *system* has any meaning is, precisely, a visual one. Not so much because 'there is no one who cannot *at the first glance* tell the difference between a woman's collarbone and the same bone in a man', but above all because the concept of system he employs in his book on woman is not organicist (implying at the very least a conception of the interaction of elements) but pictorial. His idea of a central predicate from which all other elements are supposed to derive (a centre of interest equivalent, semantically, to the vanishing-point in the formal technique of pictorial composition) may be valid for the figurative painting of a certain epoch, but not for the biology even of the eighteenth century, as is attested by Roussel's own *Fragment du système de l'homme*, where organic interactions are indeed dealt with. By reducing and finally denying the visible in his theory of beauty, Roussel is engaged in masking the very site of his own discourse and his own role as painter, or spectator.

As for the moral distinction between theory and practice, let us underline the point that what escapes woman's grasp is the great principles. On the other hand 'her imagination, overly mobile and hardly capable of a steady seat', together with woman's awareness of her own incapacity, create in her a disposition to identify with the unfortunate: a 'natural pity'. 'Everyone concurs that women have a more active kind of morality, whereas that of men lies rather in speculation.' This is an admirable summary of Rousseauian thought: to my mind, Roussel builds an interesting bridge here between the second *Discourse* and Book 5 of *Émile*. Pity, the only natural virtue, independent of reasoning, prior to all reflection, has a number of paradigms in the *Discourse*, among them the 'tenderness of mothers for their little ones', and the providential intervention by 'the Market women' in time of riot. Elsewhere, it is said in *Émile* that 'the quest for abstract and speculative truths, for principles, for axioms in the sciences, every tendency towards generalization of ideas lies outside women's scope, all their studies should belong within the practical.' And Rousseau remarks that 'the art of thinking is not itself foreign to women, but they should do no more than touch on it. Sophie grasps everything, but her memory retains nothing.' In any case, 'it is for women, so to speak, to discover an experimental morality, and for us to reduce it to a system'.

Pierre Roussel seems to have seen how all this fits together. In the *Discourse*, Jean-Jacques Rousseau offers no ground for juxtaposing his paradigm of 'woman' with animals or savages. In Book 5 of *Émile*, he credits women with no special propensity for pity. But one can establish the connection between these two texts by noticing that what is for Jean-Jacques the mainspring of pity – namely imagination, and especially *mobility* of imagination – is explicitly related in *Émile* to boys' puberty. Now there is really no puberty for Sophie, since she is always-already ensconced in sexual life – whereas the male is male only at a certain age and at certain moments, 'the female is female all her life', says Rousseau ('or at least, all her youth'). Moreover, pity, according to the *Discourse*, has as its effect 'the mutual conservation of the species', an expression not without significance. It is clear that from woman's incapacity for theory to mothers' devotedness to their little ones, passing by way of Sophie's mobility of mind, her instantaneous soul which receives every impression like soft wax and retains but little,[13] everything hangs together. For Roussel, who thus reifies Rousseauian morality in woman's body, these are all consequences of that anatomical 'mobility' necessitated by the demands of childbearing.

A pansexualization, a metonymy of difference – but one of a rather special kind: this dissemination of sex leaves a void at its centre. Roussel genitalizes the whole body, but degenitalizes sex. Thus women's thighbones, collarbones and arms can be distinguished 'at first glance' from men's, but – not the pubis:

It had been supposed that the bones of the pubis were joined only by a supple, mobile cartilage, enabling them to separate during difficult childbirths: this opinion, grounded in the idea of a supposed need, has been refuted by more exact examination, and it is now recognized that these bones are no more mobile in woman than in man. (p. 6)

A denial of difference with respect to the 'literal' point of this difference. And one can see that this negation is phrased in the typical style of a repudiation of pre-scientific beliefs: that it is precisely the qualities of mobility and suppleness (determinations which Roussel elsewhere attributes to all the rest of the body) which are denied; and that the 'supposed need' denied here is omnipresent in Roussel's style of argument with respect to women's nerves, collarbones and talents.

An image of the body, then, governed by the figure of the chiasma. Evidently this schema is not announced as such in the text itself: it is I who am drawing the connection between page 6, where (in passing) an absence of sexual difference is mentioned regarding the pubis, and the sexualizing inflation of the rest of the body, in the rest of the book. This is not the only such connection that needs to be made: Roussel also maximalizes the 'natural', physiologically grounded character of psycho-relational phenomena whose distribution is, in fact,[14] social and historical. He denies that such differences are 'an effect of women's education or mode of life'. Yet, symmetrically, he strips of its physiological and natural character a phenomenon which might never have seemed destined to be labelled as cultural: menstruation. So if women are timid, soft, hopeless at mathemetics, disastrous in politics – this comes from nature; but if they have periodic haemorrhages – this is an acquired habit, due in the last instance to a psychohistorical cause! And whereas Roussel has attributed every possible other feminine quality to a genital cause, he is at pains to show that periods have nothing to do with procreation or fertility.

Roussel starts by 'observing' that Brazilian women (??) and the females of other mammal species have no period; which proves that, 'far indeed from being a natural institution, the menstrual flow is a factitious need contracted in the social state'. This original opinion at once transports us to a Rousseauian scene, with its familiar narrative accessories,[15] its conceptual slides,[16] and its stock theoretico-dramatic ploy of undertaking to account for some phenomenon by harking back to a past state of nature in which it is non-existent, so as to construct out of this extrahistorical temporality a conjectural genesis (which Rousseau calls 'hypothetical and conditional') to account for the phenomenon's emergence and persistence.[17] (Thus, according to Roussel: one can 'conjecture that there was a time when women were by no means subject to this incommodious exaction'. The social state led to the contraction of this factitious need.[18] Once assembled together, human beings discovered conviviality, the joy of the feast. In order to 'reiterate' this gaiety,[19] they acquired the bad habit of exceeding their strict alimentary needs and consuming dishes prepared with the perfidious refinements of art. This resulted in a habitual and general state of plethora. Nature sought for a means to re-establish metabolic balance through compensating bodily evacuations. 'The effects of this disposition were common to both sexes; men and women alike found themselves in a state of chronic plethora which necessitated for each alike outflowings, different indeed in their form, but the same in their principle.')

Ergo: a phenomenon which is cultural, not physiological; alimentary, not genital; dictated by the equilibrium of general health, not specifically by the reproductive function; human, not feminine. Six pages are devoted to denying the mark of sex in this 'great inconvenience' and assimilating it to nosebleeds, the masculine form assumed by this flow. Here again we have a chiasma, since this negation counter-weighs the general movement of the text. It is quite accidental here for Roussel that this loss of blood occurs via 'the organ destined for the perpetuation of the species'. But everywhere else, it is the requirements of maternity that are invoked.

THE MIRROR OF MODESTY

The nature of the topic might certainly encourage one here to speak of repression, and of a return of the repressed, marked by a displacement, and Roussel's biography[20] indeed offers abundant justification for such a psychoanalytical interpretation. Freud, as reread by Lacan after a conversation with Jakobson? The *Système physique et moral de la femme* might well serve to illustrate the idea that human desire is constituted like a metonymy.

But while such an approach to his text is certainly pertinent, it would be illegitimate to reduce the meaning of Roussel's work to this psycho-biographical level. Does the entity called 'desire' function according the same mechanisms at every time and place? There is no doubt that a frustrated [*douloureux*] drive can find a form and a means of satisfaction in the chiasmic schema that structures the feminine image in Roussel, but this does not mean that all that is involved here is the resurgence of censored drives. In so far as this chiasmic function of displacement connects *four* terms, imposing silence on the literal meaning and drawing out to infinity its chain of metonyms and metaphors,[21] it needs to be understood also as providing a working principle for the solution of quite different questions. We are dealing here with a widespread type of intellectual mechanism, almost a commonplace of our own age. Consider, for instance, how the word 'economy' is used in the contemporary language of philosophers: one is endlessly regaled nowadays with disquisitions about libidinal economies, textual economies – even about a rather vaguely formulated 'general economy'. But would anyone dare to use the word 'economy' to signify such trivia as the price of cotton in Manchester, or the EEC's potato market? The metaphorical uses, particularly of the adjectival form 'economic', proliferate, while philosophy keeps silent about the economy in its literal sense. Similarly, one hears it tediously reiterated that 'everything is political', yet the theory of the state seems to have vanished from among the preoccupations of those very people who assert that every kind of decision (philosophical, existential, aesthetic or otherwise) *is* political. Sometimes one notices a remarkable prudery about even *naming* the political forces engaged in a conflict which is nevertheless dubbed 'profoundly political'.[22] An extraordinary prudery: the image which inescapably comes to mind, whether one looks at Roussel or at our own contemporaries, is the figleaf. Whether the topic is the economy, politics or sexuality, the distribution of silence and metaphorical loquacity is governed by a common law.

This word prudery [*pudeur*], leads us back to the question of sex. But it leads us also to another level within Roussel's text, a final chiasma which, for once, is not left unthought by the author himself. Here the practice of the chiasma no longer remains altogether unconscious, but is elaborated into a 'theory' implicitly outlined in its description of its object.[23] The attraction of women – that which founds their status as objects of desire, and bears the name of Beauty – is, says Roussel, 'the *secret*[24] whereby nature has designed to interest us (!!) in the conservation of the species'. And everything in woman is determined by the imperative of beauty. As we noted earlier, the elasticity of woman's body frees its articulations of angularity. From childhood on, all her behaviour is naturally guided by her penchant for acquiring coquettish charms.[25] Roussel waxes lyrical when he describes the 'fine, slender, soft contours of her arms', the 'rounded neck', the 'shining eyes', the skill with which the young girl chooses her adornments and learns those gestures and attitudes which are 'more than indifferently apt to please' . . . But this beauty and coquetry (positive outward faculties, centrifugal effects of sex) are accompanied by a contrary force: modesty (a negative, *centred* psychological disposition).[26] Modesty and beauty enhanced by coquetry are, says our author, two motors which, while moving in opposite directions, finally co-operate in the same task, just as a few drops of water serve to intensify a flame (?).

Womanly modesty can be understood here as the mirror-image, the emblematic projection of Roussel's own constant negative practice – the void at the centre, the silence about the 'place'. That yielding beauty which continually reminds us of woman's sexed character,[27] this body dispersed about its own surface, is a mirror of metonymy. Our author shows us, moreover, how two contrary movements work together:[28] Roussel's thoughts on the coupling of these two forces constitute a sort of theory of his own discursive practice. Whereas we were obliged to reconstruct the earlier chiasmas ourselves, here it is Roussel himself who makes explicit the complementarity of denegation and metonymic proliferation. A sort of awareness of his discourse's own procedure flickers here, albeit in unrecognized form. Roussel is not aware that what he reads in this feminine organization is the very structure of his system – but he reads it well, and the negation–metonymy relation does not escape him. (It is worth underlining here the historical character of this thaumaturgic structure linking a 'taboo' with an interminable metonymy; this is not an eternal constant of human consciousness confronted by prohibition. In the literary period of the '*précieux*', for example, an opposite schema reigned: metonymy as contagion rather than compensation. For the '*précieux*' everything amenable to association with 'gross instincts' was successively deported into the zone of silence (the word 'armchair', for example, was banned for its indecent evocation of 'backside'). Whereas in Roussel (and his historical environment), everything that is not literally pubis is developed into interminable discourse about it.)[29]

Let us relegate Monsieur Roussel for a moment to the relative oblivion into which he was consigned with the emergence, between 1830 and 1860, of a different style of gynaecology, linked to the discovery of ovulation and the female cycle. The work of this amiable, gentle, modest and sensitive man[30] has put us on the track of a phenomenon concerning not Pierre Roussel's own personal problems, but the history of mentalities. His book's considerable success – and not only among doctors – is no accident. It said something that its century wanted to hear;[31] it put forward a structuring of space so well suited to the new mentality of his time that others after him, without even necessarily having read him, were to employ this same chiasmic geometry. Others after him – others before him also: the exact relation of chronology does not concern us here. The thought is an epoch's, the authors only its witnesses.

We have identified a general form together with a particular application through which the form's workings 'theorize', symbolize and emblazon themselves. We have mentioned economy and politics. We still want to speak of the sacred, and love: let us take love first, in order to explain a fact remarked on earlier – that the metaphorical language we borrowed above to identify and describe the chiasmic structure comes itself from the lexicon of sexuality; that the term prudery [*pudeur*] seems itself to invest the question of sexuality with a central, original and *exemplary* status.

The emblems of love have their own history. The hunt, the quiver of arrows, the flame, the ardent fire, the sorceress's potion, the blind Cupid's fatal glance – each of these motifs sustains and inscribes a particular conception of love.[32] Moderns have returned to Genesis to discover (or invent) the melancholy symbolism of the leaf (opinions differ as to whether this should be a figleaf or a vineleaf). Like the other symbols, this one is linked to a *theory* of Eros, found for instance in Kant, though certainly not in Genesis. According to Kant's *Conjectural Beginning of World History*, man soon found that sexual excitement can be heightened by the effects of imagination, 'the more its object is removed from the senses'.

> The figleaf, then, was a manifestation of reason . . . *Refusal* was the deed which accomplished the passage from merely sensual to spiritual attractions, from mere animal desire gradually to love, and along with this from the feeling of the merely agreeable to a taste for beauty . . .[33]

We are not told in the Bible that the figleaf intensifies and transforms the sexual urge, nor that it creates the sentiment of the rest of the body's beauty. On the contrary, the shame endures in the Bible even after the hero and heroine have sewn their leafy loincloths: 'they hid themselves, the man and the woman, from before the face of Jahve Elohim', and

Adam says: 'I am afraid because I am naked'.[34] This dialectical theory of Eros is a modern one – as also is the museum-keepers' practice of applying figleaves to their originally nude Greek and Roman statues. And one may wonder whether these museum-keepers, in concealing the sexes of the ancient gods, were simply paying their dues to prudery – that is, performing a purely negative symbolic act – or whether they were not, if only tacitly, seeking with chiasmic logic to affirm the beauty of the rest of the body, conducting a fantasy-dialectical operation to make the Greek gods, at last, *beautiful*.[35]

It seems to me in any case that the chiasma may well be, for the spatial imagination, what dialectical logic[36] is for the conceptual. Our aim here should then be to bring out their common basis, to elicit from imagination something like a spatial logic, a poetics of space 'for our time' – or for our clan.

A certain kind of attitude to the sacred serves to illustrate this peculiarity of our modern practice of space. If we are told that 'it is because Christ's tomb is empty that the Church is universal', there must be some expectation that this formula will be understood. Yet this spatial projection of a dialectical idea is by no means theologically orthodox – one would search the New Testament in vain for this kind of causal claim. It is, on the other hand, certainly to be found in Hegel's account of the Crusades. Like the Kantian theory of Eros, this idea is thinkable and imaginable only in the modern context.

And while we are on the subject of philosophers' theology, we can hardly fail to recall that the prevailing eighteenth-century forms of pantheism are allied to a critique of the idea of the Temple (considered as a separate, particular space) and of the Church (considered as a specialized institution).

Men have banished the Divinity from among them; they have relegated it to a sanctuary; elsewhere it does not exist. Madmen that you are! Destroy these enclosures that hold back your ideas; set God free; see him everywhere . . .[37]

Set God free; and see woman's femininity, similarly, everywhere. But (at the same time): abandon the churches, and hide the precise object of your desires under a veil of oblivion.[38] The shaping schema is the same in both cases.

A HAVEN OF ALTRUISM

Cui bono? What is the advantage – and whose? Roussel's book, implausible as the ideas it advances may seem, gave satisfaction to thousands of readers over a period of fifty years and more. We must now try to explain its gratifying character.

First one should stress that the chiasma it propounds affords satisfaction for a phallocentric and phallocratic standpoint[39] by offering the figures of the pan-hysterized woman (everywhere marked by her difference) and the female eunuch. The phallocentric viewpoint *cannot* read sexual difference as genital: that would be to recognize that there are two sexes, whereas there is 'of course' only one sex with, as its 'Other', a simple absence, a blank, a silence. Erasing the genitality and femininity of feminine genitality is thus highly profitable for phallocentrism. Once Roussel has rejected the anatomical difference of the pubis and the genital, specifically feminine character of menstruation, it is clear that only the absence of a penis remains to characterize femininitude – in a purely negative, privative fashion. But, correlatively, the phallocratic viewpoint has an interest in seeing the difference of the sexes everywhere else, especially in such interesting areas as politics and intellectual capacity. The proliferation of difference to the muscles, nerves and ideas grounds woman's inferiority, or rather the necessity of male protectorate over women, globalized wardship. It also grounds woman's exclusion from competitive spheres, e.g. intellectual life and politics – this of course being what the half-century which read and reprinted Roussel liked best of all.

We have suggested that Roussel *realizes* in woman's body the philosophical ideas of his century. We shall return to this point in a moment, but here too we can already see the considerable benefits accrued. For the purposes of grounding a dogma, endorsement by science (be this 'true' or spurious) is always more useful than philosophy's. The authority of an overtly philosophical discourse was never found sufficient, even in the eighteenth century.[40] To legitimize women's oppression and provide, for women's use, an ethic of submission, religious discourse long sufficed. I am not the first to have noticed that by Roussel's time this discourse was no longer entirely able to fulfil its function, first because of its global loss of hegemony, and secondly because of its ineffectiveness in handling the new difficulties facing the phallocratic order in the eighteenth century and the new modes of exclusion which it was called on to pronounce: woman's exclusion from politics, for example, belongs to a republican problematic.[41] The Church, still living in the now insecure world of those divine and feudal rights which had enthroned queens in their day as pious Catholic sovereigns and regents, was unable to adapt itself instantly to the newly emerging form of power. For a time, at least, another form of justification was needed to take its place. Philosophy attempted to do this, but ultimately served more as a laboratory of ideas than as an instance possessed itself of adequate authority. No doubt this is because philosophy is a construction of arguments which it is always permissible to refute. Mary Wollstonecraft's demolition of Rousseau's notions about woman[42] is a perfectly normal and plausible operation in philosophy, so far as the question of authority is concerned. Quite a different situation applies for a discourse which appropriates, justifiably or otherwise, the title of science. Here, an author speaks in the name of facts; his discourse, which thus boasts an extrinsic criterion of legitimacy (as indeed religious discourse had done), can thereby occlude its own discursive operation, and so proceed to dogmatize as it chooses. What can you say against the fact that women's collarbones are more curved (or straighter) than men's? We are still not through today with this kind of mystification.[43]

And thus physiological pseudo-knowledge proved to be a more effective and reliable tool than philosophical thoughts, even if it was from the philosophers of his century that Pierre Roussel derived his ideas. The physiologization of Enlightenment anthropology takes place at a number of different points in Roussel's text. Some of these have already been noted; here are some more.

'The principal destiny of women,' writes Roussel, 'being to please by the attractions of the body and the natural graces, they would stray from it were they to run after the reputation conferred by science or wit' (p. 62).

Weakness and sensibility are the dominant and distinctive qualities of women . . . As for morality, with them everything takes the form of sentiment . . . No doubt this organization was necessary in the sex to which nature was to entrust the repository of the human species . . . The latter would have perished a thousand times, had it been reduced to the tardy and uncertain help of cold reason. But sentiment, quick as a flash, lively and pure as the fire from which it emanates, will lead a woman through flames or cause her to plunge into the waves, to save her child; even more, sentiment leads her to fulfil, with a patience one cannot sufficiently admire, and even with a sort of satisfaction, the most disgusting and tiresome tasks. (p. 29)

To please and, through sentiment, to prefer another to oneself. In either case, the same virtue: alienation. Woman does not live or act for herself but, spontaneously, for the other. Are these commonplaces? They are today, no doubt, since these ideas are still terribly alive, but when Rousseau published *Émile* such a conception of the human balance was still new: a male totally 'for himself' and a female totally 'for the other', this being the guarantee of a harmonious and orderly human relationship. This new conception of the regulation of human ties comes to displace those more sympathetic ideas which did not look to woman alone to provide the harmony: the ideas of natural symbiosis,[44] of *philia*, and, still more, of justice.[45] With Rousseau there emerges the outline of a (masculine) world dominated by the struggle for recognition, the war of self-loves, the conflict of particular interests. Certainly, the *Social Contract* envisages a possible political solution; but 'in the meantime' *Émile* suggests (for men, that is), an existing haven, a breathing-space, a relationship where this battle for recognition is suspended: the masculine–feminine relation[46] where there is no longer any struggle, woman totally recognizing man and man being totally recognized by woman ... Hence the fact that nature imposes two totally different models of education: Émile is raised for himself, taught never to pay attention to the opinion of another, to flee dependence, etc. As for Sophie – 'woman is specially made to please man', woman must know and recognize her dependence on men (a material dependence – for her needs; and a moral one – men's opinion of her matters more to her than what she really is), and it is for this reason that girls must be soon checked, accustomed from the first to suffer constraint, etc. From this obligatory alienation flow the various attributes of Rousseau's feminine ideal: weakness, incapacity for material or moral autonomy; women must receive all their moral and religious principles from men.

Following this model, Roussel is able to establish a (very coherent) relation between the qualities (pity, desire to please, love) and defects (inaptitude for reasoning) of women: in a word, between their general weakness and, on the male side, 'the sophisms of particular interest which defy almost all laws'. The total altruism[47] of women is necessary in order for the 'social bond' to be maintained, despite male egotism and egocentricity, despite the atomistic nature of the male half of man-kind – each man isolating himself in the closure of his own particular interest. Thus, at a stroke, this individualism ceases to appear dangerous or damaging to society.

Roussel's contribution here is to have conferred on what in Rousseau is merely an ideal or an 'ought' the status of a physiological fact: it is to the soft consistency of their nerves that one must attribute this marvellous feminine altruism or other-ism [*autruism*], thanks to which we do not have to live for ever in a war of all against all.

The same applies with the prohibition of learning. Rousseau simply says that an educated, reasoning woman is a monster he would want neither for a mistress nor for a friend, an unpleasing and morally repugnant being. To this Pierre Roussel adds that study is very damaging for the health of women: their temperament deteriorates, their digestion in particular is affected, the body 'languishes, declines and falls like a tender sapling planted in an arid terrain', and then there opens up 'that tumultuous scene we call the vapours'. Physical threat here takes over from moral condemnation.

Finally, leaving aside a number of other, more localized repetitions of Rousseauian discourse in Pierre Roussel's science, we must consider the asymmetry noted above: *one* feminine temperament, *several* masculine temperaments.

Involved here is an essential component of the modern imagination's categorial framework. As Colette Guillaumin writes:

The appropriation of women is made explicit by the very commonplace semantic habit of identifying femal social agents principally by their sex ('women', 'the women') . . . In whatever context, professional, political or otherwise, every appropriate qualifying noun is omitted or withheld when denoting agents of female sex, whereas of course it is these qualifiers alone which are used to designate all other agents. These phrases for instance, which I collected over the last forty-eight hours: 'a student was punished by a month's suspension, a girl was reprimanded' (news item on repression in the *École Polytechnique*); 'A company president, a croupier and a woman' (about a panel brought together to give its opinion on some current topic); 'They murdered tens of thousands of workers, students, women . . .' (Castro, on the Batista regime). These phrases, whose imprecision regarding occupation, status and social function when speaking of the women concerned we find so exasperating, are not mere lapses due to lack of information . . . On the contrary, they are shapshots of social relations.[48]

Here Colette Guillaumin admirably describes a distinction which corresponds to what I want to demonstrate; for this failure to qualify women social agents amounts to an affirmation of the unity and homogeneity of the category 'women'; to say, on the other hand, 'a croupier, some workers, a student, a company president' is to signal the plurality within the category 'men'. Guillaumin is right to stress the extreme banality of these verbal practices today, but it is not certain that they were dominant practices before the eighteenth century. In a society divided into orders (aristocracy, Church, third estate) it was impossible for a narrator to pass over in silence the status (or 'quality') of an individual, and describing a scene on the Pont-Neuf, one would say 'a Duchess, a nun, a *petite bougeoise*, a servant woman . . .'.[49] Let me just recall here that when the French Revolution 'omitted' to recognize the voting right of women (treating them thus *en bloc*), whereas the legislators drew distinctions concerning voting rights *within* the group of men,[50] this attitude, destined to become natural and 'normal' in the nineteenth century, was vigorously contested by Condorcet among others, who appealed, on this question, to the 'old system':[51] he demanded (in vain) that a distinction be drawn between women property-owners and other women! This debate documents the historic passage from one system of discrimination (by estate) to another (by sex): treatment of women as a homogeneous and uniform category is relatively recent, in its systematic form at least.

Now this bourgeois realignment was prefigured in the mid-eighteenth century's philosophical anthropology. Rousseau once again:

There is among peoples a prodigious diversity of customs, tempera-ments and characters. Man, I acknowledge, is one; but man modified by religions, governments, laws, customs, prejudices, climates, differs from himself so widely that it is no longer possible for us to seek for what is good for men in general, but only for what is good in such and such a climate and country.[52]

Not Man, says Enlightenment anthropology, but only men. Except that . . . there *is* Woman, one sole kind of woman (normal woman, that is): Sophie. One encounters this bifurcation down to and including Nietzsche. Man is a species having as yet no fixed model; but there is only one proper type of woman: an 'Eternal Feminine'.

Women, in their monstrosity, are thus 'all the same', just as all hunchbacks appear to resemble one another. According to Roussel, men differ in temperament (the bilious, the melancholic, the phlegmatic) but all women have the same temperament, which as it happens is the sanguine one. Everything fits together, our author having denied that menstrual blood was constitutive of woman's femininity.

Everything fits together above all when one sees how Roussel goes about explaining this asymmetry. If there are several male temperaments, this is because man is modified by the climate he lives in, by his habits of diet and, globally, by his conditions of life: that is to say, by a relation to the exterior. But if the same temperament is common to all women alike, this is due to the uniformity of their occupation: namely gestation. Roussel's reflection truly forms a system: the male lives in relation to exteriority *and* the consequence of sex is not, for him, a hegemonic one. The female is entirely ruled by an internal principle *and* unconnected to any physical or social milieu. Or again, there is no self-identical substance of 'man', because each man maintains an intense relation with his situation: man is a being 'in situation', not an essence. On the contrary, there *is* a substantive, immanent essence of femininity. I am insisting on this point because, rightly or wrongly, I see it as posing issues which are still alive today. Some women now assert that sexual specificity exists or ought to exist everywhere, in every domain of our life. These same people rigidly hierarchize different levels of opposition, saying that sexual difference is *prior to* class distinctions, political divisions or national differences. All this goes together and quickly leads to the idea that the determining factor is an intrinsic distinction, an inner principle, an interior cause; hence the political emphasis on the body and the refusal to take account of supposedly 'outside' factors, whether social, political or historical. To my mind this thinking entraps itself in the same pleasant reverie which Roussel offered his contemporaries – that of a womanhood enclosed in itself.[53]

From this image one can proceed, as Roussel does not fail to do, to the idea of woman's character as non-functional. Woman is a cocoon, a being hand-less by definition. Woman never enters into an operational relation with the world (her soft body prevents this); she has no effective actions, only graceful gestures. Erving Goffman[54] has noted that the representation of the female body in advertising corresponds to ideas of a similar kind: when a woman holds an object, she seems barely to caress it – the brandy-glass is in serious danger of being dropped. Her physiognomy expresses quite generally a zero level of alertness to exteriority.

CHIASMIC EXCLUSION

The fact that certain elements in Roussel's discourse remain present today in quite widespread collective representations and practices may seem to run against my initial objective of showing the specifically *literary* or *lettered* character of the imagination at work in this book which stands halfway between the *Encyclopédistes* and the *Idéologues*. Certainly, if one retraces the different elements of his theory, it is clear where Roussel is drawing on his immediate intellectual inheritance: the principle of inertia, the Rousseauist philosophy, Diderot's aesthetics and theology. But when one follows the subsequent career of this discourse, when one looks at what it afterwards became, it is clear that the system fell apart and that its different elements had different fates. Yet this very diversity is significant. ·

Certain of these component ideas[55] were adopted by the bourgeoisie after the Revolution – indeed, became functioning rules which it was not even necessary to make explicit. The history of voting rights in France well illustrates the success of the separation effected between *a homogeneous group of women* and *a group of men fissured by difference* – the political exclusion of all women not having as its correlate a global political inclusion, even in principle, of all men. Feudal law began by separating individuals into three orders, and thereafter treated the women in each order as (more or less diminished) individuals. Bourgeois electoral law begins, on the contrary, by dividing individuals into two sexual classes, and then abolishes the unity of one class by introducing internal fractures (with property-qualified suffrage). In the light of the historical success of this asymmetrical division, one can say that Enlightenment anthropology (whether reified into a medicine or not) was simply advancing the first formulation of a symbolic system of distributions which was to take the place of feudal hierarchies. Something of the kind holds true also for the non-functional character of the female body – which finds its juridical transposition in what the *Code Napoléon* calls the 'incapacity of the married woman'. The incapable, inoperative woman (incapable legally as well as corporally)' remains, to be sure, a narrowly bounded bourgeois dream. P. J. Hélias ably shows how, until quite recently, a young peasant woman's value on the marriage market was largely a function of her recognized physical vigour: that is to say, her potential as labour-power. It is likely that among the working class the *incompetence* which some recent American best-selling authors[56] have advised women to cultivate has never been regarded as an ideal.[57] The fact that Rimbaud, the poet of the Commune, sings of 'Jeanne-Marie's hands', that he designates a woman by her hands – which are strong ones – should also be included in our archive: it marks a doubtless important break with the bourgeois ideal.[58]

In contrast to the adoption of these ideas by a social group which, while narrow, was not confined only to the world of letters, other equally significant notions in Roussel seem to me to have neither struck a chord in the public imagination nor been taken up in any serious way by law or legislation. On the other hand, these latter themes have since been continually reiterated in the world of learning and letters. The non-exportable quality of these ideas suggests that they amount simply to a self-serving advocacy '*pro domo*': that they belong not just to a learned imaginary but to an imaginary of learnedness.

The first of these elements from Roussel is woman's theoretical incapacity. I gave my opinion earlier as to the coherence of the category 'theoretical'. While, from the mid-eighteenth century to our own time, the learned have never stopped repeating that the 'speculative', the intellectual life in general, are beyond women's competence, this same period is one which has witnessed the progressive establishment of the school – and has gradually opened up its different pathways to girls. Not without qualms and reservations, no doubt, but it is important to evaluate the extent of these resistances. To measure these we have available two points of comparison.

The creation of *lycées* for girls gave rise neither to such uproar as did Jules Ferry's proposed compulsory, secular state school system, nor to an interminable debate like that on votes for women. Indeed, in terms of strict chronology, it was during the Second Empire that Victor Duruy established primary schools for girls wherever these were still lacking, and secondary schooling for girls in sixty French cities – all this, in other words, taking place well in advance of the violent Third Republic debate over the principle of compulsory schooling. And the kind of resistance which did manifest itself concerned not the schools themselves, but only the certificates they awarded. The idea of women studying mathematics or experimental physics does not seem to have worried any of the politicians in charge of establishing the school system, nor the women's fathers. But for a woman to pass the *baccalauréat* did, so it seems, pose rather more problems, for a time at least, since the *baccalauréat* is a social qualification. As for higher education, there obtained a striking disagreement between the politicians who regularly supported women's demands to enter university courses, and the university men,[59] the internal institutional authorities, who for their part alleged women's total lack of 'physical, intellectual and moral' capacity[60] either to complete the same studies as men, or (most important of all) to perform the same jobs.

The discourse on women's incapacity for theory thus remained the appurtenance of a minuscule social group, that of the administrators of knowledge. And if the writings of these lettered authors do not bother with details but instead postulate a global state of female incapacity, the positions they adopt in practice themselves reveal that these managers of learning really take up arms only to defend the summits of the educational hierarchy: in other words, their own positions. Woman is intellectually incapable, but where does her incapacity begin? With the elementary-school certificate? At entry to higher education? At the level of the male PhD in mathematics? The question becomes absurd when the threshold of tolerance is a floating one; consequently doctoral discourse decrees instead a global female incapacity, a natural impossibility. And this clearly amounts to no more than a plea *pro domo*, a symbolic affirmation of the pre-eminence of the intellectual function. The ruling 'no women here' establishes not only the (fictive) identity of the 'here', but also its value. One can understand why the politicians had no use for this fiction. They had their own, which was actually its exact counterpart: women are dangerous in politics . . .

This, then, was a zone of Roussel's discourse which remained confined to learned culture. It seems to me that the same can be said of the chiasmic Eros, and more broadly of that attitude which combines silence about the thing itself with hyperbolic proliferation of metaphors elsewhere; denying the partial and the local, while appealing to the general and the global. This kind of play on the spatialization of the body can readily be seen at work is psychoanalytic theory,[61] and what the Lacanians describe using the image of the 'Gorgon's head' is, perhaps, the figure of *their* truth. One might have thought that the analysts would content themselves with possessing a partial competence, a specialized knowledge, a particular technique of cure. But it is no secret that they lay claim instead to a general competence – that, in other words, they behave as though analytical theory possessed global explanatory value and jurisdiction over a whole range of problems: metaphysical (happiness, death), ethical,[62] aesthetic, linguistic, epistemological . . . One may well wonder into what sector of the present-day encyclopaedia psychoanalysis has not intervened to hand down some pre-given certainty. There is an answer to this rhetorical question: if psychoanalysis never admits to doubt when treating of politics or morals, it becomes strikingly problematical when it comes to speaking of itself. The Lacanian polemic against scientism in dealing with the unconscious goes in tandem with the dogmatism of Lacan's disciples, and indeed of Lacan himself, when dealing with 'other' fields of knowledge. The Lacanian continually reminds us that the analytical cure is not intended to 'heal' or help (this being the practical corollary of the denial of partial knowledge). Is this not consonant with the imaginary logic founded by Roussel to sanction the export of expertise? Roussel too washes his hands of objective practice: medicine has nothing to do with the art of midwifery: this latter task can be left to the 'close friends of the parturiant' (p. 220). Difficult childbirths are not a matter of concern for those who have undertaken 'long and serious studies in physics, mechanics and mathematics'. The Gorgon's head can well and justly stand as the emblem of psychoanalysis, as the modesty–beauty couplet was Roussel's.

THE SEX IN THE BRAIN

Let us not, however, leave the hard work of chiasmizing to the Freudians alone. The reification of the chiasma of difference as a fantasy-geography of the female body can still be read in medical philosophy today. In a moment we will read it in *Le Fait Féminin*.[63] It is, admittedly, less easy to dissect the strategy of this book, in so far as the form of scientificity it lays claim to may seem to be contemporary, and therefore valid – valid here, of course, as a means of intimidation and nothing more. This intimidation is based on two techniques.

1. The citation of experiments which describes their 'result' but not the procedure employed, so that the reader is disqualified from forming even an opinion of what is being said. See, for example, Sandra Witelson's 'duly established facts' (Part 2, chapter 6). These are to do with aptitude tests: in other words with one of the most suspect areas of psychology. The conditions under which the research leading to the establishment of these 'facts' took place are not described; nor is its progress; still less the essential question as to how the tests were developed before being put into use. Such a procedure is scientifically illegitimate, worth as much and as little as a recital of a UFO sighting. But since the expert's word is valid currency, this procedure has every chance of being more effective than an account which supplied details of the techniques employed, thereby revealing their inevitable points of weakness.

2. The authors talk of gonadostimulines, the hypothalamus and the diencephalus to a public which has, at best, a vague idea of what these are, and in general has no grasp at all of this domain of knowledge. This, of course, is what founds the expertise of the expert. But what the general reader is crucially unable to evaluate is the legitimacy or illegitimacy of the expert's derivation of consequences for education and the division of labour from some discovery about hormones. This provides the expert with an *ad hoc* licence to say more or less anything, and in particular whatever happens to suit the expert's own prejudices.

The only possible adequate response to this kind of work is an outright dismissal, taking as its prize exhibit the most picturesque of E. Sullerot's fancies, one which delights me by the way it completely demolishes the rest of her laboriously scientistic *mise en scène*. Sullerot relates (pp. 284–5) that previous converging and repeated observations in the sociology of work had led her 'to formulate a number of hypotheses open to verification, among these the genetic hypothesis of a recessive gene in the X chromosome. This hypothesis attracted the interest and attention of Jacques Monod . . .' – the recessive gene in question being, as one learns on page 430, responsible notably for the musical non-creativity of women. One may as well spell it out here that any such genetic hypothesis not formulated on the basis of the most recent state of relevant knowledge is no better than a hoax, a fabrication which should never be regarded as innocent. Not only does Sullerot betray, by her recitation of her conversations with Jacques Monod, the scientifically cloaked amateurism which underlies the entire book, she also takes her place in the long line of ideologues who recruit genetics to justify some otherwise unacceptable form of exclusion or segregation. The ghost of Lombroso[64] haunts the margin of these pages, accompanied by other, more recent and atrocious memories. We have already witnessed the use of biology as an alibi for aetiologies of forms of behaviour labelled as antisocial. We know the empty hopes various racisms invested in the measuring of skulls.[65] And because all this has been resuscitated with the theory of the 'crime chromosome', someone naturally feels warranted to start fantasizing about a female handicap gene in the X chromosome.[66]

Over the dinner table, an American professor murmurs to his biologist colleague that, in the whole of his long career, the only coloured students among those the university is compelled to admit whom he has known to reach a tolerable level have been those of mixed descent. His colleague replies that this may well be so, but that the subject is a taboo which science is currently unable to examine, because of the outrage it would provoke. Likewise over the dinner table, Sullerot says to Monod that there could well be an as yet uncatalogued gene which . . . and Monod replies that were there to be a taboo on the question today, because of the feminists, that would not stop him tackling it: 'rather, it would stimulate him'.[67]

All this goes to prove is that the feminist movement in France is not as strong as the black movement in America. Everything comes down, indeed, to the relation of social forces within the decision-making consensus – the making of decisions whether or not to pursue such and such a line of 'research'. People feel authorized today to daydream about the X chromosome in the same way that in the Germany of the 1930s and early 1940s they could feel positively incited to undertake certain researches.

This much having been pointed out concerning the functioning of scientificity in *Le Fait féminin*[68] we can see how history here repeats itself. Roussel set out to restore medicine to its proper rights – which are, for him, its rights to establish the basis of proper morality.[69] 'It was time', says the blurb of Sullerot's book, 'for the biological sciences to examine the social implications of their researches and discoveries.' If the emblem in Roussel of such a manipulation of competences was a sexualized collarbone and a neutered pubis, what is the trademark of the Sullerot colloquium's sociologizing biology? Identical genital apparatuses, and a very marked 'psychosexual differentiation of the brain'. Alfred Jost[70] points out, for example, that sex difference is not to be looked for at the level of the primitive embryonic configuration of genital organs: 'The embryologists of the last century admirably demonstrated that the different parts of the two sexes' genital apparatuses develop from profiles which are initially identical in all individuals.' Identity, perhaps, at the level of the *visible*. An appearance of resemblance, to the naked eye.

This observation has as its first corollary the reintroduction of the idea of the eunuch woman, the castrated female. 'All castrated foetuses develop into females' (p.86). 'In the animal which does not receive this imprint[71] around the time of birth – in the female or castrated male – the adult libido will be of feminine type', Pierre Royer adds a little later. The second corollary is that femininity derives from an intrinsic cause, masculinity from an extrinsic one: 'The genital apparatus of the foetus has an *inherent* tendency to develop according to the feminine model, unless it is subjected to . . .'[72]

I myself have, of course, no particular opinion as to the role of the testicular hormones. My analysis is concerned here only with vocabulary and presentation: with the means, that is to say, by which a work of vulgarization is able to produce ideological effects. 'In the course of development, becoming male involves a constant struggle. The smallest testicular deficiency places the foetus at risk of being more or less feminized . . .' Such a statement (by A. Jost, p. 87) may be an echo of the present state of knowledge in embryology (though I doubt it[73]), but this echo comes back at us off a wall of prejudices and fantasy-engendering anxieties – anxieties that can doubtless be identified, though this is not my concern here. I shall content myself with remarking that in the contributions here of Jost and Royer, the action of the testicular hormone is described in a rather startling way as an outside influence on embryonic structures, a power which modifies their inherent nature: 'The foetal testicule has to actively oppose the actualization of feminine structures and impose the formation of male organs. Any testicular deficiency . . . liberates the female tendencies.'

'The inhibitive testicular hormone', 'indelible influences': and Jost concludes with 'the *inherent* tendency towards femininity' (my emphasis, again). Royer goes further: the action of the testosterone over a very short period before and after birth is an 'imprint', a term which implies the presence of a substance 'subjected to this action', *and* an external action intervening so as radically to modify this substance.

An inherent feminine, and a masculine 'by virtue of an exteriority'; Eléanor Maccoby humorously recalls[74] the cliché that woman is specially destined to remain in the home, the refuge, the domestic hearth, while men journey over hill and dale; and she notes that sociobiology has made possible a reactivation of this cliché.[75] The embryologists' very vocabulary bears the trace of this conventional opposition. From its beginnings in foetal life, 'masculinity' is a thing of drama, conflict, struggle, danger, openness to influence, relation to an Other, while 'femininity' is the tranquil, immobile unfolding of the inherent, self-closure in the same.

Tracing the pre-given imaginary pathway which invites Sullerot to invite the contributions of these various specialists, one can see why the psychosexual brain differences turn out to manifest themselves in differences of *spatial* aptitude.

It was only to be expected that since sexual difference is absent in the original form of the genital organs it would surface elsewhere, preferably in association with valorized subjects after the manner of politics and intellectual work in Roussel. From page 20 of the book there is talk of cerebral hemispheres and cognitive mechanisms, and indeed the whole book is peppered with remarks on cerebral differences. It was only to be expected that, wherever sexual difference comes into play,

Le ciel, dont nous voyons que l'ordre est tout-puissant,
Pour différents emplois nous fabrique en naissant. (p. 15)

(Heaven, whose order we see to be all-powerful
Shapes us from birth for different employments.)

Thus Molière, quoted without tongue in cheek in Sullerot's epigraph. Since the contract for the colloquium is funded by the sociology of work, and since today work is seldom purely muscular, one could anticipate some elaboration on the neuro-psychological basis of 'higher' forms of activity. But why should the ceaselessly reiterated inequality of men and women have specifically to do here with *spatial* aptitudes? One might just as well have expected an inferiority in logical aptitudes, in grasp of temporal relations, in the capacity to generalize, to find the common constructional principle for a set of examples, or whatever. Why should it be space that foots the bill for the sexist myth? To my mind, there are at least two reasons. First of all, no doubt, it is because 'spatial aptitudes' are a vague enough datum ('seeing in three dimensions') to be said to operate everywhere. An inequality of this order can have an indefinitely wide domain of application, in everyday life (driving a car, reading a map) as much as in work (the whole of mechanical industry; scientific education too [p. 281]; the professions of architecture, engineering, art [p. 298]). And as space means the right-hand hemisphere and the right-hand hemisphere means creation, if your daughter doen't compose music you can blame space for that as well . . . (Sandra Witelson, p. 298). The oft-repeated presupposition that 'individuals choose the profession for which they have greatest aptitude'[76] obliged these apologists of the *status quo* to discover a handicapping factor of great generality since, 'in fact', women have less brilliant careers in every sector of socio-economic life than men . . . A mere hump or lobe, or some single convolution of the cerebral cortex, would not have been enough. It was not sufficient to invoke some 'narrowly specialized' handicap; it had to be some general dimension of existence. Hence, a whole hemisphere.

The second reason I see for the choice of this particular incapacitating factor is a more subterranean one. In terms of simplistic philosophy and association of ideas, spatiality means exteriority. 'Over hill and dale' is at once a trajectory, a space in which one moves, and an outside-oneself. This can perhaps more easily be felt if one opposes this primary valorization of space to the poetics of time, which is regularly aligned on the side of subjectivity and the inner life of closed meditation. The man of action is a man of spaces, a Jack London hero, Klondike pioneer or South Sea navigator. The man of temporality, who never travels farther than Balbec and seldom leaves his own room, who is absorbed by introspection and introversion – wouldn't you say his was rather a feminine mode of life and sensibility?

Witelson criticizes a study by Wikin which shows that children who do well at perceptual tasks are those who have been allowed from an early age to wander farther outside their home. Witelson reverses the causal connection here, saying that it is those individuals most genetically endowed with spatial aptitudes who are inclined (and able) to wander. So it is the exploration of the external world which is at issue here. The practical consequences are easily arrived at: if small girls are less gifted at mastering spatial relationships, one would be wise to keep them at home. And if Sullerot's 'sociology of work' duly finds the same handicap in adult women, then it would be better likewise for them not to travel too far from home. The imaginary schema this implies is the same as Roussel's: woman enclosed in her interiorist cocoon, man with his relation to exteriority. 'Inherent', staying-always-close-to-itself, developing without external influence: the female embryo is already a house-wife.

PERENNIAL IDEOLOGY

'They truly see miracles whom miracles profit.'[77] This stress on the original non-difference of the genital organs, and on the major sex differences of brains: why would anyone believe or endorse such a picture, unless there were some pleasure to be gained from it? Among the group of researchers brought together by Sullerot there is one person who visibly fails to see the miracle. Michelle Perrot is a discordant voice[78] in the consort; instead of speaking about 'woman' she reflects, as a historian, on those who speak about women – and she evokes, precisely, the memory of our Roussel.[79] Here, Sullerot's response is marvellous:

> A fine example of the magical use of analogies to ratify an ideology! But I would rather we took care not to confuse an ideological discourse with the beginnings of scientific discourse, since that would be to give the impression that it was medical discoveries and scientific endeavour which gave rise to nineteenth-century attitudes to woman and femininity.

But it is just this 'I would rather we took care not to confuse . . .' which embodies the most basic misconception of what the practice of ideology is! There is not, on the question that concerns us, a scientific discourse 'on the one hand' and an ideological discourse 'on the other', since the ideology involved here consists precisely in the exportation of an expertise, the extrapolation of a scientific knowledge made malleable for the greater glory of the cause.

In what sense is this ideology? Do we mean the vague idiomatic meaning this word has acquired – 'false consciousness', 'mystification' – the idea of a conceptual phantasmagoria squalidly compliant with actual oppressions; or do we mean the historical referent of the word: the *Idéologues*, a French philosophical school influential around 1800?[80]

To simplify: the historical *Idéologie* was a movement which claimed to provide a new 'first philosophy',[81] conceived as advantageously taking the place of metaphysics. This other philosophy was to be one founded in observation and experience, based on a certain actual form of physiological knowledge: since the brain is the organ of thought (as the liver is the organ of bile), cerebral physiology was to provide the grounding of a general theory of thought – in the broad sense, embracing everything to do with human judgement, will and language: which makes this '*Idéologie*' at once a moral philosophy, a doctrine of education and a theory of the human faculties. This (in my terms) special 'knowledge', a physiology of the nervous system, provides the basis of a global conception of man.

Now the creation of the *Encyclopaedia* had already made evident the difficulties inherent in any 'general philosophy' – if, indeed, it was not the realization of these difficulties which had made the *Encyclopaedia* an appealing project in the first place. Diderot, for example, whom Roussel knew personally, had been acutely aware of philosophy's instability – whether as a global system erected by simple reflection or pure rationality, or as a retrospective totalization of partial or piecemeal knowledges; since every totalization remains precarious, and needs constant repair.

The philosopher who acts as a specialist of generalities is thus forced to acknowledge that he 'has nothing'[82] – that (as Diderot says) his only capacity is to bring local knowledges into communication one with another. This retreat of philosophy from the standpoint of a general world-view is linked to the acceptance as fact of the rather uncongenial realist criterion of science described by Diderot in his *Interpretation of Nature*:[83] one constructs by pure mental exertion a palace of systematic ideas, and then there ensues some localized discovery, 'a single part which wrecks the architecture', and everything collapses. Hence the retreat from generality, from the 'system of the world', as this proves to be an uninhabitable space. But the consequence of philosophy's abandonment of its cloudy palaces is that this space of generality is left unoccupied.[84] The *Idéologues* opted to reoccupy it, notwithstanding their new alertness to the constant danger, the nature of the stone liable to upend the giant with feet of clay:[85] the 'fatal part' is always the outcome of some particular scientific discovery.

Not the least of the paradoxes underlying this story was that the empty space was annexed by a group of savants who, possessing the limited authority conferred by a localized competence, expanded it into a right to pronounce on everything. For what enabled them to take this risk was the fact that the immediate source of danger happened to lie inside their own initial zone of competence – hence the necessity for these savant-ideologues to rein their 'specialized' knowledge well back within the limits of its potential scope. To begin with, I found this aspect of Roussel's discourse particularly intriguing. His extrapolation of physiological knowledge into considerations on morality and women's psychointellectual capacities seemed fairly unexceptional. On the contrary, what was enigmatic and needed explaining was the way this diffusion of partial knowledge left behind it a central void, and the ostentatious way in which Roussel proclaims his *definitive scepticism* concerning the most elementary questions of gynaecology. I could make sense of only half of the chiasma. It was a remark about *Le Fait féminin* by a biologist friend that set me on the right track: Jost and Royer's vague assimilation of the categories of the castrated and the female led her to comment that 'One could just as well maintain the exact opposite . . . from a hormonal point of view, a castrated woman becomes masculinized.' Of course my own private conversations are no more cogent as evidence than those of Sullerot and Monod.[86] But when I afterwards reread Diderot's exposition, in *The Interpretation of Nature*, of the process by which a localized discovery can overthrow the philosopher's palace of ideas (his general system of the world), the theoretical position of *any* savant who purports to draw global consequences from his partial knowledge came to strike me as a paradoxical one which falls under the sign of the chiasma: if the shoemaker wants to dogmatize *ad lib* over and above the matter of the shoe, he first has to neutralize the force of his local knowledge,[87] either by blurring it (vulgarization readily lends itself to this function) or by affecting a certain scepticism, even to the extent of rendering his own knowledge problematical. For if no regional knowledge can found a global world-view, a philosophy in the classical sense, regional knowledges are, on the other hand, certainly quite capable of producing disabling arguments *against* such philosophies. (The example Diderot had in mind was the wrecking of Cartesian philosophy by Newton's discoveries.)

So one does indeed need to look to the historical *Idéologie* if one is to interpret this chiasma. Roussel provided the *Idéologues* with a working model – and a mythical image to use for the writing of their own protocol. His critique of his predecessors (for supposing that woman is woman only in the one place), and his reproval of ancient medical authors for lacking proper conviction about the true rights of medicine, amount to one and the same idea, his geography of the female body ultimately yielding only a cartography of jurisdictions, an organizational plan for the manipulation of competences. The structure of the female body serves to legitimate the displacement of Ideology's legitimate field of discourse.

The simultaneously castrated and panhystericized woman can thus be read as the emblem of a discursive practice, one which can be called Ideological in the strict sense of the term, provided one recognizes that Ideology in this strict sense has long outlived Cabanis and Destut de Tracy. But why should it be specifically 'woman' who covers the costs of this chiasmic figuration of competence? To resolve the problem of this choice of symbolizing substance one would need to reconsider the strategies of all those philosophers since the mid-eighteenth century who have transcribed their anxieties about their own legitimacy into reveries on 'the feminine'. Perhaps this will be a subject for a later discussion. My aim here has been only to articulate some of the possible forms of the learned imagination.

Notes

1. Plato, *Symposium*, 221e.
2. Hegel, *Lectures on the Philosophy of History*, Introduction.
3. And that its study thus belongs to the history of themes of scholarly fable.
4. Entering upon a process of self-foundation and self-validation means already in itself setting out to build an imaginary construct. There can be no such thing as a self-founding discourse – yet to produce one is philosophy's recurring claim and ambition. This makes recourse to myth an inevitability. And the ultimate implication of my conception of the philosophical imaginary, the most drastic hypothesis for its reading that I might be tempted to make, would be this: it is in the administration of its own legitimacy, the establishment of its own value, that philosophy is drawn into defining and designing its own myths, making use of spatial or narrative plans and layouts, wielding as part of its discourse stories about pierced barrels, islands surrounded by all kinds of danger, fruit trees, and chains which must be forged or broken. It would certainly be both excessive and reductive to assert that *all* images in philosophical texts are about philosophy – for the ills of this order of discourse are not all specular in form – but this hypothesis does account for some eminently classic images which are to be found everywhere and form part of the language of the corporation (which by definition transcends its particular utterers) and which may be, just as much as certain principles, rules and misapprehensions, structuring elements of the philosophical position itself.
5. *Symposium*, 221e.
6. *Revue de Métaphysique et de Morale*, July 1896, Supplement, p. 16.
7. *Traité des Systèmes*, Chapters 1 and 5: Condillac cites the (illegitimate) use of picturesque comparisons, whether in the form of metaphor, 'popular

prejudices', or dreams: 'here one creates or rules the universe from one's bed. All this costs no more than a dream, and a philosopher dreams easily.' Even if a philosopher is dreaming, it is clear that productions of this kind have for Condillac no philosophical value. They are palliatives for ignorance, plugs to stop up a hole.

8.   Kant, *Critique of Pure Reason*, Transcendental Analytic, Book II, Chapter 3, trans. Norman Kemp Smith (London: Macmillan, 1970), p. 257.

9.   Suspecting a change of perspective or level of discourse, which is indeed easy to locate here: breaking off the critical theory of understanding, Kant turns back reflectively upon his own critical enterprise and makes its apologia. He passes from his object to his project – and to the (positive) value of his intervention in the field of his object.

10. This successive order should not be taken as a hard-and-fast rule. Let us say that there are several complementary ways of approaching the image, one in terms of system (looking for comparable or divergent uses of the image in the rest of the work), another in terms of the primary symbolic meaning of this image, another in terms of erudition, and yet another, essential one in terms of the structure of the work (reinserting the question evaded and settled by the image). The interpretation of the image lies at the intersection of these different axes of investigation.

11. *Conjectural Beginning of Human History*, 1786.

12. That is, the details which are of interest here. There are innumerable islands in philosophical texts, and the figure is not a wholly univocal one. Its archetypal dimension is certainly important, but a poetics of insularity (dealing with the most classic usage of this figure) will not suffice, since the particular configuration of this island is often rich in meanings; cf. Chapter 2 below.

13. See Chapter 5 below.

14. Regarding our example, it is important to be aware that the island has very often, if not most often, a link with the problem of the existential value of philosophy, the happiness-value of truth. It regularly accompanies the appearance of axiological reflection within the theory of knowledge.

15. A trace of this ambivalence appears in Kant's text, with regard to adventures which the navigator is never capable of refusing. Further, the island of truth is in Bacon, likewise, second in order, placed at the ending of a passage of restoration, in difference, of the lost island origin. Cf. *The New Atlantis*.

15a. Spedding's translation of the Latin text of the epigraph reads as follows: 'Of myself, I say nothing; but on behalf of the business which is at hand I entreat men to believe that it is not an opinion to be held, but a work to be done; and to be well assured that I am labouring to lay the foundation, not of any sect or doctrine, but of human utility and power. Next, I ask them to deal fairly by their own interests . . . to join in consultation for the public good; and ... to come forward themselves and take part in that which remains to be done. Moreover, to be of good hope, nor to imagine that this Instauration of mine is a thing infinite and beyond the power of man, when it is in fact the true end and termination of infinite error.' (Bacon, Preface to *The Great Instauration: Works*, ed. Spedding (Ellis and Heath, 1858, vol. IV, p. 21.) [Translator's note.]

16. One might also study the highly problematic character of what has been called Kant's Pelagianism.

17. The fact that Bacon conceives his own action by means of a host of images indicates that for him, too, the business is not without its difficulties. But that is another story.

18. *The New Atlantis* (Oxford Paperback, 1974), p. 239 f.

19. *Critique of Pure Reason*, op. cit., p. 259.

20. *De me quoque fabula narratur?* Need one answer this question?

21. 'Conjectural Beginning of Human History', in *On History*, ed. Lewis White Beck, trans. Emil L. Fackenheim (Indianapolis: Bobbs-Merrill, 1963), p. 68.

22. Where texts are concerned, doubtless the only tenable 'psychoanalysis' is that of the reader.

23. This book is the subject of Chapter 8 below.

24. The last page of the 'Architectonic of Pure Reason': *Critique of Pure Reason*, p. 665.

25. Ibid.: 'that censorship which secures general order and harmony, and indeed the well-being of the scientific community'.

26. The different sciences are of great value as means of attaining the contingent ends of humanity; if they also ultimately lead us to its necessary and essential ends, this is only when helped by metaphysics.

27. For example, it is perfectly correct that the theory calls for the abandonment of vain *hopes*.

28. 'An Old Question Raised Again: Is the Human Race Constantly Progressing?', in *On History*, op. cit., p. 151 f.

29. *Critique of Pure Reason*, op. cit. ('Architectonic'), p. 664.

30. There has been an immemorial assumption that concrete comparisons and images are pedagogical. My experience of teaching philosophy to final-year philosophy classes in *lycées* has regularly proved the opposite to me. It is as difficult to get students to understand a certain metaphor as a certain concept. The philosophical image-album is a language as technical as our jargon – and its pedagogical or didactic value is a delusion.

31. See J. Imbelloni and A. Viviante, *Le livre des Atlantides*, trans. Gidon (Payot).

32. Which considers that discourse is the conclusion, the· secondary rationalization of what I dream, an idea supported by a formulation which

appeared ten years ago in *Cahiers pour l'Analyse*: 'What I think is only the
effect of what I unthink [*de ce que j'impense*].'

33. This tells the story of a child born without father or mother on a desert
     island, who arrives all alone 'by his own powers' at wisdom. For further
     details, see my 'Irons-nous jouer dans l'île?', in *Écrit pour Vladimir
     Jankélévitch* (Flammarion, 1978).

34. Leibniz declared a great liking for this book, no doubt for wholly
     monadological reasons!

35. Selkirk was rescued in 1709 and his adventure made known in 1712 by the
     publication of Captain Woodes Rogers's book *A Cruising Voyage Round the
     World*.

36. The portrait of Selkirk by Captain Dampier, who had left him on Juan
     Fernandez, is quite different: he was the best man on board.

37. The character of Friday also follows quite faithfully a model in Ibn Tufayl,
     that of Açal. They both appear when the initial narrative device has run
     through its programme and exhausted its stock of possibilities, to relaunch
     the story. And both represent the pedagogical temptation: Açal-Friday
     will be the disciple of him who has had no master, and will prompt the
     urge to leave the island so as to go and teach the subjects of Salaman, or
     the savages: 'You teach wild mans be good sober tame mans; you tell them
     know God, pray God, and live new life', says Friday. From this angle one
     can doubtless recover one of the historical circumstances which carries the
     myth beyond its place of origin: a certain philosophical tradition
     nourished the hope of a colonization, by the philosopher, of the world of
     men. The actual colonization of the New World by Europe must have
     made possible a wider circulation for a fable carrying this meaning.

38. All that follows is pure conjecture. I am concerned only to raise some
     doubts over a notion widely accepted by philosophers today to the effect
     that, since philosophy is supposed to lay down the law for all other
     discourse and hold a hegemonic position in the cultural field, its effects are
     propagated as a matter of course.

39. I doubt anyway whether this notion of cultural domination can have any
     more than a descriptive value; further, to my mind it serves only for
     describing dual situations, binary conflicts, the collision of two cultural
     positions. When there are more than two and there is no 'situation', no
     actual meeting on a specific stage, this notion loses its meaning. One
     would be hard put to say what is culturally dominant today in France.

2: DAYDREAM IN UTOPIA

1. Thomas More, *Utopia*. I have slightly amended Robinson's classic transla-
    tion: for example, he renders the Latin *cornua* (horns) as 'corners', which
    greatly weakens the image of Utopia's crescent form.

2. *L'Utopie* (Paris: Éditions Sociales, 'Les classiques du Peuple', trans. Marcelle Bottigelli-Tisserand).
3. Hegel, *Reason in History*.
4. It is also worth underlining the fact that one never senses the presence of the sea in Utopia. Whereas in Book I Raphael gives a detailed description of the systems of navigation used by other people he has met, there is no mention of ships in the whole of Book II. There are indeed a few fish in the market at Amaurot, but the catalogue of occupations which is given does not include that of the fisherman: Utopia's economy is essentially agricultural, which is surprising for an island. Lastly, all Utopia's wars are fought on land. The island apparently does not possess a battle-fleet. How, anyway, would one get out of a harbour where no wind blows? The only solution would be by rowing; but the slaves in Utopia are not galley-slaves.
5. This capital is called Amaurot. Amaurosis means, in Greek, darkening. But there is a wider possible network of signifiers here: a-More-aut[or]: 'Thomas More not being the author' – the cancelled emblem of the writer (Thomas More practised a number of wordplays on his own name), a writer who denies being one, since he claims to be simply reporting Raphael's narrative.

3: GALILEO

1. Alexandre Koyré, *Galileo Studies*, trans. John Mepham (Harvester, 1978).
2. I intentionally choose for illustration these two school manuals, which transmitted a certain image of science to more than one generation of students.
3. For convenience of exposition I simplify the question by terming 'first formulations' laws which were formulated in immediate historical proximity to Galileo; but the pre-scientific state of the question is actually much more complex. On this see Pierre Duhem, *De l'accélération produite par une force constante* (Geneva: Congrès International de Philosophie, IIe Session, 1905) and *Études sur Léonard de Vinci*, vol. VIII.
4. In order to describe intersubjective time, Jacques Lacan has proposed a more complex model:

> 'But mathematics can symbolize another kind of time, notably the intersubjective time that structures human action, whose formulae are beginning to be given us by the theory of games, still called strategy, but which it would be better to call *stochastics*.'
>
> The author of these lines has attempted to demonstrate in the logic of a sophism the temporal sources through which human action, in so far as it orders itself according to the action of the other, finds in the scansion of its hesitations the advent of its certainty; and in the decision that

concludes it, this action gives to that of the other – which it includes from that point on – together with the consequences deriving from the past, its meaning-to-come.

In this article it is demonstrated that it is the certainty anticipated by the subject in the 'time for understanding' which, by the haste which precipitates the 'moment of concluding', determines in the other the decision that makes of the subject's own movement error or truth.

It can be seen by this example how the mathematical formalization that inspired Boolean logic, to say nothing of set theory, can bring to the science of human action the structure of intersubjective time that is needed by psychoanalytic conjecture if it is to ensure its own rigour. (Jacques Lacan, *Écrits, A Selection*, trans. A. Sheridan [London: Tavistock, 1977], p. 75)

5. *Opere di Galileo Galilei*, Edizione Nazionale, vol. VIII, p. 197. Translation (cited here) in Koyré, op. cit., pp. 95–6; full translation in Galileo, *Dialogues Concerning Two New Sciences*, trans. H. Crew and A. del Salvio (New York: McGraw-Hill, 1963,) p. 154.

6. Goethe, *Elective Affinities*, trans. R. J. Hollingdale (Penguin, 1978), p. 53.

7. The term 'affinity' may perhaps have retained the ethnological ambiguity of its etymology or, better still, have been drawn into the field of alchemy on account of the contradiction proper to its original meaning. For in classical Latin *adfinitas* is *kinship through alliance*, which says a lot in ethnographic terms: as alliance requires the absence of kinship (the incest prohibition), yet creates a sort of kinship, Lévi-Strauss has written that for every form of social thought marriage constitutes a sacred mystery; denying incest, it also 'borders on it'. One finds this same ambiguity and floating of sense in Goethe's novel, for the text hesitates – and, if I am right, cannot but hesitate – between the vocabulary of the 'same' ('each thing has an adherence to itself' [p. 52]) and the vocabulary of otherness ('Those natures which, when they meet, quickly lay hold on and mutually affect one another we call akin. This affinity is sufficiently striking in the case of alkalis and acids which, although they are mutually antithetical, and perhaps precisely because they are so, most decidedly seek and embrace one another . . .' [pp. 52–3], translation modified).

8. *La Formation de l'Esprit Scientifique*, Chapter 1.

9. These words, '*praeter spem*', in the *Dialogue Concerning New Sciences*, might to my mind serve as a title for this work's starting-point. To accept that what seems most plausible is false and that '*what is improbable at first sight*' (ibid.) can be found to be the case, and afterwards explained, seems to me one of the original points of Galileo's epistemological discourse, a discourse which carries astonishingly modern resonances when compared with the Cartesian system. Even if Galileo seldom conducts experiments, his

physicalism, which I discuss below, implies that matter has *other* laws than those which one might imagine if one kept one's eyes closed.
10. The original paper was written for a group of women physicists.
11. Galileo, *Dialogues . . .*, op. cit., First Day.
12. On Gassendi, see the *Actes du Congrès du Tricentenaire de Pierre Gassendi* (Digne, 1957), especially the fine thesis by Olivier-René Bloch, *La philosophie de Gassendi* (The Hague: Martinus Nijhoff, 1971).
13. *Theological Complements* (1453), Chapter 8. French translation by Maurice de Gandillac, in *Oeuvres Choisies de Nicolas de Cues* (Aubier, 1942), p. 457.
14. On this subject see Koyré, 'Galileo and the Law of Inertia', in *Galileo Studies*.
15. See Georges Canguilhem, *Études d'Histoire et de Philosophie des Sciences* (Vrin, 1970), p. 38.

4: THE POLYSEMY OF ATOPIAN DISCOURSE

1. The 'Moral' of the poem begins:
   Then leave Complaints: Fools only strive
   To make a Great an Honest Hive
   T'enjoy the World's Conveniencies,
   Be fam'd in War, yet live in ease,
   Without great Vices, is a vain
   EUTOPIA eated in the brain.
   Bernard Mandeville, *The Fable of the Bees, or, Private Vices, Publick Benefits*, ed. F. B. Kaye (Oxford: Clarendon, 1924), vol. I, p. 36.
2. Louis Marin, *Utopiques: jeux d'espaces* (Paris: Éditions de Minuit, 1973), Chapter 4.
3. Kepler, *Opera Omnia*, ed. Christian Frisch (Frankfurt–Erlangen, 1858–71), vol. VIII. For an analysis of the history of this piece, see C. de Buzon, 'Un Songe de Kepler', in *Cahiers de Fontenay*, 1.
4. This is not an exhaustive list; one might add to it Morelly, for one.
5. One need hardly labour the fact that the idea of community of goods is extremely variable in its meanings.
6. The title of René Dumont's book, *L'Utopie ou la mort*, is eloquent in this regard: for More, too, Utopia is a possibility presented as the only alternative to an apocalypse.
7. Besides, the Utopians' consciousness of their own happiness remains a problem for More.
8. *The Laws*, IV, 704c.
9. *Political Treatise*, Chapter 1.
10. *Social Contract*, Book II, Chapter 10.

11. Which does not mean that it cannot be taken up and reworked by virtue precisely of its polysemy. Only thus perhaps can one account, for example, for the career of the phrase *'changer de vie'*, from Rimbaud to our own time.

12. This is why I have made use of this term *atopos*, borrowed from Book VIII of the *Republic* (515a): a word applied to the allegory of the cave, marking it as exterior to the common heritage of myth and hence foreshadowing the need for a lengthy explanation.

5: RED INK IN THE MARGIN

1. This question might be broadened to cover the scientific editing of ancient writings available to us only in defective versions, partly because of careless copyists. Take, for example, Lucretius's *De Rerum Natura*, II, 257. The passage is about the *clinamen*, the swerving of atoms. The O and Q manuscripts read here *'fatis avolsa voluptas'*, pleasure snatched from the fates. Scholars generally reject *'voluptas'* (pleasure) and substitute *'potestas'* (power) or *'voluntas'* (will), and no doubt have sound reasons for so doing. Perhaps *'voluptas'* is a mistake by a Benedictine copyist in the ninth century. But should it be rejected without further discussion? It is, at all events, a curious error, for even if 'pleasure snatched from the fates' makes the sentence's meaning incoherent, this does not make the idea incongruous relative to the poem as a whole. Certainly Lucretius does several times offer mechanical explanations for pleasure (the smooth round atoms, for example). But he also sings of sweet feelings which are not linked to a hard-and-fast causal explanation; Lucretius's writing, within which the attribution of sweetness happens unpredictably, itself suggests the idea of a causal indeterminacy of pleasure, as though pleasure were that small varying of perception, that almost-nothing [*nec plus quam minimum*] which all things are capable, at some unspecifiable place and time [*incerto tempore incertisque*], of representing. And did not Lucretius give to this slight departure without which nothing would exist another name, that of her but for whom nothing would accede to ˙the divine shores of light: Venus? Lucretius's writing is not a systematic treatment [*mise en cause*] of pleasure: perhaps this is what suggested the reading *'fatis avolsa voluptas'* to the copyists: a *lapsus calami* which is thus not devoid of sense.

2. D'Alembert, article on 'Cartésianisme' in the *Encyclopédie*.

3. Hamelin, *Le Système de Descartes*, p. 376. This is a course of lectures delivered at the École Normale Supérieure in the rue d'Ulm in 1903 and published by Robin in 1910, after Hamelin's death. All the emphases in passages quoted in this essay are added by the author.

4. Cf. the Summary of the *Discourse on Method* in this edition:

> The *Discourse on Method* contains the germ of the whole Cartesian philosophy: the First and Second Parts of this treatise contain an abstract of the rules of logic, which the author developed later [*sic*] under the title of *Rules for the Direction of Mind*. In the Third Part he lays the groundwork of his morality, and his letters to Elizabeth add nothing fundamental to this theory.

Thus the problem is not yet engaged.

Moreover, the expression 'definitive morality' as used by Garnier does not expressly refer to the perfect morality of the *Principles* (the tree), but to later formulations which are considered more elevated, concerning beatitude, God's goodness, etc. I commit, in passing, to the annals of the history of philosophy the tabular scheme of Descartes's philosophy given in the Introduction to this edition, which subdivides Descartes according to the chapter headings of the then official programme for philosophy teaching:

> Chapter 1: Descartes's psychology.
> Chapter 2: Descartes's logic.
> Chapter 3: Descartes's morality.
> Chapter 4: Descartes's theodicy.

5. One should say that it is not the moral thought of Descartes *as such* which interests the author of this edition, but the fact that the famous philosopher Descartes had proclaimed his submission to the Christian religion:

> 'Doubtless this will suffice to confound those writers who have the temerity to say that sincere belief in the truth of the Christian religion can only be the lot of lesser minds. But will their confusion not reach its height when it is proved that . . . the Christian religion finds, marching humbly under its colours, the four great chiefs of all modern philosophy?'

These four great chiefs are Descartes, Bacon, Leibniz and Newton.

6. Letter to Mersenne, 18 March 1630.
7. The *provision* can be challenged only through an appeal hearing; thus judgement *par provision* is already a part of the definitive judgement.
8. *Discourse*, Part III.
9. *La Morale de Descartes* (Paris, 1957), p. 3.
10. Op. cit.
11. Reply to the Second Objections.
12. *Discourse on Method*, Part VI, p. 168.
13. *Principles*, Part IV, §. 205.
14. p. 345 in the Garnier reprinting of Bayles's *Recueil de Pièces curieuses*, contained in vol. IV of the *Œuvres philosophiques de Descartes*. This is thought to have been a text addressed to the king in September 1678, together with the draft of a (pedagogical) concordat between the Jesuits and the Oratorians.

By this concordat the Oratorians undertook, especially in the domain of physics, to cease teaching Cartesian philosophy.

15. *Revue de Métaphysique et de Morale*, January 1937, p. 166. On this point I would note that while the present essay several times quotes Henri Gouhier's essay in an approving spirit, I cannot of course follow him in viewing the transcription of '*par provision*' as 'provisional' as a simple modernization of vocabulary.

16. Who in 1867 translates John Stuart Mill's book *Auguste Comte and Positivism*.

17. Publisher's announcement, Paris, 19 Moise 110 (19 January 1898), reproduced in the classic edition (Vrin, 1974).

18. Ibid., p. 111. We may also note that Bréhier 'Descartes selon le Père Laberthonnière', *Revue de Métaphysique et de Morale*, 1935) speaks of 'Descartes's positivist ideal'.

19. Jules Ferry, *Lettre aux Instituteurs*, 17 November 1883.

20. I wish here to record my debt to an exceptionally well-documented and as yet regrettably still unpublished work by Marie Ymonet: *Les Modèles Kantiens dans l'enseignement de la morale à l'école primaire sous la troisième République*, a *Mémoire de maitrise* completed under the supervision of Jean-Toussaint Desanti. I wish to thank Marie Ymonet warmly for providing me with the manuscript.

21. Ministerial Instruction of 27 July 1882, cited in the *Dictionnaire de Pédagogie*, article on 'Laïcité'.

22. *Lettre aux Instituteurs*, op. cit.

23. Article on 'Morale' in the *Dictionnaire de Pédagogie*.

24. The article is entitled 'La Crise du Libéralisme', *Revue de Métaphysique et de Morale*, 1902.

25. Ferry, *Lettre aux Instituteurs*, op. cit.

26. Charles Adam writes, concerning this ethical conversion, that provisional morality is 'destined to disappear before the light of science' (*Vie de Descartes*, Adam and Tannéry XII, p. 58).

27. Espinas, *Descartes et la Morale* (Paris, 1925), vol. II, Chapter 1.

28. I have simplified the situation by presenting it as an opposition between politico-pedagogues and university men. This is true in an overall sense, but two additional points need to be noted: there was never unanimity in the world of university philosophy, no more so at the time we are concerned with than at any other, and no more regarding the question of philosophy than over any other issue. The academics I refer to are those one might call the adherents of the philosophy, more or less explicitly inherited from Victor Cousin, which forms the dominant current of thinking in the university. But there are also the Positivists, who understand the rejection of *philosophy* by Ferry in terms of the censure of *metaphysics* by Auguste Comte, and who consequently support the Minister. Belot devotes four

long articles to 'the positive morality' in the *Revue de Métaphysique et de Morale* in 1905 and 1906; I reproduce here their significant opening lines:

One might with much truth apply the law of three stages to the evolution of morality in our European and Christian world. First almost exclusively theological, it became and has generally remained metaphysical. Almost everywhere – or at least where, not satisfied with the traditional formulae and dogmas of the catechism, morality aspires to self-understanding and reflection in the books of pure philosophers or the teaching of educators – it generally stops short at a metaphysical doctrine.

But one can say that contemporary thought, almost even public awareness itself, is today searching for a positive morality, and that an effort is being made in that direction comparable to and doubtless connected with the work of secularization which has been pursued, above all in France, for several decades past.

The second point of qualification to be made, connected to this first one, is that one should not suppose that Jules Ferry is proceeding against philosophy in its entirety from a position located altogether outside philosophy – that he is in reality the barbarian against whom Brochard, as sacred goose of the Capitol, proposes to defend the philosophical citadel. There is a philosophy at work in his discourse also. Ferry is, to a manifest degree, a Positivist.

29. The Écoles Normales of Saint-Cloud and Fontenay at this time recruited their students exclusively from the Écoles Normales Primaires (which had a very different syllabus from the *lycées*), and trained them to become either schoolteachers or heads of these same Écoles Normales Primaires. The students did not take the university faculty examinations but were given, over two years, a rapid general education to a rigorously 'structured' format. The importance accorded to the creation of a public and secular primary-schooling system had as its correlate a quite systematic ideological preparation and training of this system's future personnel.

30. Foreword, p. viii.

31. 'Du rapport de la morale à la Science dans la philosophie de Descartes', *Revue de Métaphysique*, 1896, p. 502.

32. Ibid., p. 503.

33. Ibid., p. 504.

34. 'I fear indeed that the writings I have published are not worthy that she should stop to read them . . . Perhaps, *if I had dealt there with morality*, I might have had grounds to hope they would be more agreeable to her; but this is what I must not meddle with writing about. Messieurs the Regents are so vehement against me, because of the innocent physical precepts of mine they have seen, and so angry because they can find no pretext there for

calumnying me, that if I were to deal after this with morality, they would leave me no peace.'

35. *The Interpretation of Dreams*, trans. James Strachey (Penguin, 1976), p. 196.

36. 'Though Monsieur Descartes applied himself to the study of morality as much as to any other part of philosophy, we yet have no complete treatise by him on this matter' (op. cit.).

37. Pascal, *Pensées*, Section VII, no. 425.

38. '. . . by eradicating from my mind all the wrong opinions . . .' (conclusion of Part II); 'I rooted out from my mind all the errors . . .' (Part III); 'I have already reaped from it such fruits . . .' (Part I); 'rather than the fruits of study' (Part I).

39. 'I know well that there are spirits who hurry so much and use so little circumspection in what they do that, even if they had firm foundations, they would be unable to build anything sure.'

40. Prefatory Letter to the *Principles*.

41. Sixth Meditation.

42. Diogenes Laertius, *Lives of Eminent Philosophers*: the life of Zeno.

43. On this matter, François Chatelet's book *La Philosophie des professeurs* is still pertinent.

44. We should, however, be careful not to exclude the possibility that something else is at work in these corrections: political and philosophical views comparable to those which produced the original misappropriation of meaning. Could it be that those in charge of philosophy teaching today might prefer to abandon morality to an extra-philosophical approach; might they, that is, wish to protect ethics against philosophy? Consider the *Capès* Examiners' Report for 1973: this time, the emphases are added by the author: 'The examiners can only note that the majority of candidates desiring to teach philosophy . . . do not have a sense of *morality* or even of *concrete politics* in their immediate everyday existence' (p. 20).

6: LONG HAIR, SHORT IDEAS

1. Needless to say this theoretical practice, though necessary, is also completely insufficient.

2. The deliberate exclusion of *women* from philosophical work is not necessarily explicitly stated. This is not true, however, of the exclusion of *the 'feminine'*.

3. This problem is further explored below in Chapter 8.

4. The *agrégation* is the top-level competitive examination for recruiting teachers for French secondary schools.

5. In France, philosophy has traditionally been taught in the *lycées* as part of

the *baccalauréat* (taken at the age of eighteen, the *baccalauréat* is required for university entrance).

6. Friend and correspondent of Diderot.
7. Of course, Auguste Comte has in mind the chronology of the masculine situation: a boy having first his mother, then a sister . . .
8. *L'Ange* is a book by the *nouveaux philosophes* Lardreau and Jambet which was causing a brief stir at the time this article was written (1976).
9. The *Capès* is also a competitive examination for recruiting teachers, at a somewhat lower level than the *agrégation*.
10. 'Ten years ago' means 'in the 'sixties', the article having been written in 1976.
11. The author broached this question some years later in a kind of short story, 'Spécial-Femmes, un grumeau sur la lange', published in *Alidades*, no. 1 (Paris, 1982).

8: PIERRE ROUSSEL'S CHIASMAS

1. Jean-Jacques Rousseau, *Émile* (Garnier), p. 450.
2. Thanks notably to the work of Y. Knibiehler. Cf. 'Les médecins et la nature féminine au temps du Code Civil', *Annales* ESC, 1976, no. 4.
3. Failing this allegorical coronation, Roussel at least enjoyed a marked success with the cultivated public of his time. The *Décade Philosophique* published extracts in four of its issues. As Marc Régaldo writes: 'Intimate with Bordeau, acquainted with Helvétus, Pierre Roussel was a precursor of Cabanis and Moreau. His *Système physique et moral de la femme*, first published in 1777, was reprinted by Alibert in 1803, and again in 1805 accompanied by a *Système physique et moral de l'homme* and an *Essai sur la sensibilité*. Despite the unfavourable juncture, the work reached its seventh edition in 1820.' (*Un milieu intellectuel: la décade philosophique*, doctoral thesis published by the University of Lille III, vol. II, p. 632.)
4. Cf. *Système physique et moral de la femme*, p. 130. The edition cited here is the 1820 *Complete Works*, ed. J. L. Alibert, first doctor-in-ordinary to the king. To summarize: among the peoples of the North, whose chilly imagination displays objects to them only with their real qualities, the hymen is taken for what it in fact is: an encumbrance. Among the peoples of the South, however, where the sentiment of love has prodigious energy, men, not content with the present alone, desire to enjoy the past as well.
5. Op. cit., p. 8.
6. *Essais sur la peinture*, Chapter 6. Note that the term 'a system of deformities' relates in Diderot to the notion of a *visual* system.
7. Indeed, the term itself was invented only in 1830.

8. All these and many other organs being absent from the *Système de la femme*. One might suppose that in Roussel's eyes whatever is not sexualizable in women does not exist.

9. 'This spreading of the thighbones must needs increase the breadth of the hips. It follows that the muscles anchored to these bones, being thus less compressed . . .' (p. 7).

10. Woman's sex subjects her to numerous revolutions (pregnancies, births): 'it was thus necessary that woman's organs should be structured so as to yield to the impulsion' of external causes – i.e., soft. This teleological passage is immediately followed by an analogical transposition: in the sphere of human relations too, 'yielding' is a very feminine attribute; and a 'certain weakness contributes to the perfection of woman'.

11. 'In geometry, when one knows a side and two angles of a triangle, one also knows the other two sides. The ideal in anatomy would be that, having seen the state of certain parts, one should be able to judge the state of the others' (p. 9).

12. So much so that his method cannot properly be described in epistemological terms, and I have had to borrow an 'appropriate' (?) term from rhetoric, that of metonymy.

13. Let us note in passing that the projection on to sexual difference of the generalized theory–practice opposition is a commonplace of modern philosophy. Even a (self-styled) 'defender' of women like John Stuart Mill devotes some long and peremptory pages to this division (see *The Subjection of Women*, Chapter 3).

    These projections seem to me overdetermined primarily by the fact that the radical opposition of theory and practice is so untenable that projection on to a differential paradigm is the only possible means of founding it: sex difference serves as a phantasmagorical guarantee of this unstable opposition. In the second place, the writer himself is not a neutral party in the affair, as adherent of one of the sides of the opposition, the 'theoretical': situating women 'elsewhere' amounts to excluding them from the domain which the writer is purporting to administer. No women *here*: the fact that women may not enter *here* is the only way of assuring the identity of the place – that of the theoretical in general which, putting it briefly, I would say is a chimera. The existence of acts of theorization in different fields of knowledge does not suffice to license the postulation of a sphere of pure and undifferentiated 'theory'.

14. This is not just my own assertion but that of many of Roussel's women contemporaries, notably Madame d'Épinay – and perhaps that of everyone except the *Philosophes* and their disciples. We may recall the contradictory criticisms provoked by Thomas's essay *Sur le caractère, les mœurs et l'esprit des femmes*, a text read and admired by Roussel. While Diderot blames it for not

going far enough in sexualizing women and constructing a specifically feminine 'subject', Madame d'Épinay protests, in the name of the obvious: 'He continually attributes to nature that which we manifestly owe to education or institution' (cf. Michèle Duchet, *Revue des Sciences humaines*, no. 168).

Moreover, this rooting in nature of women's psychological or intellectual attributes is a paradox for eighteenth-century philosophy, for this philosophy labours to show that all humanity's observable characteristics are cultural, historical, variable between different societies – and that almost all of them depend on education. And now, at the very moment when Rousseau and others are developing this leading idea, they produce its contrary, its paradoxical exception: it is nature that makes your daughter dumb.

15. Or narrative operators: the feast, idleness, pernicious spices in cookery, sedentary life, city life, etc.

16. Principally, the opposition *bounded* natural need/*unbounded* factitious need.

17. This genetic process works on the global, not the detailed, level; it concerns the species rather than the individual. Roussel emphasizes that plethora (which, as we shall see, requires counteraction through menstruation) is not an individual matter ('many women have periods without being plethoric'). There is a causality here which operates via 'the human race', the collectivity, so that in individual cases the cause may be absent, but its effect present none the less. Civil man, says Rousseau, is only a fractional entity whose value lies in the whole, namely the social body. For Roussel there exists, in a non-metaphorical sense, a collective body of the human species.

18. And 'when the human species has once contracted some new vice or affection, this vice or affection is transmitted from generation to generation, and perpetuated until some contrary cause arises to destroy it'. 'Furthermore, a woman may be subject to menstruation even though the primitive cause which creates this need is no longer present in her' (p. 121). The way Roussel conceives of process and history draws on a *precise* reference to mechanics, the principle of inertia, and then mixes up with it the factitiousness and contingency of the contract. There is an inertia of the factitious which makes what has once been contracted definitive. This mixing happens in Rousseau too: it makes it possible to conceive how a denaturation can function like a nature.

19. Another dynamic schema inherited from Rousseau's philosophy of history (or historical narration): a secondary benefit, a bonus of pleasure, is fortuitously met with in some activity, which leads to the repetition of the experience, to procure the pleasure in more than its necessary dose – and thereafter it becomes a *de facto* nature or natural need.

20. Cf. the *Éloge historique de l'auteur* by J. L. Alibert, op. cit., p. xxxii. Roussel had 'so to speak, a general tenderness' for women, but he could never resolve himself to marry a particular one.

21. The metaphor–metonymy distinction is not always a pertinent one for commenting on Roussel's work, since he sometimes associates analogical transposition and contiguity. For instance, when he proceeds from the (soft) consistency of organs to the (likewise soft) consistency of ideas, there is at once a contiguity (ideas being carried by the nerves) and an analogical transposition.

22. Prudery in naming exists in anatomy as well: in Roussel's time certain bones in the pelvic basin were called *innominés* ('unnamed'); cf. also the artery which medicine today officially terms the *artère honteuse* ('shameful artery'). Cf. Roussel, p. 6: 'Among the bones comprising the lower part of the trunk, those which one calls *innominés* . . .' When one wants to speak of something whose name means that it has none, everything becomes a periphrasis . . .

23. I would add this much to my comparison between Roussel and present-day philosophers: they too describe their discursive practice in terms of a privileged object: metaphor. The metaphor presupposes the literal meaning, but (we are told) since there is no literal meaning, there is nothing but metaphor and thus one is always-already installed in a detour. This evidently serves to invalidate in advance the critique of the philosophers' metaphorical evasions when faced with the 'literal meaning' of certain conflictual objects.

24. Author's emphasis.

25. 'A vague desire to capture the attention of all men' (p. 103), due to the 'mobile character' of women.

26. Roussel gives his term *pudeur* here an extremely precise sense which is in fact the modern one, and only the modern one. In the classical age, *pudeur* is a sense of shame which a person of honour will necessarily feel at the idea of committing an unworthy, base or cowardly act. The particular meaning 'discomfort about sexual matters' became established only later. As a doctor, Roussel further considers that this refusal due to *pudeur* brings a secondary advantage: 'a certain delay contributes to the appropriate preparation and maturation of the materials employed by nature in the production of a new being'.

27. Cf. note 10 above.

28. Certainly, but for what purpose? To incite the desires of men and render them more durable, as the text affirms, or doubly to efface a disagreeable object? One may ask whether this beauty deriving from the genital ever returns there. As far, at least, as Roussel's personal life is concerned, it is certain that it did not. Only once did his love separate out from the diffused

tenderness he felt for women in general and fix itself on a particular person. But 'of course', despite Alibert's exhortations, he divulged nothing of this to the lady concerned, dissimulated his sentiments and – as his biographer and friend records – contented himself with shedding a flood of tears when the girl eventually married.

29. What is basically involved is an exorcistic technique symmetrical with that of the scapegoat. In the latter procedure a global, diffused malaise is localized and contained in one 'part' of the social body, which is thus made into a sort of artificial abscess induced in order to avert the onset of general gangrene.

30. Alibert, again.

31. A century which perhaps is still not ended.

32. I regret presenting this idea here without going into detail or grounding it in a precise analysis. But Erwin Panofsky's admirable study of blind Love (and the Cupid who takes off his blindfold) seems to me so persuasive that its citation here is worth more than a long disquisition on my part. Cf., then, E. Panofsky, *Studies in Iconology* (London: 1939), notably Chapters 4 and 5.

33. Kant, *Conjectural Beginning of Human History*, trans. E. L. Fackenheim, in *On History*, ed. L. W. Beck (Library of Liberal Arts, 1963), p. 57.

34. Genesis 3: 8.

35. Sarah Kofman has established an analogous structure in Freud's aesthetic. From the metapsychological point of view, the genesis of the sense of beauty is linked to the inhibition of interest in the genital parts (cf. her *L'Enfance de l'Art*, pp. 150 ff.).

36. Understood summarily as the notion of a process of negation issuing in a positive result.

37. Diderot, *Pensées philosophiques* (1746), section 26.

38. The *decentring* invoked by this conception of Eros has as an effect a style of *designation* whose precision only the medical alibi suffices to preserve from bad taste. One finds in all these texts a paradoxical logic of the sign which might illustrate Deleuze's views in his *Logique du sens*: just as, in saying that Alice is growing, one says at the same time that she was small, in the same way the insistence on the negation of the 'place' amounts to a pinpointing of just what is being denied, and finally to the exact localization of that which one purports to diffuse. The violent, not to say exceedingly crude, quality of the imagination thus proposed is made tolerable in Roussel only by the neutralizing efficacy of the work's 'scientific' framework. In Kant's texts this dimension is lacking, and so they scandalized more than one commentator.

39. Phallocentric point of view: the idea that there is only one sex, the male one, the other half of heaven being eunuch. Phallocratic point of view: the ideological justification of the exclusion of women from valorized social

fields, and the project of maintaining in existence all forms of social domination and inferiorization of women.

40. 'No doubt I have restored medicine to its true rights. I have always been persuaded that only in its breast are there to be found the foundations of good morality ... The ancient doctors were not perhaps sufficiently persuaded of this truth.'

    Roussel goes on to say that there were few links between these ancient medical authors and the ancient philosophers, this being a reason why both groups fell into error. For one cannot evaluate the moral faculties of man without knowing the influence on them of his physical organization. Beyond the thesis of the body's influence on the soul, one can read in this section of the Preface a reflection on the superiority of medicine in matters of 'good morality' and thus, implicitly, a cautious invalidation of the purely philosophical. This reading is further corroborated by the fact that in this same Preface Roussel praises Jean-Jacques only on one single point: that he 'more or less based his views on the principles of medical science' – which is in my view an inverted image of the real relation of influence, but not absurd as to the question of underpinning: Roussel himself indeed provides (albeit retrospectively) a medical underpinning for Rousseauist ideas.

41. The Salic Law which in certain European countries excluded women from royal power (except for the not unimportant power of regency) involved a principle which was not immediately convertible into a justification of the exclusion of the class of women in the framework of a republican political system.

42. The *Vindication of the Rights of Woman* appeared in 1792.

43. Cf. the comparison below with *Le Fait féminin*.

44. Nature invites mortals to give one another mutual aid. One finds this Stoic idea at least down to More's *Utopia*.

45. Which Plato clearly explains *not* to be be alienation, a foreign good, a virtue profitable to the other, not to the just individual.

46. This work on Roussel was undertaken in the course of a seminar held at the École Normale Supérieure de Fontenay-aux-Roses from 1976 to 1978. The group's discussions of various papers read drew echoes from the work of many of the participants. The present discussion of Rousseau, for instance, owes a good deal to the work of Martine Feldman, and that of *pudeur* was clarified through Colin Gordon's reflections – and I record here only the more readily identifiable contributions. More globally, the exchange of ideas during these two years was of crucial value to me.

47. I use this term here in a very broad sense which includes within it the idea of alienation, since French lacks a word to designate, positively or negatively, the state of being 'wholly for the other', an idea encompassing equally altruism, alienation and the effort to please or to concur (a certain form of

seduction; a certain form of submission): in Roussel's text, coquetry and pity are two parallel effects of the same subjective position. I propose below the term *autruisme* ('other-ism') to designate this manner of being.

48. Colette Guillaumin, 'Pratique du pouvoir et idée de nature', *Questions féministes*, no. 2, p. 6; Éditions Tierce.

49. With an important exception, however: religious discourse rails against 'women' *en bloc*.

50. The proposal of a property-qualified suffrage, distinguishing between 'active' citizens and others.

51. Feudal law did not treat women '*en bloc*' but contained a number of particular provisions for marginal 'cases', treated more or less pragmatically. It provided, for instance, for the case where a fief came into the hands of a woman; and regulated the status of the corporation of Market women, within the condition of the third estate.

52. Rousseau, *Lettre à d'Alembert*, Garnier-Flammarion edition, p. 67.

53. This representation of woman as completely 'in herself' of course contradicts the idea, also developed by Roussel, of woman's total *autruisme*. To hold this contradiction against our author would be to postulate – which is impossible – that the site of his discourse is that of rationality.

54. Erving Goffman, *Actes pour la recherche en sciences sociales*, 14 (1977).

55. Either these or analogous formulations by eighteenth-century authors. I am not of course purporting here to measure the historical impact of Roussel's book – that would be to suppose that a person's thought can in itself determine the course of things. Our author's ideas, the basic schemas which he puts into operation, are sufficiently shared by the philosophers of his time for it to be clear that he should be regarded only as an active witness, albeit no doubt a privileged one in that he produced an easily consumable book, a work of semi-vulgarization, and gave the warranty of science to values and distinctions which had still been fragile in the mid-eighteenth century.

56. Helen B. Andelin's *Fascinating Womanhood* is the most important of these.

57. One can find pointers in this direction, regarding the plebeian image of woman, in Eric Hobsbawm's article 'Sexes, symboles, vêtements et socialisme', *Actes pour la recherche*, 23 September 1978.

58. *Les mains de Jeanne-Marie* (1871).

59. This emerges notably from an extremely well-documented study by Marguerite Cordier, published in *Diplomées*, no. 106, 1978. Government ministers (Duruy, Paul Bert), the Empress Eugénie the Prefect of the Seine in 1886, parliamentarians, a law passed in the Senate, all backed the demands of the 'women pioneers'. Ferociously hostile to them, on the other hand, were the faculty doyens, the interns of the Faculty of Medicine, the society of lawyers, etc. Each victory of the pioneers rests on an auth-

oritarian decision by the central power, taken in the face of recrimination by the local power.

60. These are the terms of a petition of the Paris hospital interns in 1882, directed (naturally) against the admission of women as interns.

61. Cf. Sarah Kofman, *L'Enfance de l'art*, and Freud, *Three Essays on the Theory of Sexuality*.

62. The works of Françoise Dolto are exemplary in this respect. The most conventional and threadbare morality imaginable receives fresh protection and legitimation in this expert's discourse. And no doubt psychoanalytic expertise needs to possess a considerable authority to be able to resuscitate the value-system of *La Semaine de Suzette*.

63. *Le Fait féminin*, ed. Évelyne Sullerot (Fayard, 1978). [Note added to the English translation: the French sociologist Évelyne Sullerot is the author of a significant body of research into the situation of women, undertaken at a time when such work was neither academically nor politically fashionable: *La Presse féminine* (1963), *Histoire de la presse féministe des origines à 1948* (1966), *Histoire et sociologie du travail féminin* (1968). In the 1970s, apparently disenchanted with the militancy of the emerging French women's movement, Sullerot veered towards the political Centre-Right and, as representative of an officially 'acceptable' feminism, assumed a role during the Giscard presidency as a quasi-technocratic adviser, regularly consulted by the French government and the EEC.

Le Fait féminin ('the feminine fact') was one of a series of colloquia organized at the Royaumont 'Centre for the Study of Man', founded in 1972. Other discussion themes included 'the unity of Man' and a debate between Piaget and Chomsky. Sullerot's volume can in this context be seen as representative of an increasingly influential philosophical current in France (perhaps destined to emulate the recent media success of the '*Nouveaux philosophes*') made up of such writers as Edgar Morin, Serge Moscovici, Atlan and Monot, and with connections to the work of Le Roy Ladurie, Michel Serres and Cornelius Castoriadis; its goal might be stated as the reconstruction of a unified intellectual world-view, synthesizing the 'new science', 'new culture' and 'new politics' . . .

Le Fait féminin appears to have met with a sympathetic readership among various 'crypto-essentialist' groups: men who see the male – female distinction as symbolically rich, and hence as a suitable means of counteracting the desicated abstraction of modernist intellectual life; some radical lesbians, favourable to any position which emphasizes the substantive difference between men and women; and all those circles which consider the 'scientific' treatment of any problem desirable in itself. On the other hand, the tone of the book provoked a hostile reaction from the two main feminist currents: egalitarian feminists saw it as reactionary because positing an (inferior) essence of femininity; while the 'new femininity' current, preferring a more intuitionistic, impressionistic, 'body'-orientated style of discourse, disliked its excessive scientism.]

Évelyne Sullerot has also edited the anthology *Women on Love* (London/ New York, 1979).

64. Lombroso's theory of the 'born criminal' follows on from the work of Gall. During the first quarter of the nineteenth century F. J. Gall did research in orphanages, asylums, prisons, and even – or so he said – at the foot of the scaffold. From his palpation of all these skulls, together with those of individuals 'taken from the lower classes', he 'deduced' a craniological chart. Thus, the organ of circumspection is located in the middle parietal region, that of the religious sentiment behind the frontal region – which enabled Gall to explain, on sight of his portrait, why Saint Thomas was Saint Thomas. Any individual with highly developed lateral regions is liable to end up on the scaffold, this being the 'bump' of the carnivorous instincts of theft and trickery. Gall and Lombroso are the ancestors of the 'crime chromosome', a particularly dubious hypothesis formulated around 1965.

65. The ratio of the transverse and front-to-back dimensions of the skull. One can usefully consult G. Olivier's article 'anthropologie physique' and A. Memmi's article 'Racisme' in the *Encylcopedia Universalis*.

66. This gene being supposed responsible for women's lesser aptitude in mastering spatial relations – and for the greater verbal competence of little girls. This female 'superiority' mysteriously evaporates as children grow older – so that by adulthood only the spatial handicap remains; it also accounts for 'women's lesser place in (musical) creation'. The considerable disparity between the word-stock of a three-year-old working-class child (of either sex) and a middle-class one is not even mentioned here, neither are the sensory-motor differences between peasant and town children. Despite the extremely problematic character of all such tests, including those which tend to show the inequalities and differences I have just mentioned, one is entitled to feel astonished at the book's silence on the influence of the ecological and social environment.

67. Cf. the portrait Sullerot traces of Jacques Monod, p. 21.

68. I have contented myself here with a formal critique of the way hypotheses are developed and the methods of proof used in this book – polemics against the content of theses it advances having already been brilliantly carried out by others. See *Questions féministes*, no. 5 (Elizabeth de Lesseps's article) and *La Revue d'en face*, no. 4 (Eliane Navarro's contribution).

69. Cf. note 40 above.

70. A. Jost, 'Le développement sexual prénatal', in *Le Fait féminin*, pp. 85 ff.

71. p. 99: this concerns the action of testosterone.

72. p. 86. emphasis added.
73. Once again, this cannot be judged from a work of vulgarization, whose imprecision necessarily opens the door to arbitrariness and mystification. What does 'more or less' mean here anyway? And what is feminization? A matter of morphology, or hormonology?
74. 'La psychologie des sexes', op. cit., p. 248.
75. Maccoby's intervention, nuanced and critical of the general tone of the book, is violently rejected by Sullerot (pp. 280–1), who uses a very interesting argument: Maccoby, says Sullerot, has denigrated the importance of these spatial aptitudes by assuming that male superiority in these matters produces only 'banal and narrowly specified' aptitudes. Sullerot protests: these small, seemingly narrow differences can take on decisive importance in certain socioeconomic conditions – that is to say, of course, our own. The fact that men see better than women in three dimensions may be of little consequence in New Guinea (read: among savages), but in our industrialized societies this fact can take on considerable importance, and justify inequalities of status. I conclude from this that for Évelyne Sullerot, the subordination of women belongs not so much in remote ages as in the future. If she says so, it must be true; and this time I am willing to accept her word, since her word has a certain small performative value: if the government specialist in the sociology of female work says that there are excellent neuropsychological reasons for women to occupy only low-grade jobs in the watch industry (for example), then there is not much chance of the career orientation of our technical schools being shaken out of its sexism.
76. Sandra Witelson, p. 298, and *passim* in E. Sullerot's notes.
77. Saint Augustine, cited by Pascal's letter of September 1656 to the Duke and Charlotte de Roannez.
78. She is not the only one. More than one participant shows some reticence about endorsing the colloquium's presuppositions. But the matter is firmly kept in hand by Sullerot, who encases all the contributions' opinions in 'notes towards a sociological reflection', introductions, conclusions, etc.
79. p. 433.
80. The *société d'Auteuil*, Madame Helvétius's circle, was the sociotheoretical intermediary between the *encyclopedistes* and the *Idéologues*. Roussel was a regular frequenter of the society; it was at Auteuil that Cabanis was to meet him.
81. That is to say a general theory of first principles, rather than a doctrine about some particular object.
82. 'Diogenes, the philosopher who has nothing', is an important figure in Diderot. In his correspondence with Sophie Volland, he even speaks of identifying himself with this Diogenes.

83. *De l'Interprétation de la nature* (1753), notably paragraph XXI.

84. When, in the words of the proverb, I feel tempted to say to a Roussel or a Sullerot 'shoemaker . . .!', this is not because I want to defend a higher domain, *my* professional 'place', against outsiders' pretensions, but because I think that this sphere of generality ought to be left vacant.

85. Again, a Diderot metaphor.

86. And masculinization seems to be a notion as doubtful as feminization, so long as one has not strictly defined what one means by it.

87. In the group of invited participants at Royaumont, one person did sense that his colleagues were labouring to discredit *their own* theoretical tools. Cf. op. cit. R. Zazzo, pp. 120 ff.

Index